Being Genuine

Being Genuine

Stop Being Nice, Start Being Real

THOMAS D'ANSEMBOURG

PuddleDancer
PRESS

2240 Encinitas Blvd., Ste. D-911, Encinitas, CA 92024
email@PuddleDancer.com • www.PuddleDancer.com

Being Genuine
Stop Being Nice, Start Being Real
©2007 PuddleDancer Press
A PuddleDancer Press Book

Originally published in French by Les Editions de L'Homme
©2001, Les Editions de L'Homme
une division du groupe Sogides

PuddleDancer Press, Permissions Dept.
2240 Encinitas Blvd., Ste D-911, Encinitas, CA 92024
Tel: 760-652-5754 Fax: 760-274-6400
www.NonviolentCommunication.com email@PuddleDancer.com

Ordering Information
Please contact Independent Publishers Group, Tel: 312-337-0747; Fax: 312-337-5985; Email: frontdesk@ipgbook.com or visit www.IPGbook.com for other contact information and details about ordering online

Author: Thomas d'Ansembourg
Translated by: Godfrey Spencer
Editor: Dan Shenk, CopyProof, ShenkCopyProof@aol.com
Index: Phyllis Linn, Indexpress

Manufactured in the United States of America

24 23 22 21 20   7 8 9 10 11

ISBN: 978-1-892005-21-2

Publisher's Cataloging-in-Publication
(Provided by Quality Books, Inc.)
D'Ansembourg, Thomas.
     Being genuine : stop being nice, start being real /
Thomas d'Ansembourg.
        p. cm.
     Includes bibliographical references and index.
     ISBN 1-892005-21-2
     ISBN 978-1-892005-21-2

     1. Interpersonal communication. 2. Nonviolence.
     I. Title.

     BF637.C45D36 2007   158.2
                                    QBI07-600002

I flit from perch to perch, in an ever-shrinking cage, the door of which is open, wide open.

GYULA ILLYÉS
Hungarian poet

The story of my life began on the day I decided not to live it as if I was going up the down-escalator.

PASCAL DE DUVE
Belgian poet

ACKNOWLEDGMENTS

My gratitude goes first of all to Marshall Rosenberg with whom I trained in Nonviolent Communication (NVC). Meeting Marshall and learning what he taught brought me back to life at a time I was becoming a *nice, dead* person! Through his clarity, coherence, and integrity, this process of understanding oneself and others has contributed to changing—through and through—both my professional and emotional life.

My gratitude next goes to Anne Bourrit, a Nonviolent Communication trainer, in whose company I was lucky enough to decipher and clarify in myself the fundamental challenges that were making life so difficult for me. Valérie, my wife, and I keep Anne close to our hearts.

My deep gratitude also goes to Guy Corneau for his preface to this book and for his constant encouragements to write it. During many years of shared work and friendship, I have been touched and inspired by his great compassion for human beings and by his faith in life itself. He conveyed to me his desire to translate into simple language the psychological challenges that can seem so complex, as well as to contribute in this way toward enabling all, through a better understanding and a greater love of self, to become true co-creators of their lives.

My gratitude also goes to Pierre-Bernard Velge, the founder and living spirit of the nonprofit Flics et Voyouz (Cops and

Hoods) organization. In the work we did with young people in difficulty over a period exceeding ten years, he awakened in me an ability to listen from the heart: listening without judging, listening to understand and love more.

And certainly my gratitude also goes to all those who placed their trust in me at workshops, private consultations, and conferences. It was out of the authenticity of our encounters and the beauty of the transformations undergone that my project of writing this book arose.

I further am infinitely grateful to Liliane Magi for patiently decoding my handwritten notes.

Finally, my gratitude goes to all of the NVC trainers in Switzerland, France, and Belgium with whom I have been privileged to work . . . for their friendship and support.

*To Valérie
and our children, Camille, Anna, and Jiulia,
with love, affection, and respect*

CONTENTS

Chapter 7

Epilogue

PREFACE

Moving From Being Nice to Being Genuine

Expressing one's truth while respecting others and respecting oneself . . . that is the journey on which attorney and author Thomas d'Ansembourg invites us to accompany him. This is the invitation he extends to us in this book by suggesting that we plunge straight into the heart of how we enter into dialogue with ourselves and others. In it, we learn how to reprogram the way we express ourselves. Once that has been done, there comes the joy of being closer to others and closer to ourselves. There is the joy of being open to others. And at the heart of this process lies the possibility of giving up the familiar, even comfortable, confusions with which we so often content ourselves, instead of gaining access to a universe of choice and freedom.

What finer prospect, what finer program? This isn't about skimming the surface, like dragonflies flitting above a summer pond. Rather, the method of communication put forward by Thomas d'Ansembourg calls into question our psychological makeup, inducing us to delve more deeply into ourselves and our relationships.

- It is a demanding venture because in order to succeed in clearly formulating what is alive in ourselves, we often need to search out unconscious conditionings.
- It is a revolutionary venture because along the road we discover that our plan to express our true self plainly puts our vulnerability on the line, puts our pride to the test.
- It is a daunting venture because it highlights our propensity to leave things as they are for fear of upsetting others—and for fear that others might upset us in turn if we truly speak out.
- Finally, it is a venture as challenging as it is stimulating, for it invites each of us to work on changing ourselves rather than expecting anyone and everyone else to change.

I personally became aware of the potential of Nonviolent Communication when I was traveling in the Sahara Desert. With the assistance of Jean-Marie Delacroix, I was guiding a group of twenty-four men who were taking part in a program called The Inner Flame. At Thomas d'Ansembourg's suggestion, I had accepted responsibility for some young people from the Cops and Hoods organization, as well as some of its adult facilitators to provide us with technical assistance during this adventure. Some years earlier, I had learned that this organization was involved with street children. Pierre-Bernard Velge, the founder, and his right-hand man, Thomas d'Ansembourg, had invited me to join them as psychological counselor for a desert expedition in which the troubled youngsters were taking part. I had subsequently persuaded the twenty-four men to join us in our program, and I'd gotten really caught up in this venture, which was designed to help the men with their social reintegration.

I had indeed gotten caught up in the program, but I began to regret it when one young member of the program threatened an adult with a knife. We were hours away by motor vehicle from any sign of civilization, and danger was now staring us in the face. In absolutely no way did I want to jeopardize the people I was responsible for and could think of only one solution: Pack the whole group and head home as soon as possible. In fact, that was an easy way of getting rid of the problem for myself.

I told Thomas about my intentions. Without rejecting my proposal, he asked me for a few hours more time. Long discussions took place on the sand dune, at a slight distance from the campground. To my great surprise, the conversations led to unity among the entire group. Moreover, no further problems occurred to mar our trip. While admiring Thomas's patience, I was telling myself that the Nonviolent Communication technique he was using would be worthwhile studying.

Subsequently, Thomas became an assistant and a regular cofacilitator at my workshops. Within the *Cœur.com* association, I still often call him in to settle tricky situations. I attended his introductory Nonviolent Communication workshop, and the basic principles of this discipline became those of my own seminars.

Why? Because I realized that most of us, first and foremost myself, are still in our infancy when we endeavor to communicate. We are inclined to assess others, to judge them and to label them without disclosing to them our own feelings and without daring to express our *true self*. Who among us can boast of having taken stock of the feelings that underlie our judgments before we enunciate them? Who takes the trouble to identify and name the needs that have been forced back and camouflaged behind the words we speak? Who tries to make realistic, negotiable requests in their relationships with others?

In my view this way of communicating, based on realistic and negotiable requests, is all the more interesting as it complements what has already been proposed by other methods, among others those of Jacques Salomé and Thomas Gordon. They all rightly stress the need to learn to express ourselves using "I" messages, based on our own life experience and to admit that our needs, in and of themselves, are legitimate. However, such legitimacy has its limitations. It needs to find expression in the formulation of negotiable requests made to others, unless we want to enclose ourselves in a bubble of egocentricity; for although our needs are justified, they cannot all be met. Compromises acceptable to all parties must be sought. In my view it is here that Nonviolent Communication shows its true colors.

Such a technique would make miracles in politics. Moreover, it should be taught to schoolchildren as soon as they go to primary school in order to help them steer clear of the bad habit of losing touch with themselves and with their own modes of expression. As for couples, where friction between human beings is sometimes painfully and dangerously intensified, NVC truly comes into its own to prove its efficacy. Nonviolent Communication to me appears to be the antechamber to psychology and also what makes it possible in the psychological understanding of our human challenges to find day-to-day applications of a very practical nature.

In truth, although the principles of any communication method are in general easy to grasp, it's always practice that remains the difficulty. Bearing this in mind, the book you hold in your hands is a genuine reference manual. It shows the talent and openness of the mind of the author, who provides the world with an approach to feelings and needs in which one can see two aspects of his long practice at the bar: rigor of analysis and a down-to-earth concern for effectiveness.

Among the relatively few people who have been bold enough to speak *their true selves*, Thomas d'Ansembourg is for me the one who succeeds with the greatest agility. This poet of communication, this explorer of inner and outer deserts, has understood that in order for there to be true communication between human beings, it is necessary to give up power relationships and take the risk of expressing one's own truth. I saw him transform himself and, in a few years, move from being a nice little boy, afraid of committing himself, to becoming an amorous husband and a devoted father. I witnessed him gradually withdrawing from his lawyer's and banking consultant's world in order to be faithful to himself—and to help others become so as well.

I am happy to see him at his best in this book, written to teach us that in the final analysis there is no intimacy with others unless there is intimacy with oneself . . . and no intimacy with oneself unless there is intimacy with others. With the gentleness and elegance of Saint-Exupéry's *The Little Prince*, Thomas d'Ansembourg reminds us that we can join others without ceasing to be ourselves.

Guy Corneau

INTRODUCTION

I have no hope of getting out of my solitude by myself. Stones have no hope of being anything but stones. However, through collaboration they get themselves together and become a Temple.

ANTOINE DE SAINT-EXUPÉRY
French writer

I was a lawyer, nicely and "oh, so politely" depressed and demotivated. Today, it is with enthusiasm that I lead conferences, seminars, and private consultations. I was a bachelor terrified at the idea of emotional commitment, and overwork gave me solace in solitude. Today, I'm a husband and a father and am overjoyed to be so. I was living with a well-concealed but constant inner sadness. Today, I am filled with confidence and joy.

What happened?

I *became aware* that by ignoring my own needs for such a long time I was inflicting violence upon myself, and I tended to deflect this violence toward others. Then, after experiencing the insights and power of Nonviolent Communication, I *accepted* that I had needs, that I could listen to them, differentiate between them, establish priorities among them, and take care of *myself* rather than complaining about no one taking care of me. All the energy I had previously devoted to complaining, rebelling, and being nostalgic, I little by little gathered together, *re-centered,* and placed in the service of inner transformation, creation, and relationship. I also became aware of and accepted the fact that others also have their needs and that I am not necessarily the only person with the skills and availability to meet such needs.

The process of Nonviolent Communication was and continues to be for me an inspiring and reassuring guide in the transformation I sought to undergo. I hope it will inspire and reassure readers in understanding their own relationships, beginning with the relationship with themselves.

Through this book, I wish to illustrate the process that Marshall Rosenberg[1] developed in the spirit and the line of thought of the works of Carl Rogers. Those acquainted with the work of Thomas Gordon also will find notions they are familiar with. I hope in this way to show my trust that if each of us accepts our own violence, the violence we often exert unconsciously and very subtly on ourselves and others (often with the best of intentions)—and takes care to understand how the violence is triggered—each will be able to work toward defusing it. We will then be able to create more satisfying relationships . . . relationships that are both freer and more responsible.

Marshall Rosenberg calls his process Nonviolent Communication (NVC). I myself refer to it as conscious and nonviolent communication. Violence in fact is a consequence of our lack of consciousness. Were we more aware inside of what we are truly experiencing, we would find it easier to find opportunities to express our strength without committing aggression against one another. I believe that there is violence as soon as we use our strength not to create, stimulate, or protect but to constrain, whether the constraint is in regard to ourselves or to others. Our strength may be emotional, psychological, moral, hierarchical, or institutional. Thus subtle violence, the kid-glove violence (especially emotional violence), is infinitely more widespread than the violence that expresses itself through blows, crimes, and insults, and it is all the more insidious for not being named.

If the violence is not named, it is because it is hidden within the words themselves we use—innocently and sometimes not so innocently—each day. Our vocabulary is violence's day-to-day vector. Indeed, we translate our thoughts and therefore our consciousness mainly through the intermediary of words. We therefore have the choice of communicating our thinking and our awareness through words that divide, oppose, separate, compare, categorize, or condemn—or through words that gather, propose, reconcile, and stimulate. Thus by working on our consciousness and our language, we can suppress the interference that hampers communication and generates ordinary violence.

There is, therefore, nothing new about the underlying principles of Nonviolent Communication. For centuries, they have been part and parcel of the wisdom of the world, a wisdom so little implemented because it doubtless seems impractical in most cases. What I think *is* new, and what I have been able to verify each day in its genuine practicality, is the way the process proposed by Marshall Rosenberg is articulated.

On the one hand, there are the concepts of communication and nonviolence. These two notions and the values they convey, however attractive they may be, often leave us feeling helpless: Is it always possible to communicate without violence? In our dealings with others, how can we make both real and concrete the values to which everyone adheres in thought: respect, freedom, mutual compassion, responsibility?

On the other hand, there are the components and challenges of communication. Through a four-point process, we are invited to become aware that we always react to something—to a situation (point 1, observation); that this observation always produces a feeling in us (point 2, feeling); that this feeling corresponds to a need (point 3, need); that this need invites us to make a request (point 4, request). This method is based on the fact that we feel better when we clearly see what we are reacting to; when we understand properly both our feelings and our needs; and when we manage to formulate negotiable requests while at the same time feeling safe in being able to receive others' reactions, whatever they may be. This method also is based on the observed fact that we feel better when we clearly see what others are referring to or are reacting to, when we understand their feelings and needs and hear a negotiable request that allows us the freedom to be in agreement or not—and to seek together a solution meeting the needs of both parties, not one to the detriment of the other. Thus, beyond being a method of communicating, Nonviolent Communication leads to an art of living in relationships, as well as respecting oneself, others, and the world at large.

In this computer era, more and more people communicate faster and faster but less and less well! More and more people are suffering from loneliness, a lack of understanding, meaning-lessness, and a loss of reference points. Organizational and operational preoccupations take precedence over the quality of our relationships. It is a matter of urgency to explore other ways of relating.

Many of us feel tired regarding our inability to express ourselves genuinely and be truly listened to and understood. Even though (using modern technology) we exchange a great deal of information, we are still handicapped when it comes to *true* expression and listening. Out of the resulting powerlessness are born fears that trigger old fallback reflexes: fundamentalisms, nationalisms, racisms. In the excitement of technological conquest—particularly worldwide means of communication in the totally new context of the interweaving of cultures, races, religions, fashions, political and economic paradigms that these means allow for—are we not running the risk of missing out on what is intimate and true? This intimacy and truth are so invaluable that any other quest might well prove fruitless, even pointless: The end purpose here is encounters, true encounters between human beings, with no games, no masks, no interference from our fears, habits, and clichés that don't carry the weight of our conditionings and old reflexes—and that subsequently bring us out of the isolation of our telephones, our screens, and our virtual images.

It would appear that here lies a new continent to be conquered, little explored to this day, that strikes fear into many: *a true relationship between two individuals who are free and responsible.*

If this exploration strikes fear into our hearts, it is because many of us tend to be afraid of losing ourselves in a relationship. We have learned to alienate ourselves from our true self in order to be with another.

What I am proposing is to explore a hypothesis for genuine relations between human beings who are free and responsible at the same time, a hypothesis that I will characterize by a twofold question that, it seems to me, is so often at the center of the existential difficulties many experience: *How can one be oneself without stopping being with another, and how can one be with another without stopping being oneself?*

While writing this book, I regularly had a concern in the back of my mind. I know that books can inform and can contribute to our evolving. However, I also know that intellectual understanding can never "in and of itself" transform hearts. The transformation of the heart is born out of emotional understanding, that is, experience and practice over the duration. This book itself is an example of that: It is largely based on experience and practice.

Since my first contact with Nonviolent Communication, I have striven to consolidate knowledge through practice, exercising wariness toward theoretical knowledge that often leads us to believe that we have understood it all—which perhaps is true intellectually—whereas we have taken nothing at all on board. Such an illusion enables us to skirt any opportunity to transform ourselves in any true or durable manner.

This is why I have no reference works to propose, except for Marshall Rosenberg's book *Nonviolent Communication: A Language of Life,* although I realize and am thankful that the notions I am tackling here also have been explored by other authors. In addition, I quote the wisdom of dozens of sages and great thinkers.

I am taking a risk by committing to the pages of this book words and notions that are necessarily static regarding what is actually learned through *experience* in workshops or seminars, role-plays, integration time, listening to emotions, feedback, silences, and the resonance of a group. The risk is that the process may appear simplistically utopian. I accept this risk because it is a process and not a trick; it is a state of consciousness to be practiced as one practices a foreign language. And everyone knows that a read-through of *Simple French from A to Z* will not win a person a speech-making competition in Paris. Nor will that person dare to step into the arena of a conversation in French at a party! First of all, one modestly plays one's scales. So in the end, does not the word *utopia* offer us a taste of another place to strive toward?

This book seeks to speak precisely to those who are heading for another place, a place of *true* encounters between human beings. My work allows me to meet such people—top executives in business, couples and families from every walk of life, individuals on welfare, persons in education or in hospitals, young people in distress—every day in the most diverse of environments. And each day I can bear witness that this place does exist—if only we want it to.

CHAPTER 1

Why We Are Alienated From Ourselves

Our intellectual world is made up of categories, it is bordered by arbitrary and artificial frontiers.

We need to build bridges, but for that there is a need for knowledge, a greater vision of man and his destiny.

YEHUDI MENUHIN
U.S. and British violinist
and conductor

Preamble

I have no words to describe my loneliness, my sadness, or my anger.

I have no words to speak my need for exchange, understanding, recognition.

So I criticize, I insult, or I strike.

Or I have my fix, abuse alcohol, or get depressed.

Violence, expressed within or without, results from a lack of vocabulary; it is the expression of a frustration that has no words to express it.

And there are good reasons for that; most of us have not acquired a vocabulary for our inner life. We never learned to describe accurately what we were feeling and what needs we had. Since childhood, however, we have learned a host of words. We can talk about history, geography, mathematics, science, or literature; we can describe computer technology or sporting technique and hold forth on the economy or the law. But the words for life within . . . when did we learn them? As we grew up, we became alienated from our feelings and needs in an attempt to listen to those of our mother and father, brothers and sisters, schoolteachers, et al.: "Do as Mommy tells you . . . Do whatever your cousin who's coming to play with you this afternoon wants . . . Do what is expected of you."

And it was thus that we started to listen to the feelings and needs of everyone—boss, customer, neighbor, colleagues— except ourselves! To survive and fit in, we thought we had to be cut off from ourselves.

Then one day the payment comes due for such alienation! Shyness, depression, misgivings, hesitations in reaching decisions, inability to choose, difficulties to commit, a loss of taste for life. Help! We circle 'round and 'round like the water draining from a sink. We are about to go under. We are waiting for someone to drag us out, to be given instructions, and yet, at the same time, recommendations aren't exactly welcome! We're snowed under with "You must do this . . . It's high time you did that . . . You should . . ."

What we need most of all is to get in touch with ourselves, to seek a solid grounding in ourselves, to feel within that it is we who are speaking, we who decide and not our habits, our conditioning, our fears of another's opinion. But how?

I like to introduce the process that I advocate by using the picture of a little man born of the imagination of Hélène Domergue, a trainer in Nonviolent Communication in Geneva, Switzerland.

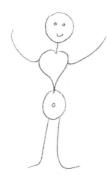

- *Intellect*
  (or observation)
- *Feelings*
- *Needs*
  (or values)
- *The request*
  (or concrete and negotiable action)

1. Intellect (or observation)

Intellect

- Judgments, labels, categories
- Prejudices, *a prioris,* rote beliefs, automatic reflexes
- Binary system or duality
- Language of diminished responsibility

The head symbolizes *mind.* The main beneficiary of our educating is the mind. It's the mind that we have honed, toned, and disciplined in order to be effective, productive, and fast. Yet our *heart,* our emotional life, our inner life, has not enjoyed such attention. Indeed, we learned to be good and reasonable, to make well-thought-out decisions, to analyze, categorize, and label all things and place them in separate drawers. We have become masters of logic and reasoning and, since childhood, what has been stimulated, exercised, refined, and nuanced is our intellectual understanding of things. As for our emotional understanding, it has been encouraged little or not at all, if not overtly reproved.

Now, in the course of my work, I observe four characteristics of the functioning of the mind that are often the cause of the violence we do to ourselves and others.

Judgments, labels, and categories

We judge. We judge others or situations as a function of the little we have seen of them, and we take the little we have seen for the whole. For example, we see a boy in the street whose hair is orange and combed into a crest; he has his face pierced in various places. "Oh, a punk, another rebel, a dropout feeding off society." In a flash, we have judged, faster than the sun creates our shadow. We know nothing about this person, who is perhaps passionately engaged in a youth movement, a drama troupe, or computer research and who is thus contributing his talent and his heart to the evolution of the world. However, as something about his looks, his difference, generates fear, mistrust, and needs in us that we're unable to decipher (perhaps the need to welcome difference, the need for belonging, the need to be reassured that difference does not bring about separation), we judge him. Look how our judging does violence to beauty, generosity, the wealth that may well lie within this person whom we have not seen.

Another example. We see an elegant woman dressed in a fur coat, driving a large car. "What a snob! Just another woman who can't think of anything better to do than display her riches!"

Again, we judge, taking the little we have seen of another for her reality. We lock her into a little drawer, wrap her up in cellophane. Once again, we do violence to the whole beauty of this person, which we have not perceived because it lies within. This person is perhaps quite generous with her time and money, and she may be engaged in social work, giving support to destitute people, or pursuing other unknown endeavors. We know nothing about her. Once again, her looks awaken fear, mistrust, anger, or sadness in us and put us in touch with needs that we don't know how to decode (need for exchange, need for sharing, need for human beings to contribute actively to the common good) as we judge, so we imprison others within a category; we close them away in drawers.

We take the tip of the iceberg for the whole, whereas another part of us realizes that 90 percent of the iceberg is under the surface of the sea, out of sight. It is worth recalling the words of Saint-Exupéry, author of *The Little Prince*, "We only see well with our hearts; what is truly important is invisible to our eyes." Do we really look at others with our hearts?

Prejudices, *a prioris*, rote beliefs, automatic reflexes

We have learned to function out of *habit*, to *automate thinking*, to presumptively have *prejudices* and a prioris, to live in a universe of concepts and ideas, and to fabricate or propagate *unverified beliefs*:

- Men are macho.
- Women can't drive.
- Officials are lazy.
- Politicians are corrupt.
- You have to fight in life.
- There are things that have to be done, whether one wants to or not. That's the way it always has been done.
- A good mother, a good husband, a good son . . . must . . .
- My wife would never put up with me speaking to her like that. In this family, one can certainly not raise an issue like that.
- My father is someone who . . .

These are expressions that basically reflect our fears. Using them, we enclose ourselves and others in beliefs, habits, concepts.

Once again, we do violence to the men who are anything but macho, who are open to their sensitivities, their kindness, the nurturing "feminine" that lies within them. We do violence to the women who drive much better than most men, having both more respect for other motorists and greater safety in traffic. We do violence to the officials who give of themselves generously and enthusiastically through their work. We do violence to the politicians who do their jobs with loyalty and integrity, working idealistically and selflessly for the common good. We do violence to ourselves and others regarding all the things that we dare not speak or do, whereas they are truly important for us, as well as for the things we believe we "have to" do without taking the time to check whether they indeed are a high priority or whether we might better take care of the true needs of the people concerned (those of others or our own) in some different way.

Binary system or duality

When all is said and done, most of us have gotten into the all-too-comfortable habit of expressing things in terms of black and white, positive and negative. A door has to be open or closed; something is good or bad; one is right or wrong. This is done or that is not done. It is fashionable, or it is obsolete. It is just great or absolute rubbish. There are subtle variations on the theme: You are intellectual or manual, a mathematician or an artist, a responsible father or a free spirit, a social butterfly or a couch potato, a poet or an engineer, a homo or a hetero, "with it" or a fuddy-duddy. This is the trap of *duality, the binary system.*

Most of us have gotten into the all-too-comfortable habit of expressing things in terms of black and white, positive and negative.

It's as if we could not possibly be both a brilliant intellectual and an effective manual worker, a rigorous mathematician and an imaginative artist, a being both responsible and fanciful, a sensitive poet and an earnest engineer. It's as if we could not possibly love ourselves beyond our male/female sexual duality, be conventional in some areas and highly innovative in others.

Stated another way, it's as if reality were not infinitely more rich and colored than our poor little categories, these tiny drawers into which we try to stuff reality because its mobility, diversity, and enchanting vitality disconcert and frighten us. In order to gain reassurance, we seem to prefer to lock everything away in apothecaries' pots, carefully labeled and placed on the shelves of our intellect!

The logic of exclusion and division is something we practice on the basis of *or.* We play at "Who is right, who is wrong?"—a tragic game that stigmatizes everything that divides us rather than extolling the value of what unites us. Later we will see to what extent we allow ourselves to be trapped by the binary system and what violence it perpetrates on ourselves and others. The most frequent example is the following: Either we take care of others, or we take care of ourselves, with the consequence that either we are alienated from ourselves, or we are alienated from others—as if we couldn't possibly take care of others *and* take care of ourselves while being close to others without ceasing to be close to ourselves.

Language of diminished responsibility

We use a language that allows us not to feel responsible for what we're experiencing or for what we are doing. First of all, we have learned to project onto others or onto an outside agency most of the responsibility for our feelings. "I am angry because you . . . I am sad because my parents . . . I am depressed because the world, the pollution, the ozone layer . . ." We take little or no responsibility for what we are feeling. On the contrary, we find a scapegoat, we make heads roll, we off-load our negative energy onto someone else who serves as a lightning rod for our frustrations! Then we also have learned not to take responsibility for our acts. For example: "It's the rule . . . Orders from above . . . Tradition has it that . . . I wasn't able to do otherwise . . . You must . . . I have no choice . . . It's time . . . It is (not) normal that . . ."

We will see to what extent this language alienates us from ourselves and from others and enslaves us all the more subtly as it appears to be a language of diminished responsibility.

2. Feelings

Through this traditional way of functioning, which sets mental processes at a premium, we are cut off from our feelings and emotions by something as effectively as by a concrete slab.

Perhaps to some degree you will recognize yourself in what appears below. Personally, I learned to be a good and reasonable little boy, ever listening to others. Speaking of oneself or one's emotions in regard to self was not well-received when I was a child. One could describe with emotions a painting or a garden, speak of a piece of music, a book, or a landscape, but speaking of oneself, especially with any emotion, was tantamount to being tainted with egocentricity, narcissism, navel-gazing. "It isn't right to be busy with oneself; it is others whom we should attend to," I was told.

If one day I was very angry and expressed it, I might hear something like: "It isn't nice to be angry . . . A good little boy doesn't get angry . . . Go to your bedroom and come back when you have thought things over." Back to reason.

I thought things over with my head, which wasted no time in judging me guilty. So I then cut myself off from my heart and put my anger in my pocket and went downstairs to redeem my place in the family community by displaying a contrived smile. If another day I was sad and unable to hold back my tears, suddenly shaken by one of those heavy moods that can fall upon you without understanding why, and I just needed reassuring and comforting, I would hear: "It's not nice to be sad. Just think of everything that is done for you! And then there are people who are really unfortunate and who don't have nearly as much as you do. Go to your room. You can come back when you have thought things over." Dismissed again!

I would go to my room, and the same rational process would predominate: "It's true, I have no right to be sad. I have a father, a mother, brothers and sisters, books for school and toys, a house, and food. What am I complaining about? What is all this, this sadness? I'm so selfish. Useless idiot!" Once again, I judged myself and found myself guilty, alienating myself from my heart. Sadness went off to join anger in my pocket, and I went to redeem my place in the family, displaying another contrived smile. So you can see how early we learn to be nice rather than genuine.

Finally, another day when I was brimming over with joy, exploding with happiness and expressing it by running around, playing my stereo full blast, and singing and talking nonstop, I would hear the following words: "What's wrong with you? Life is no spring picnic!" My goodness, that was the death knell! Even joy wasn't welcome among adults! So what did I do then as a ten-year-old lad? I entered the following two messages on my internal hard drive:

- To be an adult is to cut oneself off as much as possible from one's emotions and use them only once in a while to produce the right effect in a party conversation.
- To be loved and have my place in the world, I must not do what I feel like doing, but what others want me to do. To be truly myself runs the risk of losing the love of others.

This data-entry operation generates several factors of conditioning that we will explore further in Chapter 5.

Yes *but,* I hear you say, is it really necessary to give a warm reception to all these emotions? Might we not run the risk of being manipulated by our emotions? You are doubtless thinking of some people who have been angry for fifty years and who have been wallowing in their anger without taking a single step forward—or others who are sad or homesick and dwell incessantly and morosely on their perceived problems, with little hope of escape. Still others rebel against everything and drag around their rebellion like a ball and chain, without ever finding peace. Indeed, swimming perpetually in one's feelings brings no development and may even induce nausea.

Our emotions are like waves of multiple feelings, pleasant or unpleasant, that are useful to identify and distinguish. It is useful to identify our feelings because they inform us about ourselves and invite us to identify our needs. Feelings operate like a flashing light on a dashboard, indicating that something is or is not operating properly, that a need is or is not being met.

As we are so often cut off from our feelings, we tend to have few words to describe them. On the one hand, we may feel good, happy, relieved, relaxed; on the other, we may feel fearful, rotten, disappointed, sad, angry. We have such a paucity of words to describe ourselves, and nonetheless we still function. In Nonviolent Communication training sessions, a list of more than two hundred fifty feelings is handed out to participants to enable them to expand their word power and, in so doing, broaden the consciousness of what they are feeling. This list doesn't draw its words from an encyclopedia or thesaurus. Rather, it is a glossary of common words that we read daily in newspapers or hear on television. However, a sense of propriety and reserve handed down from generation to generation in most families prevents us from using them when speaking about ourselves.

> **Developing our vocabulary expands our ability to deal with what we are experiencing.**

Much of what we learn from infancy onward plays a part in developing our awareness of subject matters or fields of interest that lie outside ourselves. As noted in the preamble, we become quite proficient at learning history, geography, and mathematics, and later we can specialize in plumbing, electricity, data processing, or medicine. We develop a vocabulary in all sorts of areas, and we thus acquire a certain mastery, a certain ease with which to deal with these matters.

Acquiring vocabulary goes hand in hand with developing awareness; it is because we have learned to name elements and differentiate among them that we can understand how they interact—and modify such interaction as necessary. Personally, I don't understand much about plumbing, and when my water heater doesn't switch on, I call a plumber and tell him what the problem is. My level of awareness of the elements at play and my ability to act on them are pretty close to zero. As for the plumber, he will identify what is going on and express that in practical terms: "The burner is dead" or "The pipes are scaled up, and the gas injector has had it." This gives the plumber power to act and, in this case, power to repair.

When I was still a practicing lawyer and received people in my office who were muddled, confused, and powerless when faced with legal difficulties, I experienced pleasure in sorting out the *matters at stake*, seeing how they interacted, defining priorities, and thus being in a position of strength to propose a way forward. Power of action is therefore tied to awareness and the ability to name elements and differentiate among them. Each of us has thus learned to exercise a degree of power of action in areas outside ourselves.

However, when in our education did we learn to name *what was at stake* in our inner life? When did we learn to become aware of what was going on within us, to distinguish and sort through our feelings, as well as our basic needs, to name those needs and then simply and flexibly make concrete and negotiable requests, taking into account the needs of others? How often do we feel helpless, even rebellious, at the powerlessness we experience relating to our anger, sadness, or nostalgia—feelings overflowing within us, poisoning us like some venom—without being able to react? To our feelings of being ill at ease and angry, sad or nostalgic, are now added discomfort and helplessness: "Not only am I unhappy or angry, I also don't know what to do to get out of it."

Often "to get out of it" we can only blame someone or something: Daddy, Mommy, the school, buddies, colleagues, clients, job, the state, pollution, the slump. Having neither understanding of nor control over our inner lives, we find a party outside ourselves to serve as a scapegoat for our pain. "I am angry because *you* . . . I am sad because *you* . . . I am disgusted because *the world* . . ."

We export our difficulty, we off-load it onto someone or something else as we are unable to process it ourselves. On the other hand, to be able to process what is happening within us, we need to develop a vocabulary of feelings and needs in order to become more at ease with the method. Little by little we gain mastery, which is not suffocation of our true needs and feelings. Instead, it is appropriate management of them.

Feelings act like a blinking light on a dashboard or control panel. They inform us about a need: A pleasant feeling shows that a need is being met; an unpleasant feeling indicates an unmet need. *It is therefore invaluable to be aware of this key distinction in order to identify what one needs. For, rather than complaining about what I do not want and often asking someone incompetent to help, I will be able to clarify what I want (my need rather than my lack) and to inform a competent person in order to get help—this person most often being "yours truly"!*

> **Feelings act like a blinking light on a dashboard; they tell us that an inner need is or is not being met.**

Here is an example I give at conferences: I am driving my car along a country road, and I may find myself in one of the following three situations:

1. I am driving an old car with no control panel, like a Model T Ford of the early 1900s. I'm driving along confidently, using up all the reserve gasoline and have no concern for my need for gas (since there is nothing to alert my awareness). Sooner or later I run out of gas in the middle of the countryside—no signal, no awareness of the need, no power to act.

2. A more conventional scenario: I'm driving a modern-day car that has a fully equipped dashboard. At some stage, my gas gauge shows me that I'm on reserve. So I complain: "Who forgot to put gas in this car? It's simply unbelievable; it always happens to me! Isn't there anyone

besides me in this family who can think about filling up?"
I complain and complain, so much so that I'm totally
absorbed by my complaining and fail to see all the gas
stations I drive past. Sooner or later I run out of gas in the
middle of the countryside. There had been a signal, I
became aware of the need, but I undertook no actions
to remedy the situation. I devoted all my energy to
complaining and seeking a guilty party and someone on
whom to vent my frustration.

3. A scenario advocated by Nonviolent Communication:
I'm still driving a modern-day car that has a fully
functioning dashboard/control panel. The gas gauge
shows that I'm on reserve. I identify my need: "Aha, I'm
going to need fuel, but I don't see a gas station right now.
What am I to do?" I then take concrete and positive
action. I will be *alert* to the next gas station I come across.
I'll go there and take care of my need. I provide the rescue
service myself. Being *aware* of the need I have voiced, I
awaken myself to the possibility of coming up with a
solution. The solution does not occur immediately, but as
I have become aware of the need, there is a much greater
chance I will come up with a solution than if, as in the
first scenario, I have no awareness.

If I sorted things out myself by filling up, this doesn't
mean I'm going to forgo my need for consideration or respect.
Back home, I may say to my teenage child or spouse: "I'm
disappointed at having had to fill up after you used the car
(feeling—F). I have a need for consideration of my time and
respect for having loaned you my car (need—N). In the future,
would you agree to filling up the tank yourselves (request—R)?"

Indeed, we are often alienated from our feelings through
our education or habit. This is even more so when it comes
to our needs.

3. Needs (or values)

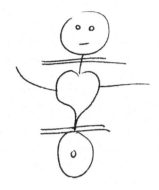

Most of us nowadays are to a large extent cut off from our feelings, and we are almost completely alienated from our needs.

I sometimes like to say that a concrete slab separates us from our needs. We have been taught to try to understand and meet the needs of others rather than listen to our own. Listening to oneself has long been synonymous with sin, or at least egocentricity or navel-gazing: "It is not right to listen to oneself like that. Oh, another person who listens to himself." The very idea that we might "have needs" is still very often perceived as problematic.

Now it's true that the word *need* has often been misunderstood. It does not mean a passing desire, a momentary impulse, a whim. We are referring here to our basic needs, the ones that:

- Are required simply to maintain life.
- We meet for the sake of balance
- Relate to our most basic human values: identity, respect, understanding, responsibility, liberty, mutual aid.

The more I practice NVC principles, the more I'm aware of the extent to which better understanding our needs enables us to better understand our values. I will expand on this issue a bit later.

In a workshop I was running, a mother was complaining how she failed to understand her children. A state of war reigned in the household, and she said she was exhausted at "having to require them to do a thousand things that either they appeared not to understand or that made them feel like doing exactly the opposite." When I asked her if she could identify her needs relating to this situation, she exploded and said:

"But it is not here on earth that we are meant to look after our needs! If everyone were to listen to their needs, war would break out all over. What you are offering is dreadful selfishness!"

"Are you angry (F) because you would like human beings to be attentive and listen to one another (N) in order together to come up with solutions to meet their needs?"

"Yes."

"Is your wish (N) that there should be understanding and harmony among human beings?"

"But of course."

"Well, you see, it's difficult for me to believe that you will ever be able to listen properly to the needs of your children if you don't begin by listening sufficiently to your own. It's hard for me to believe that you will be able to understand them in all their diversity and contradictions if you don't take the time to understand yourself and love yourself with all your multiple facets and your own contradictions. How do you feel when I say that to you?"

She was speechless, on the brink of tears. Then it was as if something clicked in her heart. The group stayed with her in silence, a moment of profound empathy. Then laughing, she observed: "It's incredible. I'm just realizing that I never learned to listen to myself. So I don't listen to them either. I just demand that they obey my rules! And of course they rebel. At their age, I rebelled too!"

Can we genuinely give proper listening attention to others without genuinely giving ourselves proper listening? Can we be available and compassionate toward others without being so toward ourselves? Can we love others with all their differences and their contradictions without first of all loving our own differences and contradictions?

> **If we cut ourselves off from our needs,
> there will be a price to pay—
> by ourselves and others.**

If we cut ourselves off from our needs, there will be a price to pay—by ourselves and others. Alienation from our needs generates "invoices" in various ways. Here are the most frequent ways:

- It is difficult for us to *make choices* that involve us personally. At work we usually manage to. But in our emotional, intimate lives, when it comes to more personal choices, how difficult it is! We hesitate, not knowing how to choose, hoping that eventually events or people will decide for us. Or we force the choice upon ourselves ("That's more reasonable . . . That's wiser"), helpless as we are to listen and understand our deeper yearnings.

- We have an addiction: the way others see us. Unable to identify our true needs, those that are personally our own, we become dependent on the opinions of others: "What do you think about that? . . . What would you do if you were in my place?" Or, worse, we fit perfectly into the mold of their expectations, such as we imagine them to be, without checking them and simply adapting or over-adapting to them: "Whatever will they think of me? . . . I absolutely must do this or that . . . I must behave in such and such a way, otherwise . . ." We wear ourselves out being dependent on others' recognition and, at worst, we become fad addicts ("Everyone does it like that . . . I'm going to behave like everyone else"). We become the playthings of various addictions (money, power, sex, television, gambling, alcohol, prescription drugs and other drugs, and now the Internet) or formal instructions (submitting to the authority of a demanding company, a directive political movement, or an authoritarian cult or sect). I have met many people suffering unconsciously or consciously from addictions recognized as such. In my view, the most widespread and the least recognized is the addiction to how we appear to others. We are not aware of our needs, and for good reason, since we weren't taught to recognize them. We therefore expect our needs to be met through drugs, alcohol, people. We become dispossessed of—and disconnected from—our deepest and truest selves.

- We have been taught to meet the needs of others, to be a good boy (or good girl), polite, kind, and courteous—the "good fellows," as Guy Corneau calls them, listening to everyone except oneself.[2] So, if one day, despite all that, we confusedly observe that our needs are not being met, then there is necessarily a guilty party, someone who has not bothered about us. We then get into the process of *violence by aggression or projection* referred to earlier, that is, a process where criticism, judgment, insults, and rebukes loom large. "I'm unhappy because my parents . . . I'm sad because my spouse . . . I'm feeling down because my boss . . . I'm depressed because of the economic situation or all the pollution . . . I'm in a bad mood because [name sports team] keeps losing . . ."

- More often than not, we have experienced being subservient to the needs of others (or we have feared not being able to have our needs met) to such an extent that we bossily impose our needs on others—and no questions asked. "That's how it is. Now, go and clean your room—and at once! . . . Do it because I said so, that's why." We then get into a process of *violence through authority*.

- We are exhausted at trying to get our needs met and forever failing. Finally, we capitulate: "I give up! I give up on myself. I close in on myself, or I run away." Here, the violence is directed against ourselves.

Yes, I hear you say, but what is the good of being aware of one's needs if it means living in perpetual frustration? And doubtless you are thinking of persons who have indeed identified their needs for a sense of community or some sort of recognition and who haphazardly spend life seeking to belong and be recognized, going from cocktail parties to meetings, from sports clubs to humanitarian activities, never satisfied.

Others, who so need to find their place, their identity, or their inner security, run to and fro from workshop to therapy, never finding real respite.

In the next chapter we will see how the very act of identifying our need, without it even being met, already produces relief and a surprising degree of well-being. In fact, when we are suffering, the first level of suffering is not knowing what we are suffering from. If only we could identify the inner cause of our discomfort, we would come through the confusion. Thus, if you do not feel well physically, if you have suspect stomach pains, headaches, or backaches, you get worried: "What is happening? Maybe it's cancer, a tumor . . ." If you see your doctor and he identifies the cause, pointing out that you are suffering from indigestion, that your liver is overloaded, or that you have twisted your back, the pain does not go away. However, you feel reassured in the knowledge of what is happening, and you cut through the confusion. The same is true of *need*. Identifying it makes it possible to get out of the confusion that only adds to our misery.

A key reason for us to be interested in identifying needs is that as long as we're unaware of our needs we don't know how to meet them. We often then wait for others (parents, spouse, child) to come along and meet our needs spontaneously, guessing what would please us, whereas we ourselves find it difficult to name those needs.

> **A key reason for us to be interested in identifying needs is that as long as we're unaware of our needs, we don't know how to meet them.**

Here are two examples of couples who came to me for consultations to sort out their relationship difficulties:

But first, notes on examples quoted

1. The examples from real life quoted in this book are deliberately abridged to avoid the length and detail of storytelling. I have endeavored to maintain the essence of the interaction because the exchanges took a lot longer than what appears here. Too, the time devoted to silence and inner work cannot be conveyed very well by the text, even though contemplative disciplines constitute a basic component of the work.

2. The tone or the vocabulary might at times seem naïve. I do this deliberately in many of my consultations in order to get to the heart of the matter, avoiding as much as possible any thinking or intellectualizing about what is truly at stake that might interfere with listening and inner awakening.

   In an atmosphere of openness and profound mutual respect, the simplest words and tone often have the greatest impact. I have observed that simplicity sharpens consciousness, because attention, being required only a little or not at all for intellectual understanding, is available for emotional understanding.

3. People's names have been changed, and sometimes roles have been reversed in order to respect confidentiality.

   In the first example, a wife is complaining about her husband's inability to understand:

   "He doesn't understand my needs."

   "Could you," I suggested, "tell me a need of yours that you would like him to understand."

   "Oh, no! He's my husband after all! It's up to him to understand my needs!"

   "Are you saying that you expect him to guess your needs, whereas you yourself find it difficult to determine them?"

   "Precisely."

   "And have you been playing this guessing game for a long time?"

"We've been married for thirty years."

"You must feel exhausted."

(She bursts into tears.) "Oh, I am! I'm at the end of my rope."

"Are you exhausted because you have a need for understanding and support on the part of your husband, and that is what you've been waiting for so long?"

"Yes, that's exactly it."

"Well, I fear you may wait a long time unless you clarify your needs for yourself and then tell him."

Then, after a long, tear-filled silence, she said: "You're right. I'm the one who is confused. You see, in my family, we were not allowed to have needs. I know nothing about my needs and, of course, I chide him for usually being wrong, without being able to tell him what I really want. Basically, I think he's doing his best, but in the heat of the moment I seldom tell him that. And then of course he gets angry, and I sulk. It's hell!"

With this couple, therefore, we did lengthy work on understanding and clarifying the needs of both. People who have always expected others to take care of them without doing much for themselves find it difficult to accept responsibility for themselves, and taking that initiative can be painful. However, it's only through work on the relationship with oneself that the relationship with others may improve.

In the second example, the husband is the one doing the complaining.

"My wife doesn't give me recognition!"

"Are you angry because you need to hear her express recognition?"

"Yes."

"Could you tell me what you'd like her to say or do to express the recognition you need?"

"I don't know."

"Well, she doesn't either! So it seems to me that you're

fervently expecting her to express recognition to you without you saying, in the most practical of terms, how you envision such recognition. It must be exhausting for her to sense on your part that there's a strong request for recognition, yet faced with it, she feels helpless. I suppose the more recognition you ask of her without saying specifically what that means, the more she flees."

"Yes, that's exactly how it is!"

"Then I suppose you're tired of this never-ending quest."

"Actually, exhausted."

"Exhausted because you want to share with her and feel close to her?"

"Yes."

"Then I suggest you tell her how you would like to receive recognition, in concrete terms, and in relation to what."

With this couple, we worked not on the need but on the practical request. This man felt wounded because he was not receiving the approval and recognition he wanted for the efforts he had made for years to provide the household with financial security, despite physical and professional circumstances of a trying nature. So he got stuck in complaining to his wife: "You fail to take the full measure of the efforts I've been making. You have no idea how hurtful that has been to me." And she, shutting herself off from each criticism, was incapable of reaching him through all the bitterness. Finally, I suggested the following:

"Would you like to know if your wife has taken the full measure of the efforts you made and if she appreciated your profound commitment?"

"Yes, that's exactly what I would like to ask her."

"Well," I turned to his wife, "you have heard that your husband would like recognition for his efforts. In more concrete terms, I would like to know if you're aware of the efforts he has made and whether or not you appreciate them."

"But of course I'm aware, and of course I appreciate them. I simply no longer know quite how to tell him. In the long run, I fear he can't hear me. It's true, I no longer respond, and I rush away to do something else."

"Do you mean that, in your turn, you would like him to be able to hear that you're not only aware of his efforts but also touched by them?"

"But of course, most touched, even moved, but he seems to be so hurt that he can no longer 'recognize' my appreciation."

Turning to her husband, I asked, "How do you feel when you hear that your wife is touched, even moved, by your efforts?"

"Very moved, in my turn, and relieved. I'm becoming aware that I was actually obsessed with my complaining and feeling I was not receiving the recognition I was expecting, and I was no longer aware of the affirmations that in fact she gave me regularly. I myself am shut away in a cage."

This awareness lightened the relationship and removed from it a weight that had, in effect, anesthetized the couple to the caring that each had for the other.

This second example makes two things clear:
a) As long as we fail to explain in concrete terms to the other party how we wish to see our need met, we might well see our request crushed under the weight of an insatiable need. It's as if we were to have the other person carry the full responsibility for this need. Faced with a threat like that, the other person goes slightly berserk and says, "I cannot on my own assume responsibility for this huge need (love, recognition, listening, support, etc.), so I take flight or shut myself off" (in silence or sulking). This is precisely what Guy Corneau describes with these words: "Follow me, I flee; flee me, I follow you."[3] The husband is clearly desirous of recognition. The wife is just as

desirous of escaping from the request. And the faster she takes to her heels, the more he chases after her.

Of course, this works in the other direction too. For example, a wife deeply wishes for tenderness and intimacy. Her husband panics when faced with such an expectation and seeks escape in work, sports, his papers. The farther away he goes, the more pressing her request. The more pressing her request, the farther away he moves. What he fears, perhaps even on a subconscious level, is having to meet a need for love unmet since childhood. That is too much for one man on his own. Were the situation reversed, it would be too much for a woman as well.

The lesson from this story: If needs aren't followed by a concrete request in an identifiable time and space (e.g., need for recognition: "Would you agree to thank me for specific efforts I've been making for thirty years?" . . . need for intimacy and tenderness: "Would you agree to take me in your arms for ten minutes and gently rock me?"), it often looks to the other person like a threat. The other person wonders if he or she will have the capacity to survive such an expectation and remain themselves, maintain their identity, and not be swallowed up by the other person.

It's worth remembering that we are often caught in the binary-thinking trap. Not knowing either how to listen to another's need without ceasing listening to our own or how to listen to our own need without ceasing listening to the need of another, we often terminate the relationship. We cut off the listening primarily to protect ourselves. When I perceive listening to another's need as a threat, I cut myself off from it and flee, or I take refuge in silence.

> **When I perceive listening to another's need as a threat, I cut myself off from it and flee, or I take refuge in silence.**

By expressing our practical request to the other party (e.g., "Would you agree to take me in your arms for ten minutes and gently rock me?"), we make the need less threatening ("I need love, tenderness, intimacy—help!") because we "materialize" it into reality, into our day-to-day existence. This is no longer a virtual need, apparently insatiable and threatening. Rather, it's a concrete request, well-defined in terms of space and time. In relation to a request like that, *we are able to position ourselves* and adopt a stance.

b) Another issue the above example clarifies is this: As we are obsessed by the idea of our need not being recognized, we aren't open to observing that it is so. The wife had striven to recognize her husband's efforts. Yet he was so caught up (or bogged down) in the notion of not being understood, that he couldn't hear her. This is a common phenomenon. By dint of repeating to ourselves the thought that we aren't being understood or recognized, that we are the subject of injustice or rejection, we give ourselves a new identity, to wit: "I am the one who is not understood, not recognized; I'm the one who is the subject of injustice or rejection."

We get caught in the rut of this belief to such an extent that the outside world may well send us messages of warmth, understanding, and belonging—but in vain for we can't hear them or see them. We will return to this matter in Chapter 3.

In these instances, it's necessary to work on fundamental needs. The questions we may be asking ourselves, among others, are as follows:

1. Am I able to provide myself with the esteem, the recognition, the warmth, the understanding that I'm so fervently expecting others to give me?
2. Can I begin to nurture these needs myself rather than maintain myself in a dependent position regarding the approving opinions of others?

And above all:

1. Am I able to experience my identity other than in complaints and rebellion?
2. Am I able to feel safe and secure in ways other than leaning on something or someone, other than by justifying myself or objecting?
3. Am I able to feel my inner security, my inner strength of and by myself, outside the domain of power and tension?

Once we have identified our need, we are going to be able to make a concrete, negotiable request designed to meet it.

4. The Request (or concrete and negotiable action)

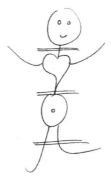

By formulating a request, or making a practical and negotiable proposal for action, we free ourselves from the third "concrete slab" that hampers us and prevents us from taking steps to meet our needs. By making a practical request, we release ourselves from the often intense expectation that another person should understand our need and accept the "duty" or challenge of meeting it. Such an expectation can last a long time and prove very frustrating.

Making a request means we assume responsibility for the management of our need and therefore assume responsibility for helping to meet it. Too often, though, we fall into the trap of mistaking our requests for fundamental needs.

The following example illustrates the distinction between a basic need, which forms an integral part of ourselves in most circumstances, and a practical request, which will vary according to circumstances.

The example of Terry and Andrea

During a workshop, I raise the issue of needs, stating that, in my view, human beings basically have the same needs. Doubtless they do not always express them in the same way, nor do they experience them in the same way at the same time. That is what lies behind marital, domestic, or school misunderstandings, the day-to-day battlefields of needs, not unlike wars waged with machine guns and missiles. To date, out of all of the behaviors I have observed, even the most frightening and the most appalling, I have been able to detect needs common to the whole of humankind.

Obviously, this is the basic hypothesis of my work, and it is based mainly on experience. In no way am I claiming to put forth a universal, comprehensive truth.

A participant, Terry, interrupted me and said: "I completely disagree with you. My wife and I do not have the same needs, and that has been the cause of so much tension that we're on the verge of divorcing. We've come together to attend your workshop just to make sure we've done everything we can. We'll be able to say to ourselves that we've left no stone unturned, but it's without much conviction, especially when you start out by stating that basically human beings have the same needs."

I suggested he come up with an actual situation where he

got the impression that he did not have the same needs as his wife. This was his answer:

"Well, it happened a few months back. Things just exploded between us. You need to know that we both work outside the home, and we have three children. One weekend, the children had been invited to stay with their cousins. I came home on the Friday evening after work, tired and . . . whew (a long sigh), I really needed to go out to a restaurant with my wife. Do you think she did? Not in the least! She needed to stay at home and watch a movie. I then told her that she had no understanding at all about my needs, and she said it was exactly the same for her. We both flew into a rage, and in the end I went to bed in the children's room. Since then, we continually have the impression that we do not share the same needs."

"When you came home that evening, what feelings were alive in you?"

"Whew (another sigh). I was tired."

"It looks like an unpleasant feeling to be experiencing at that time, and it shows that a need was not being met. Could you tell us what that need was?"

"That's easy—a need for rest, of course. Hence the idea of going out to eat that evening. No meal to get ready; no washing to do!"

"So your feeling of fatigue shows a need for rest, for relaxation at that time. At the same time, I observe your sighing, a reference to your tiredness. You twice gave a long sigh. My impression is that the sigh is the expression of another feeling. What lies behind that sigh? If you go down a bit into your 'well,' what other feeling was with you then?"

Terry stopped for a moment to think.

"Well, I think that in addition to the fatigue of the week (it was Friday, and we had been on the run since Monday), there was an older tiredness. We have been running around for months—years—with work, the children, the house, and we don't see much of each other."

"A feeling of lassitude, being used up?"

"Yes, lassitude, deep lassitude, and a kind of listlessness."

"And what unmet need did this unpleasant feeling point to?"

Once again Terry listened within. "I believe I just said it: My wife and I don't see each other anymore. I need time to be with her, to connect. I need time for us to join with each other again and share intimacy."

As Terry was expressing his needs, his wife, Andrea, sitting not very far from him in our circle, bursts into tears. "It's crazy," she said. "I had exactly the same need! I had gone to buy a prepared dish and a bottle of wine both of us like. I went to the video store to rent a movie we had never had the time to go see and, for once, the children were not at home. I was preparing for us to spend a happy little evening together as lovers, precisely to be able to get together for a few hours and share some intimacy!"

So what happened? What was it that occurred that led this couple, lucky enough to have the same need at the same time, to declare war on each other? Well, they mistook their requests for fundamental needs, and the needs became an obsession. Terry mistook his request to go out for a meal for a basic need, and Andrea did not listen. Andrea mistook her request to stay at home for a basic need, and Terry did not understand! Both Andrea and Terry stuck to their guns—and both were unconsciously trapped in their little cage! It wasn't so much the wife failing to listen to the husband as the husband not having listened to himself before opening his mouth. It wasn't so much the husband not understanding the wife as the wife not having taken the time to understand herself before opening her mouth.

I suggested re-enacting the scene. Terry and Andrea had had some practice and were aware that underlying their request, which was their present wishes, there was a basic need. If we listen to this basic need and understand it, we give ourselves the freedom to formulate a variety of requests to explore various wishes and to release ourselves from the trap into which the need/request confusion can plunge us.

To facilitate understanding of the example, I have again shown in parentheses the abbreviations for the components of the process: observation (O), feeling (F), need (N), request (R).

The role-play began.

"Darling," Terry began, "this evening I'm tired (F). I just need to rest. I don't feel like cooking or anything else (N), and I would like to know if you are in agreement for us to go out for a meal (R)?"

"Honey, I'm dead beat too. I'm happy (F) that we have the same need for rest (N). At the same time I feel sad (F) that we've both been so busy in recent times. I need to spend some quiet time with you, just the two of us (N), and I'm so afraid (F) that if we go out to dinner, we'll be bothered by the waiter or distracted by friends. So I prefer to stay quietly at home. Everything is already on the table for the meal. We can dine, just the two of us, and then afterward, if you like, we can watch a movie I've rented that we haven't had time to see yet (R)."

"You're making me aware that I have the same need: to regain some lost intimacy with you, to spend the evening together, just the two of us, and that's why I suggested going out for a meal this evening. At the same time, when I hear your proposal to stay at home, I feel a bit disappointed (F) because I also need a change of scenery, to get out of the house for once when the children aren't here (N). So now that we have set out the criteria of what is at stake for us [formerly that would have been called a conflict!]— need for relaxation, need to get together, and have a change of scenery—what solution, what concrete action could we come up with to meet these varying needs?"

During that workshop, once Andrea and Terry had played out their exchange and deciphered it, they found that what would please both of them most that evening would be to go for a walk to the end of a lake in their area, taking a picnic basket with them and a little wine. In the old days when they were in love, they often went there, arm in arm. And then they got caught up by their working lives to such an extent that they forgot to even think about it. Yet this walk would have truly nurtured their need to get together, to relax, and to have a change of scenery!

This example sheds light on four main points:

1. We fall into the trap ourselves—and tend to drag the other person in too—when we don't take care to differentiate our true need from our request. By seeing what underlies our request and identifying our need, *we give ourselves freedom*. We note, for example, that we can meet our need for intimacy and getting together with our spouse or our need for rest (restaurant, walk, movie) in all sorts of different ways. We escape from the fallacy that there is only one solution.

2. By taking care of our true need instead of haggling over our request, we together free ourselves from the trap, and *we give ourselves a space to meet, a space to create!* Andrea and Terry, harassed by the pace of their lives, had not taken time to get together or to be creative to make their evening truly satisfying. The solution they finally came up with, after looking at their needs together, proved much more innovative and satisfactory than any they had hastily come up with previously on their own.

> **By taking care of our true need instead of haggling over our request, we give ourselves a space to meet, a space to create!**

3. In this spirit, it is useful to observe that we often skip to the "quickly done, poorly done" solution. For a long time I worked as a legal adviser to an American company where the expression "quick and dirty" was the common way of describing a quick solution to meet an emergency when there wasn't enough time to look for the best solution.

   Thus Terry, coming back tired from the office, decided on the quick-and-dirty solution to take his wife out for supper. Andrea, in the same way, coming back from her work completely drained, hurriedly buys a dish from the corner take-out and rents a video. Both of these initiatives of course have their value. However, it can be seen that neither he nor she really took the time to ask, "Deep down, how am I feeling this evening, and what would truly do me and my partner the most good? What would meet our real needs?"

This is one of the consequences of our education: seeking intellectually to solve things—and solve things fast!—using our intelligence, our performance capabilities, getting immediate results, moving as quickly as possible from seeing the problem to solving it without *taking the time to listen to what is truly at stake.*

Some time ago, I was emptying our dishwasher and putting away the utensils in a kitchen drawer. As I was closing the drawer, it stuck halfway. Bang! With a swing of the hip, I tried to close it by force. But it refused to budge, and I wound up with a painful hip, a damaged drawer, and a bent fork! Quick and dirty indeed. I was bowled over. What old "force to solve" pattern was alive in me? I thought I had released myself quite considerably from my own violence, but I still had some way to go when it came to acceptance and listening. Observing that the drawer is stuck, pulling it out, bending over, observing what is blocking the drawer, suggesting to the wayward fork that it lie down quietly among its kin, then simply closing the drawer . . . Thank you, fork, for having taught me to listen and accept before looking for a solution.

Since that time, I have truly believed ever more deeply that violence is a habit, an old reflex we can get rid of if we really want to. I'll cover this in greater detail in the last chapter.

4. *Our misunderstandings are often "mis-listenings,"* themselves resulting from "mis-expressions," "ill-spokens," and "unspokens." We are capable of learning to speak with sensitivity, force, and truth.

Remarks

1. Terry and Andrea as a couple were lucky enough to have the same need at the same time. This of course facilitated the negotiation of requests and the adoption of a common satisfactory solution. Having had the opportunity to clarify this misunderstanding in a way that finally pleased them, they went deeper into their training and found pleasure again in joining each other in the life they led together.

   To be sure, not all disputes work out like that one. I can quote the example of spouses who had gotten to the stage of throwing plates at each other before they went to a training session together. After some practice they learned to listen to each other. It was even agreed between them that in their drawing room there would be two "nonviolent armchairs." When a tiff occurred in the household, they would cry: "Stop! Armchairs!" As in a game of musical chairs where children chase each other, they placed themselves in a Nonviolent Communication zone where the instruction was "Here each takes turns to speak and to listen."

   After a while they observed that they didn't operate at all at the same pace, that their respective needs were doubtless the same but seldom at the same time, and this made life together very difficult and, finally, unbearable. So they decided to split, to go arm in arm to see a lawyer and then the judge. They went as friends who loved and respected each other. One day after their divorce they told me they spent at least one evening a week together, and there they finally nurtured the friendship, the trust, and the transparency between them that they had always dreamed of. Such a relationship, however, had been impossible to achieve living under the same roof.

   It's often difficult to observe peacefully, with esteem and compassion, that we aren't in agreement. Difference and therefore disagreement are frequently perceived as a threat.

2. We tend to be justly proud of our language and its wealth of nuances. However, verbal language represents but a tiny percentage of communication. Nonverbal language, according to the specialists, is thought to make up some 90 percent of our communication, while a mere 10 percent comprises verbal language! Being aware of that enables us to be attentive to our own body language (our tone of voice, our speed of delivery, our facial expressions, our body positions), as well as the body language of other people. To become aware of this, note the impact, the power of a single reproachful look or, on the other hand, a look of approval coming from someone close (parent, spouse, child, hierarchical superior, teacher).

   In secondary school, we had a Latin and French teacher we liked very much, particularly on account of his humor and volubility. When he would tell us, once a month, that he would start the first lesson in the afternoon ten minutes late because he had a meeting, each time he told us mischievously, "And when I do come, I'll be listening to hear nothing!" We loved the way he used words; he stimulated our young grey matter and made us appreciate the finer points of language. Returning from his meeting (we carefully respected his instructions, out of affection and respect for him), he came in from the back of the classroom and went right up to the blackboard without a word. He looked us up and down approvingly, one hand cupped behind his ear to show he was listening and hearing not a sound, the other hand showing with thumb and index joined that he appreciated the quality of the silence we had respected. When he reached his desk he started teaching at once. We had no need for any other sign of recognition for our efforts to be silent. Although I was highly amused by each of these little rituals, I was astounded at the strength and sobriety of his presence alone, where not a word was spoken. Nor did it need to be.

CHAPTER 2

Becoming Aware of What We Are Truly Experiencing

> *I do not at all like those who claim
> that there is merit in having worked
> painfully. Were it painful, better had
> they done something else. The joy that
> one finds in one's work is the sign of
> owning it. The sincerity of my pleasure,
> Nathanaël, is my most precious guide.*
>
> ANDRÉ GIDE
> French author, Nobel Prize winner

Wearing Oneself Out Doing Good

A man came up to me in a workshop and said: "I'm not one for feelings, and even less for needs. Now my wife, she has feelings and needs. So do my children and my boss—but not me, not a thing. Duty, yes. Obligations, yes. I'm familiar with them."

"And what makes you say that?"

"It so saddens me . . ."

"So you see you can recognize one feeling: sadness."

"Oh, yes!"

"And why does it sadden you?"

"Because I would love to live like that too. It seems to be a more 'alive' way of life."

"Can you see? You too can identify basic needs: the need for sharing and the need for being more alive."

"You're right," he said, tears suddenly welling up in his eyes. "I have so often heard that a man doesn't cry, that a man represses his feelings, that a man does his duty. I couldn't so much as dare think that I might want something, have a personal craving."

Although we often are not aware, we cannot be feeling-free. Even if we were to believe that we only listen to the needs of others, we cannot be need-free. And more than that, we devote the greater part, if not the whole, of our time attempting to meet needs we know so little about.

If we think we can listen only to the needs of others and not our own, we are simply unaware that we are acting in the service of one of the strongest and most pervasive needs among human beings: to take care of others, to contribute to their well-being.

The old and unfortunate habit of binary thinking has made us believe that taking care of ourselves means ceasing to take care of others and then, in order to take care of others properly, one has to "forget oneself"!

Why should there be this mutual exclusion between care for others and care for ourselves?

When I think of the human beings—so many of them—who have forgotten themselves and either pay the price for that themselves or make others pay for it, my own sadness is boundless. My sadness tells me how much I would like human beings to understand that their own joy and well-being are first and foremost as they care for others. If this isn't the case, it would be better for them *and* others if they did something else.

How many people—particularly in welfare and education (teachers, social workers, doctors, nurses, therapists)—have not overextended themselves and worked themselves to the bone, even going so far as a nervous breakdown, helping others while disregarding themselves? They often do themselves so much damage doing good that they're no longer capable of doing much of anything. They have so cut themselves off from themselves to such an extent that their energy and vitality have run out; a spring has broken. Sometimes it's only through a jolt (depression, an accident, grieving, loss of job) that life itself brings them back to themselves. Those parts of ourselves that we fail to listen to ultimately have ways of giving us vigorous reminders that they exist. Thus, violence, often unconsciously directed toward ourselves, causes life to react violently. If we live in violence toward ourselves and toward life (demanding, controlling, overworking, feeling guilty), we run the risk of producing a violent reaction from life itself (an accident, disease, depression, mourning).

> **Those parts of ourselves that we fail to listen to ultimately have ways of giving us vigorous reminders that they exist.**

As noted above, some people unconsciously make others pay for this failure to have regard for themselves. How many people in social work are so overloaded that they lose their receptiveness, their humor, their humanity? Despite their concern to "do good," they often wind up doing more harm than good. Thus, in the medical world exhaustion can too often bring about negligence in care or attention—and in the educational world saturation in the wake of too many demands can bring about rejection or closure toward a pupil requiring special attention.

Having been a committed volunteer for some ten years in an association looking after young people with various addictions, delinquency, anorexia, depression, prostitution, and so on, I can state two things:

1. In order to survive, it is a matter of urgency to clearly distinguish between taking care of and taking responsibility for. I will come back to this.

2. The only sustainable way of taking proper care of anything, in my view, is by deriving deep pleasure from it, feeling great satisfaction for the other person at the accomplishments and steps taken. If even a part of us is acting out of duty, out of sacrifice, because "I must"—and feels such things as obligation, constraint, and guilt—this part eats up our energy and vitality and sooner or later turns on itself by coming through in the form of anger, rebellion, or depression.

On this subject, I remember what someone said about a hike we were organizing for some thirty troubled young people in the Sahara Desert, "Basically you have a good time during these trips, so what's the merit in going on them?"

A dialogue ensued, starting with my reply, "Do you feel concerned because you would like to be reassured that we take proper care of the young people who go with us?"

"Yes, because if you do go, it's because you have a good time."

"Is it difficult for you to imagine that one can both have a good time and please others, take care of your own well-being and the well-being of others *at the same time?*"

"Right. I've always seen those two things as mutually exclusive. Either I take care of myself, or I take care of others and disregard myself."

"And how do you feel when I tell you that what I enjoy about organizing this trip is that I'm nurturing *both* my need for discovery, space, and exploration *and* my need to share what I love, contributing to the well-being of others by bringing them along for this adventure?"

"I hadn't seen things like that before. That's new for me. In fact, it's a relief for me to get out of the middle of the opposition between the two."

"For me, not only is it a relief, it mobilizes my energies at the same time. My whole being is invested in this adventure, all my vitality. There's not a single part of me that says, 'Whoa, I'd just as soon stay at home and read a book by the fireplace, or I'd rather go skiing with friends.' No. Aware that my needs are not mutually exclusive, I am fully into whatever I'm doing, and the young people are aware of my availability to them and the joy this inner unity brings about. It awakens in them their own need for unity, vitality, commitment, a taste for life."

But let's come back to needs. We can often cut ourselves off from our feelings and our needs, that is, prohibit ourselves from feeling them and listening to them, then "bury them in concrete." However, we're unable to be feeling-free and need-free, even though we're often quite unconscious of the fact. Our consciousness is invaluable because to an ever-greater extent I believe that the fact of feeling and sharing is what nurtures human nature at the deepest level. Thus, our most intimate and most essential well-being is born of the quality of the relationship we maintain with ourselves, with others, and with the environment in which we live.

Do we not feel the greatest joys when we are communicating clearly with ourselves and those close to us? . . . when we are connected to ourselves and those we love? . . . when relationships are based on esteem and trust, what I call "together-well-being"? Conversely, do we not feel the greatest pain when we fail to see clearly within ourselves? . . . when we feel alienated from ourselves? . . . when we no longer have clarity regarding a relationship and feel cut off from a person we love? Thus, our happiness, our well-being, does not come from *what* we possess, nor from *what* we do, but from *how we live* our relationship with others, our activities, and the world around us.

Since I have been seeking to understand and give meaning to the difficulty of being, I note that the people who radiate deep well-being, a joy of living in this world, are those who give precedence not to the number of things they do, nor their possessions, but to the quality of the relationships they have with others, with their environment, and with what they do—beginning with the quality of the relationship they have with themselves. These people don't seek to fill their lives with things to do or people to pass time with, but to fill life with the relationships they nourish and the things they care about doing.

So it seems to me that our truest wealth, our heritage, the source of our deepest and most sustainable joys lies in our ability to establish nurturing and meaningful relationships with ourselves, with others, and with the universe around us. And doubtless that is both the most obvious and the most difficult thing! And small wonder . . .

1. *We are seldom connected to reality, as it actually is.* Most of the time we relate to reality as we believe it to be or, more to the point, as we fear it to be. So we will see how to relate as objectively as possible to reality as it actually is and not just as we see it (compare "Observing Without Judging or Interpreting," p. 54).

2. *Our reactions tend to be based on our impressions, beliefs, and prejudices* rather than on what we truly and personally feel. This means frequently we aren't listening to ourselves properly. We will therefore see how to listen to our own feelings, the ones that lead us where we go, differentiating them from those that involve blame or criticism toward another (compare "Feeling Without Judging or Interpreting," p. 69).

3. *We act as a function of outside criteria*: habit, tradition, duty, imposed or presupposed ("I believe I have to . . ."); and fear of the judgments of others (social pressure) where the others may be parents, spouse, children, social and professional environment, or, more simply, parts of ourselves we aren't well-acquainted with, which we fear will judge us and make us feel guilty. We will see how to listen to our fundamental needs, how to identify them, differentiate among them, establish priorities (compare "Identifying Our Needs Without Projecting Them onto Others," p. 80).

4. Finally, because we're unable to understand and process our

own needs easily and flexibly . . . and correspondingly unable to understand and process the needs of others easily and flexibly, *we often sacrifice our own needs to please others,* to "be nice." Exasperated at having been nice for so long or anxious at not having our needs recognized, *we impose our needs on others,* or we expect others to guess the needs we have neither expressed nor even identified. And if they do not do so, we criticize them for this and judge them. Sometimes this dynamic is termed the "martyr complex."

> ## We often sacrifice our own needs to please others, to "be nice."

We will see how to make clear and precise requests that make it possible for our needs to be met day by day, also taking into account the needs of others (compare "Formulating a Concrete, Realistic, Positive, Negotiable Request," p. 98).

In this chapter, we will endeavor to develop as much as possible our awareness of what we are experiencing at each of the following stages:

- OBSERVATION. We are reacting to something we observe, we hear, or we're saying to ourselves.
- FEELING. The above observation generates within us one or more feelings.
- NEED. The feelings guide us to our needs.
- REQUEST. Aware now of our needs, we can make a request or implement concrete action.

These four stages can easily be remembered by using the acronym OFNR.

You can see that the idea is not to lose one's head but to put it back in the right place! We need to say to our head, to our mental processes: "Thank you for the good services rendered. I often need you (to check the restaurant bill, to file my tax return, to draw up a contract, to analyze a situation, to manage my budget), but not all the time. I do not want you to be in charge of every part of my life, to make choices for me as if you were in a control tower. I also need to trust my intuition, listen to my feelings, deal with my needs at my own pace and with respect. Basically, *I need to feel whole and reunited; I don't want to be divided anymore, split between my head and my heart.* Stating it a bit crassly, I don't want to be little more than a brain on legs!"

Observing Without Judging or Interpreting

To paraphrase the words of the Indian philosopher Krishnamurti, distinguishing between the observation of a fact and the interpretation thereof constitutes one of the highest levels of human intelligence. It is certainly one of the most difficult and least "natural" things to do: differentiating between the fact, such as it is, and the emotion it generates in us. We often completely distort the facts. The way we decipher facts means that they take on the color of fear, hope, projections, and so on. We are therefore no longer in contact with reality, the factual truth, but rather with our own preoccupations and interpretations, with the more or less fictional film of this reality that we're showing—and we can even build our entire lives on that basis: all of our attitudes and thoughts on a subjective reading of reality. We do so without understanding the misery of misunderstandings and cross-purposes that such an attitude can drag us into.

On the contrary, I am seeking to invite people to get out of the interpretation/projection trap by verifying the facts.

Ping-Pong escalation

I may believe that I'm making an objective observation when I say, "My friend has been giving me the cold shoulder for days now." I'm running a strong risk of feeling blame, railing against him, or perhaps being peevish with him in turn. In any event, I'm feeling as ill-tempered as hell, probably with no good grounds. Therefore, on the basis of a highly subjective interpretation, I trigger a process of verbal violence.

In fact, how do I really know he's ignoring me? Perhaps he's sad or preoccupied for completely different reasons. Possibly he has a migraine. But I, because this observation worries me, decide that he's giving me the cold shoulder without checking that out with him. The scenario I invent is totally disconnected from reality.

My little drama involves two risks:

1. I get into a state to no avail, and it burns up most of my energy.
2. I might well aggress my friend and generate violence myself. I might, for example, approach him, saying something like "I'm fed up with you being in a huff."

To which he might well retort: "Don't be silly. I'm not in a huff."

"Of course you are."

"No, I'm not."

Or, quite common too: "Of course I'm giving you the cold shoulder and naturally it's your fault," and we might get into another game of argumentative Ping-Pong: "You are wrong, I am right."

The cornerstone of the method being recommended here is making observations that are as neutral as possible: State facts (quotes, body positions, facial expressions, tone of voice) just like a camera would. We have to be so attentive to how we "enter" into conversation with another person.

Remarks

To make the process easier to understand, here's an abridged version of it:

1. I *observe* that my friend has not spoken to me since the beginning of the meal and has left the room without speaking (O).
2. This observation generates a *feeling* in me: I feel concerned, irritable, helpless (F).
3. This complex of feelings shows I have a *need*: I need to know if something is wrong, need to understand, and perhaps need to be ready to offer my help (N).
4. In practical terms, my *request*, my *action*, will be to check how he feels—to see if he has concerns and if I can do something to lighten his load (R).

   I approach him, saying, "When I saw that you left the room during the meal without speaking (O), I began to feel concerned (F), and I would like to know if something is on your mind and if I can help (N + R)."

   This is a formulation that may appear naïve and somewhat impractical in ordinary life! It could be made more plausible and less academic by saying: "It seems to me that you are more quiet than usual. Is something wrong?" What I observe is that this way of "opening" a conversation, approaching an issue without judgment or interpretation, not only makes us better disposed to listen to the other person, it also extends an invitation to the other individual to talk to us from the heart about what they are feeling, without any sense of being criticized.

"You are so sloppy!"

Here's another example I often test out on schoolchildren.

Let's imagine you're a twelve-year-old child. You come home from school about four in the afternoon. It's raining. The bus was late, and your mother welcomes you in the first thirty seconds with: "You always leave your shoes on the stairs. You've thrown your jacket on the sofa and your backpack into the middle of the living room. Anyone would think you're the only person living in this house! Go and clean it all up, and be quick about it! And while you're at it, your room is like a war zone. You can clean that up too, right now!"

Ask yourself how you feel now, and see what state of mind you're in.

With children, I often receive one of the following two reactions:

1. "Well, if she screams like that, I'm certainly not going to clean up anything. I'm going to get mad. And it won't be any fun. Both of us are going to sulk the whole evening."
2. "Well, I won't have any choice. I'll put my stuff away. But I'll make sure I slam all the doors, bang my feet on every stair up to my room, and turn my boom box all the way up (with the music she hates most) to get back at her." (The latter would be an illustration of the classic passive-aggressive response.)

I then suggest to the schoolchildren the substitute formulation below. The circumstances are the same. It's four o'clock in the afternoon. It's raining. The bus was late. Your mother welcomes you, saying: "When I see your shoes on the stairs, your jacket on the sofa, and your backpack on the living room carpet (O), I feel sad and disheartened (F) because I took so much time and energy cleaning up the house, and I need respect for the work I do and would like others to cooperate in keeping the house clean (N). I would like to know if you would agree to clean up your things now (concrete, negotiable R)?"

I usually get one of two reactions:

"Well, if my mother always asked me to do things like that, I would do them right away."

"Why?"

"Because I hate being told to do things without any reason. But if I'm told why and am given the choice, often I do with pleasure what I'm asked to do. I like the house to be clean and neat when I come home."

"Well, it's more pleasant to hear that than the first version. It's great to have a clean house, and I like to help. But when I come back from school, what I want most of all is to be left in peace for a while to unwind."

So we do a role-play. I play the mother.

"So you're saying you're willing to clean up, but you've had a tiring day (F), and you'd like a bit of a breather first (N)?"

"That's right. I want to have a can of pop, then I'll clean up afterward."

"Basically, I want to be reassured more than anything else (F) that you will think about it later so that I'm not the only one who sees to it that the house is cleaned up (N). Can you understand that?"

"Yes, of course."

"When you say, 'Yes, of course,' and start heading to the kitchen, I'm not sure (F) that you have understood my needs (N) and the things I'm saying. I would therefore like to know if you would be willing to repeat them (R)."

"OK. You want to be sure I don't forget to clean up everything—and you're not the only one to keep the house neat. Is that it?"

"That's right. Thank you."

Remarks

1. Children are often hypersensitive about how a conversation starts. They haven't yet acquired protective armor against the brusqueness of adults' usual manner of conversation. So, in the first version, when the mother uses such phrases as "You always leave your shoes lying around" and "You've thrown your jacket on the sofa again," children feel like answering: "That's not true. Two days ago I put my shoes away and my jacket too, and I had never left it there before!" Once again, we're

up against "Yes, but" and "No, not at all." And once again we run the risk of Ping-Pong escalation ("It's always the same way with you . . . You're always picking on me . . . You let my sister do anything . . . You only see what I do *wrong*!").

The neutral observation of the second version ("When I see your shoes on the staircase and your jacket on the sofa . . .")—with no judgment, no interpretation, no criticism, neither in tone of voice nor in facial expression (beware, this is difficult; nonverbal expression is powerful)—makes it possible to *open* the dialogue in a way that makes the following outcomes possible:

Expressing our feelings and needs in a clear way *such that they can be heard by the other party.*

The other person being able to open up and listen to us in order to understand. This empowers us to move forward together toward a satisfying solution *for each party*, not just for the mother, as would have been the case had she made her need for order into a requirement without listening to her child's need for respite—and not just for the child, as would have been the case had the mother repressed her need for order and collaboration so as to be "nice" to her child.

Stating the observation in a neutral way doesn't mean we're repressing our feelings. It means we start the conversation in a way that respects reality and the vision that the other person has of it (which may be quite different from our own), and that enables us to communicate to the other person the full force of our feeling without judging or aggressing.

> **Stating an observation in a neutral way doesn't mean we're repressing our feelings.**

2. When I do this exercise with children, the reply regarding coercion is almost always the same. In the final analysis, whether adult or child, we generally hate doing things out of obligation. We need to (1) understand the meaning and (2) act freely. *Meaning* was provided in this particular situation by mentioning the needs: "I took care to clean up the house, and I need respect for the work I do."

As for *freedom*, it is ensured by the way the request is formulated. It is expressed in negotiable terms (otherwise it ceases to be a request and becomes a demand; we then fail to establish the quality of connection we wish to have): "I would like to know *if you would agree* to putting your things away now." *This stage is the most difficult*: accepting that the other person may not agree to what we want! It's worth remembering that often, as long as our needs are not recognized, we make them into requirements: "Go clean up your room immediately!" This is not a negotiable request but a demand that doesn't leave the other person free. So either the other person will submit, or they will rebel. What is often the case is that others will not act willingly and joyfully to contribute to our well-being! You may say: "But sometimes there are things that have to be done, boundaries to be imposed. You can't give free rein all the time." Indeed, I hear your need for structure, to have solid reference points. We'll be expanding on that issue later.

I can state that I have not yet met anyone, whether adult or child, who fundamentally does not enjoy contributing to the well-being of others, even if such willingness is well-hidden, buried in a corner of the heart or transformed into aggression through bitterness. I, for example, have met young people with aggressive tendencies, particularly toward elderly people, speaking tearfully about their own parents or grandparents who are sick or in difficulty. So I am confident that we're fully able to join them in that common need: contributing to the welfare of others.

Experience also has shown me that this need can be hampered or stifled if other needs, perhaps ones more vital for the person concerned, are not met: recognition, being welcomed, having one's place, being loved for who one is rather than for what one does, being respected, considered to be a whole human being, and so on. Many refusals are an expression of the fact that one or another of these needs is not being met. For example, children don't want to clean up their things because sloppiness is practically the only way they have come up with to express themselves, to express their differences or their identities, to draw attention to themselves, to get more consideration than the little sister or the big brother. As Guy Corneau says in *The Tragedy of Good Boys and Good Girls,* "If I haven't learned how to get it right or have failed to be recognized for getting it right, then I prefer to get it wrong."[4]

3. When I do the exercise with mothers, I notice they are practically always willing to listen and respect the child's need for a breather and to have a snack before putting things away *so long as* their own needs for order and support in the organization of the household are recognized, shared, *and* taken into consideration in concrete ways. In fact, it's not that they really want the tidying up to be done at once, it is rather that they are tired of being the only one in the family to put things away— the shoes, the books, everyone's toys—and moms are the only ones who feel concerned about order. And most of the time they have come up with no way of getting what they want and need other than by demanding it.

   I have seen radical changes take place in family or marital systems once the individuals concerned are careful to clarify their respective needs with compassion for the other party and with confidence in themselves—and by ensuring that they have been understood by the other person.

4. In the expression "You always leave all your things lying around," which many believe is an objective observation,

there is perhaps just one objective word—and that might be *you!* And worse, the sentence is spoken in a tone easily interpreted as *accusing*.

- The word *always* allows the same tiredness to show. Obviously, what just occurred does not occur always, and the other person, of course, will not miss the opportunity to retort: "That's not true! Yesterday, I put everything away." And he would be furious that I had judged him unjustly and not recognized his efforts of the previous day, even if his toys, shoes, and sports gear are embellishing various parts of the house.

- The word *leave* judges an attitude more than it observes a behavior: I'm tired of seeing others' things in places where I would like to see something else, so I deem that the items have been thrown down, whereas the other person is perhaps happy with where the things have ended up.

- The word *all* is used inaccurately here. Obviously, it is not a question of all, and the other person, of course, will not fail to point that out to me: "That's not true! Yesterday, I cleaned up all my mess." He will be furious that I failed to appreciate this gesture, even if his toys, shoes, and sports gear are embellishing various parts of the house.

- The expression *lying around* is too strong. He will instantly think, then say: "I live, I play, I create, and I'm alive, right? And all you can say is that I leave things *lying around*. You're not in touch with reality, are you, you grown-ups?!"

As you can see, virtually every word in this sentence generated resistance, opposition, and defiance in the other person. By starting a dialogue in this way, we can count on the *noncollaboration* of other people who feel themselves judged and criticized as a matter of course. They will then be putting their energy into justifying themselves, attempting to save face rather than listening to our need. Indeed, in our often almost desperate quest for another's approval, we tend, when there is conflict, to strive to re-establish unanimity as soon as possible by argument, control, or even submission.

By contrast, if we start dialogue with a neutral reference to something that is preoccupying us (neutral observation: "I see your stuff lying on the carpet in the drawing room, your shoes on the hall carpet, and your toys on the staircase"), we take advantage of the opportunity to inform the other person of our need. And, so that it will not be heard as criticism or an obligation that will exclude freedom of action, we take care to formulate an open and negotiable request. For example: "I feel sad and upset because I need order and help when it comes to keeping the house clean (F, N). I would like to know if you would agree to putting your things away in your bedroom (R)."

Using this approach, our thinking head, with its intelligence, has been of great value to us in making an assessment of the facts.

Exercise

Try the following exercise: observing without judging, *then* listening to what is happening to you in terms of feelings and needs.

Do not say:	Say rather:
"You're late; it's always the same with you! You can never really be relied on."	"We had an appointment at eight in the morning. It's now half past ten. (O)."
	"I feel angry and worried (F)."
	"I need to understand what's happening, to be reassured that I can count on you in the future (N)."
	"Would you agree to talk to me about that now (R)?"

"I'm in it right up to my eyeballs. It's hopeless. The bottom has fallen out of my world. I might as well throw myself in front of a train."	"I've just lost my job, and my wife has announced that she wants to leave me (O)." "I feel panicky, powerless, and disgusted as I never imagined I could be (F)." "I really need time to see things more clearly, and I have a huge need to trust myself and to believe that I'm capable of getting through this (N)." "I'm going to take the time to try to fully comprehend all this before deciding what to do (R)."
"You are such a loser! You'll never get anywhere. You're just a hopeless case!"	"When I look over your school report and I see F for math, D for chemistry (O) . . ." "I feel really worried (F)." "I need to know that you see there is meaning in studying these subjects, that you enjoy learning, and that you feel well-integrated in your class (N) . . ." "And I would like to know if you would agree for us to take time to talk about how you feel and what you want in this regard (R)."

"I am very emotional."	"When I experience a strong emotion (O) . . ." "I feel upset and ill at ease (F) . . ." ". . . because I need to have a better understanding of my feelings in order to be able to make better use of them and have greater self-control (N)." "Next time I feel a strong emotion, I'll plan to take time to bring it on board within and listen to what it's telling me about myself and about the needs it's calling to my attention (R)."

To conclude this section on the importance of observing without judging, I would like to share three thoughts with you:

1. Differentiating the telling of facts from an interpretation of them is common practice in police inquiries and court procedures. Before looking at the facts in the light of societal values as expressed through laws, all of the parties concerned (police authorities, courts, perpetrators and victims, plaintiff and defendant, third parties, et al.) need *first of all* to agree on the facts. The same applies to the armed forces. When I did my military service, I took a radio course called "Observe and Report," which teaches that to be sure the facts are described such as they really are—subjective feelings not allowed!

   Imagine an observer reporting in wartime: "We've been surrounded; the enemy is advancing over us in a most powerful way. We have been invaded." It will not be easy to come up with an appropriate military response. By contrast, if the observer describes what he is truly seeing ("A column of fifteen tanks is moving from the south toward the north, six miles from the front. Some one hundred men are moving up the left bank of the river and three XY-type aircraft have flown over the coast, flying east"), doubtless there would be somewhat more of a chance that the chosen response would be appropriate! I am certainly not making a plug for the armed forces. I am simply stating a principle of basic security and clarity for effective action: establishing the facts and agreeing on their sequence in order to ascertain more precisely what we're talking about *before* interpreting or reacting.

Out of respect for the same values of security and effectiveness, it will prove most useful to work on the way we observe, not to cut ourselves off from our feelings and needs, but rather to give them their full weight.

2. Judgments place others in boxes. In fact, they place those who judge in boxes. Judgments cut us off from the other person, from reality, and from ourselves, wrapping the object in cellophane like a bubble-wrapped commodity, making of it a small, closed, isolated parcel ready to be put into the deep freeze of preconceived ideas, beliefs, and prejudices. When I judge, I question neither myself nor the other person. On the contrary, I cut myself off from my deepest self and from the depth of the other person by remaining in my mind-space. Judgments are static; they deep-freeze reality. Judgments enclose reality in a single aspect of its nature and stop it dead in its tracks.

Judgments place others in boxes. In fact, they place those who judge in boxes.

Life is movement. From the infinitely large movements of the planets and the cosmos to the infinitely minute movements of atoms and electrons, everything is moving all the time. The only immovable thing on this planet was devised by man, who came up with the notion of fixed ideas! In the realm of nature, there is nothing fixed. Man is the one who conceived the idea of final judgments. In nature, nothing is final. Nature is all about seasons, transitions, and transformations. Even mountains are on the move.

3. As conscious beings, we have a deep-seated need to *place ourselves in relation to things and beings* and to exercise our discernment. What I mean by "placing ourselves in relation to things" is knowing:

- Where we are.
- If we're enjoying it or not.
- If what we're experiencing or seeing is in keeping with our values, our vision of the world.
- If we wish to stay put or change.
- What we can do to change.

We also have a deep-seated need to *share values*, mainly the value of meaning. We need life to be meaningful.

Yet in our attempts to meet these two needs, we tend to fall into the old, unfortunate habit of judging mentally rather than welcoming things into our hearts.

In this book, my desire is to show how we might place ourselves in relation to things without judging; see the challenges at stake, the values and the priorities without criticism, without aggression, without imposing; and find and share meaning with neither constraint nor rejection. The first stage of this process therefore will be to *verify what is happening*: What are the facts? What, indeed, is reality?

A Chinese tale

To illustrate how easy it is for us to be completely wrong when we judge, let me suggest that you read the following Chinese tale. This story sheds light on the first stage of the process, the *observation*. That is, taking in and perceiving reality such as it is (ever-evolving) and not such as we fear it might be or think it is.

NOTE: This tale does not go into the feelings, needs, and requests that show us how to *position ourselves* in relation to things and events without judging them. The old Chinaman may look cold and emotionless. Nonetheless, I like to quote this tale because he does not allow himself to be locked into a rigid and unyielding vision of reality. He never stops evolving, welcoming whatever comes his way. His attitude, when you compare it with the panicked noisy villagers, is one of great silent and trusting peace.

Here is the story that Lao-Tseu, Chinese philosopher and founder of Taoism, was fond of telling.[5]

A poor Chinaman inspired jealousy among some of the richest people in the land because he owned an extraordinary white horse. Whenever he was offered a fortune for the animal, the old man replied: "That horse is much more than an animal for me. He's a friend. I cannot sell him."

One day, the horse disappeared. The neighbors gathering around the empty stable gave voice: "Poor fool. It was obvious that someone would steal that beast from you. Why did you not sell him? Oh, what a calamity!"

The owner of the horse was more circumspect: "Let us not exaggerate. Let us say that the horse is no longer in the stable. That's a fact. The rest is only conjecture on your part. How can we know what is fortune or what is misfortune? We only know a fragment of the story. Who knows how it will turn out?"

The people laughed at the old peasant, for long since had they considered him to be simple-minded. Two weeks later, the white horse came back. He had not been stolen. He had simply gone out to graze, and he had brought back a dozen wild horses from his escapade.

Once again, the villagers gathered 'round: "You were right. It was not a misfortune but a blessing."

"I wouldn't go that far," said the peasant. "Let us only say that the white horse has come back. How can we know whether this is good fortune or bad? It is but an episode. How can one get to know the content of a book by reading just one sentence?"

The villagers went their way, convinced that the old man had lost his mind. Receiving twelve fine horses was indubitably a gift from heaven. Who could deny that? The peasant's son began to break in the wild horses. One of them threw him to the ground and trampled on him.

The villagers came once again and gave their views: "Poor friend! You were right. These wild horses did not bring you luck. Look at your only son, disabled for life. Who will give you succor in your old days? You really are to be pitied."

"Hold it!" retorted the peasant. "Not so fast. My son has lost the use of his legs. That's all. Who can know what that will bring? Life is presented to us in small segments. No one can predict the future."

Sometime later, war broke out, and all the young men in the village were enrolled in the army, except for the invalid.

"Old man," the villagers lamented, "you were right, your son may no longer be able to walk, but he has stayed with you while our sons have gone off to get killed."

"Please," answered the peasant, "do no judge hastily. Your young people have enrolled in the army; my son has remained at home. That is all we can say. God alone knows if that is good or bad."

Feeling Without Judging or Interpreting

"I feel that" vs. "I feel"

Generally when you ask someone "How do you feel?" in relation to a preoccupying situation, the person will reply: "I feel that this absolutely must be done . . . I feel that it's time for our leaders to do this or that . . . I feel that it's hopeless . . ."

People answer, therefore, with a thought, a concept, or a comment, *not a feeling*, whereas in fact the question was an invitation for them to position themselves in relation to their feelings. Doubtless, such individuals would be convinced that they have informed you of their feeling since they began by saying, "I feel that . . ."

Once again, it is the old habit of thinking rather than feeling that holds sway. It is an ancient reflex. It is not, however, unchangeable.

So if we want to get more information about ourselves, to ascertain what we are truly experiencing in relation to a situation, it is in our interest to listen to our feelings by wording the sentence like this: "I feel worried, sad, disappointed, etc." As noted previously, our feelings will lead us to our needs and help us identify them. If we can do that, we will be able to position ourselves in relation to situations or persons without judging them, without criticizing them, and without off-loading onto them the responsibility for what we are experiencing. As long as we ascribe to another the responsibility for what we are experiencing, we are acting irresponsibly. As long as we give them the keys to our well-being (and our ill-being), we are caught in a trap we have set for ourselves. It is, therefore, quite useful in our feelings vocabulary to distinguish between the words that constitute an interpretation or a judgment of what another has said, done, or is—and those that do not.

Indeed, very often, in the belief that we are using "I" statements, assuming responsibility for our feelings, we use such words (commonly considered as feelings) as: "I feel betrayed, abandoned, manipulated, rejected." True, these words do express feelings. At the same time, however, they convey an image of another person, an interpretation, a judgment. Between the lines we read: "You are a traitor, a manipulator; you have abandoned me; you reject me." Stated differently, people sometimes confess to others that they have bad or negative feelings toward them because they have done *such and such and such*. The "confessor" then uses this as an opportunity to convince the other person that they are to blame for how the "confessor" feels. Thus, the "confession" becomes a thinly veiled excuse for establishing the other person's guilt.

At the end of this book, you will find a list containing the words often used as feelings but that also include an assessment or judgment of a third party. Why is it useful to make this distinction? It seems to me to constitute a key differentiation that this process highlights. There are two benefits from distinguishing true feelings from feelings that constitute an interpretation.

> **There are two benefits from distinguishing true feelings from feelings that constitute an interpretation.**

The first benefit relates to our desire to set off on a path toward ourselves as securely as possible, by giving up scenarios where we are victims and plaintiffs. The freer our language is of any dependency on what another does or doesn't do—and the more, therefore, our awareness is free of it too—the more we'll be able to become aware of our needs and values, then take initiatives to make sure that they're honored.

Here is an example.

Thirty-six years old, Peter comes for consultations and regularly complains about his relationship with his partner:

"I always feel manipulated by my companion."

"Could you tell me what you observe when you have this impression of being manipulated?"

"She says to me: 'You don't ever understand me. We're just not made to get along.'"

"If you now listen for the feeling that is alive in you behind this impression of manipulation, what are you feeling?"

"Anger. Fatigue. I get the impression that it's always me who has to do the understanding—always me who has to understand her—otherwise, I'm worthless. In fact, I'm only worth something in her eyes if I always understand her."

"And if you listen to the needs that the anger and fatigue point to, what comes to mind?"

"A need for respect. Respect for myself, a need to be accepted just as I am and not for what she wants me to be."

"Is that a well-known impression for you, one you've already experienced? Not being fully accepted for what you are?"

"Naturally, I'm back in front of my mother, in front of my judge, being accused unjustly, both indignant that my identity should not be recognized and powerless to get it recognized."

"When you say that, how do you feel?"

"Tired and disappointed."

"Do these feelings of fatigue and disappointment show that you have a need to accept yourself more, to make more space for yourself, to allow yourself to live your own identity more fully?"

(Moved.) "Yes, precisely."

"If these needs indeed sound accurate to you, I suggest you say them again aloud to give yourself an opportunity to take them on board, to experience them from within."

(After a silence . . .) "OK. I need to accept myself more, to give myself more space, and to allow myself to live my own identity more fully."

Remarks

To people who are working with me, I often suggest they say their needs aloud. Experience has shown me that people who hear themselves say a need that fits with what they are experiencing will have a tendency to say:

"That's right. My need. I must come back to that after the consultation. I've noted it."

And the need remains virtual, like a therapeutic method read in a book or in an article, which one never actually experiences.

(Then, as if continuing the sentence immediately . . .)

"But in any case, that's the way it has always been. I don't see how things could change. There's no solution. So what's the good of identifying my needs?"

By so doing, they bury under negative thoughts the need that was trying to emerge in their consciousness. They don't even allow it the luxury of existing and being identified before repressing it.

So I'm aware of these two risks and often urge the individual, very gently, to take time to reformulate the need aloud after having checked that it rings true with them.

For some people, this is an easy and joyful exercise that they engage in willingly, grateful at last to be able to identify and express their needs clearly. The feelings they most often come up with are relief and well-being, while the need met is one of clarity, understanding, and openness to exploration. For others, this step proves very difficult. The taboo against having needs and, even more, expressing them in front of someone else weighs on many people to such an extent that they're unable to repeat the simplest of sentences, such as, "I need respect for my identity." It's almost impossible; the words just do not come out. So then what is needed is gentle coaxing, which can take several sessions until the person feels at ease expressing the needs, talking about them, making comments on them, refining them, therefore, understanding them and owning them.

Whether such instances are easy or difficult, I experience their sacred nature. The individual involved takes ownership of their own life—and gets grounded and collected. And can it be anything else than sacred for them to come back to life, to the zest for life, to observe the vitality in themselves that they can listen to and allow themselves to be guided by?

We will see later, after identifying needs, how concrete action, the request, is triggered. However, let us come back to Peter and the key differentiation made between a true feeling and a feeling tainted with interpretations. As long as Peter's consciousness takes the form of "I feel manipulated," he remains dependent on the behavior he ascribes to another. It is the other person who bears the responsibility for his ill-being. The word *manipulated* suggests the interpretation that another is doing the manipulating. And perhaps indeed the behavior of his companion may give him the impression of being manipulated. However, that is not the question.

What is of interest is to observe that Peter begins to get beyond complaining ("She's manipulating me. I am her victim.") when he gets to his true feelings ("I am sad and angry.") and his own need ("I need respect for my identity."). *It is when he begins to refer truly to himself that the work begins.* As long as he is commenting directly or indirectly on what his companion is or is not doing, he makes little headway. But as soon as he starts speaking truly of himself, he forges ahead. That is what French psychoanalyst Jacques Lacan said to a patient: "Once you have said to me a word that truly speaks of yourself, you will be healed." This approach is echoed in the work of Swiss psycho-analyst and writer Carl Jung who noted that the best gift one can give a significant other is genuine *self*-understanding.

In doing support work, which one can consider to be an attempt at conflict resolution between the conscious and the subconscious, it is this word that we seek together, not for the word itself, of course, but for the awareness it releases. Thus, Peter was able to gain greater awareness of what he was experiencing, what would enable him to start the true work necessary to break free from his negative maternal complex, and finally open up to accepting and respecting himself. During two years of therapy, I saw him evolve from being a victim and an alcoholic to having success with women and success in his career, moving to autonomy and responsibility.

The second benefit that comes from distinguishing true feelings from feelings tainted with interpretations is that this allows us to be better understood by others, using words that generate the least possible discomfort, fear, resistance, opposition, objection, argument, or flight. It's worth recalling that our intention is to establish a quality connection with others. We want them not only to hear our words, we want them to listen to and see what is alive in us. Just as we in turn listen to them, we'll want to hear not only the words they say, but also what is alive in them.

> ## We will be alert to purging our language and our consciousness of anything that generates opposition, division, or separation.

We therefore will be alert to working on our language and our consciousness to purge them of anything that may generate opposition, division, or separation and to cleanse them of anything that is—*or could be heard as*—a judgment, interpretation, rebuke, criticism, prejudice, cliché, test of strength, or comparison. We do this *because* we know from experience that if others hear what we say as a judgment, criticism, reproach, or fixed idea about them, *they are no longer listening*. They block their ears—sometimes oh, so politely—and generally are preparing an answer, a retort. They do not connect with us, with what is alive in us. They are devising a counterattack or self-defense.

The example of Peter

In a usual conversation, Peter says to his partner, "When you say that to me, I feel manipulated." His partner might well answer: "Not at all. I'm not manipulating you. You always think you're being manipulated. What a bore that is!" What has she done? She has justified herself, she is arguing, she is contradicting. Therefore, she isn't listening to Peter and is not listening to herself either. She is stuck in her head.

She also might react like this: "But you are the one who is manipulating. Have you seen the way you react?" What did she do? Since she interpreted Peter's behavior as an attack, she counterattacked, she retaliated. Consequently, she listened neither to Peter nor herself.

If we apply the method described earlier, Peter might say to his partner: "When you tell me that you never understand me and that we aren't made to get along (O), I feel tired and angry (F) because I need to be accepted as I am and not as what you'd like me to be. I also need recognition for the understanding I regularly display. And finally, I need security in our relationship and to be reassured that, even though I don't always understand you (at least not as well or as quickly as you would like), we still matter to each other and love each other (N). I'd like to know how you feel when I say that to you (concrete, negotiable R).

For his partner, hearing Peter say he feels tired and angry because he has three unmet needs that he clearly names—and regarding which he asks her to take a stance with neither judgment nor constraint—will prove less threatening than seeing herself described as a manipulator, as was the case in the first scenario. Besides, this brought no clarity to what was truly at stake in this relationship. More than in the first scenario involving Peter, his behavior is more inviting to an in-depth conversation about what is basic to the relationship:

- Respect for the identity of each partner.
- Recognition and mutual esteem for the pace at which each one manifests their attention, as well as the way in which that happens.
- Deep inner emotional security being made less dependent on outward signs of approval.

Exercise

Try to decipher for yourself your true feelings underlying your "labeled" feelings. Here are a few proposals:

- **"I feel abandoned"** (in other words, "You have abandoned me").

    Would it not be more accurate and true to say: "I feel lonely and unhappy. I need to be reassured that I matter to you, that I have a place in your heart, even if for the moment you're choosing to do something else rather than be with me or show that you care."

- **"I feel betrayed"** (in other words, "You have betrayed me").

    Would it not be more accurate and true to say: "I'm afraid. I'm truly worried. I have such a need to be able to rely on the mutual trust and frankness there is between us. I need to know that the things we agree on and the commitments we undertake are respected and, if they cannot be honored, that we will talk about it openly."

- **"I feel rejected"** (in other words, "You have rejected me").

   Is it not more enlightening, more informative for oneself and for the other person, to hear this? "I feel unhappy, disappointed, and tired (F). I need somehow to take my place (in my relationship, my family, in a group, in society, at work) and to give myself permission to take my place in the world. I also need others to understand that it's difficult for me and that it's important for me to get their help and encouragement (N). What can I say or do in concrete terms that will nurture these needs (seeking the R)? What can I put in place myself to operate the change I want?"

   As we shall see later in the chapter on *the request*, this type of consciousness makes it possible for us to get out of the rejected-victim scenario, for it clarifies what we can do in practical terms to obtain the support of others. It also clarifies the way forward (R and action) in concrete strategies that we can implement in order to bring about change.

- **"I feel excluded"** (in other words, "You have excluded me").

   Does it not enhance our sense of responsibility and stimulate us when we become aware of the following feelings and needs? "I feel alone, helpless, and sad. I have a deep need for integration, exchange, and belonging. Concretely, what can I put in place that will contribute to meeting these needs? What can I change by myself that will make it possible for me to begin to nurture these needs?"

   You see, when we use a true feeling, one that truly informs us about what is occurring in us, we give ourselves more of an opportunity to ground ourselves and to take ourselves in hand—and we give the other person a greater opportunity to remain centered on what we are saying about ourselves, to take into consideration what we are experiencing. Our ability to "talk true" stimulates the ability in the other person to "listen true." We'll look at this in greater depth at the outset of Chapter 3 in the communication section.

Aggressing, fleeing, or connecting with one another

In a play I saw in Montréal in 1999 (sorry to say I've forgotten both the title of the play and the name of the author), I heard this: "When you hear that the neighboring tribe has taken arms against yours, you have three possibilities and only these three: Take flight as quickly as possible; take up arms yourselves to be able to attack as quickly as possible; or walk toward the opposing army with no weapons and hope you will embrace each other."

In our marital, family, or school squabbles, as in our ethnic, religious, political, or economic wars, we have the same choice: flight, fight, or connect with the other side.

In all such situations, we can see how the resulting conflicts are examples of an epiphenomenon, a symptom of a larger reality. Underlying their complaints are genuine needs. To tackle the symptom without going back to the cause means that at best you get nothing—or merely an external change of attitude (one will say that all is well, or one will start working like crazy to compensate). This doesn't resolve the basic issues. At worst, the symptom could intensify: "I'm not understood. My needs are not considered. What must happen for them to really understand me? Stop cooperating? Then stop communicating altogether? And then perhaps have a proper nervous breakdown, or go to war?!" And that is how the mechanics of violence are triggered around noncommunication . . .

"I don't let you know what I'm truly experiencing. You don't seem interested in listening to what I really feel. I moan. You get scared. I rebel. You control. I rebel even more. You reinforce the control. I explode. You repress . . . Tell me, aren't you tired of this game, so perfectly orchestrated for centuries? And what if we were to genuinely listen to each other?"

Naturally, listening to another and connecting is no easy matter. It is something that arises from a deep desire within to connect with another human being. Then, finally, it is a question of constant practice, like when you learn a new language or a new art form.

Concerning our feelings

At the end of this book you'll find a list of feelings (page 254). There is nothing magical, exhaustive, or comprehensive about it. The list has resulted from observing feelings commonly identified during dozens of NVC workshops. The conventional distinction between positive feelings and negative feelings does not exist in conscious and nonviolent communication because such a distinction is irrelevant. Both sadness and joy inform us about ourselves. Anger is an invaluable signal for us since it shows vitality in ourselves or another. It is the *consequences* of feelings that may be perceived as positive or negative, not the feelings themselves. We, therefore, suggest making the following type of distinction among feelings:

Feelings that are pleasant to experience and that let us know that needs are met.

Feelings that are unpleasant to experience and that let us know that needs are not being met.

You also will see a list of feelings tinged with evaluations, which are important to see as impressions, images, and sensations rather than feelings, so that we can listen to the genuine feeling that is alive in us (behind the impression), a feeling not distorted by the intentions we ascribe to the other person.

There isn't always an absolutely clear distinction between the words designating true feelings and those designating feelings with a hint of interpretation. Once again, what is important is to clarify our intention, which will tell us whether we're making a comment on what someone has done or not done or on our attempts to understand ourselves.

Identifying Our Needs Without Projecting Them Onto Others

Are fear, guilt, and shame tools for getting what we want?

Remember that as a good boy or a good girl, what we learned first was to listen to Daddy's, Mommy's, Granny's, little brother's, neighbor's, teacher's . . . needs, listening to everyone's needs except our own. We therefore got into the habit of believing that we were *almost always* and *almost totally* responsible for the well-being of others. So doing, we got the confused and almost constant impression of guilt in respect to others rather than any enlightened sense of individual responsibility.

At the same time, we got into the habit of believing that others were *almost always* and *almost totally* responsible for our well-being. Thus we got the confused and almost constant impression of others' guilt and debt toward us rather than any enlightened sense of individual responsibility.

> Growing up, we got the confused and almost constant impression of others' guilt and debt toward us rather than any enlightened sense of individual responsibility.

So we often expect another person to take care of our needs while we ourselves have not even identified them, or we make requests of the individual that sound like demands without saying what our need is, or we have needs that encompass someone else. For example, I need:

- *You* to do this or that.
- *You* to change.
- *You* to be like this or like that.

If the other person doesn't react as we wish, we try to manipulate the situation by using criticism, rebuke, or judgment:

"You might at least try to . . . When I think of all I do for you . . . You really are a selfish monster when you . . . If you go on the way you are, I'm leaving you, or I'm going to punish you."

These formulations don't say much about ourselves and provide little information for the other person. They keep us dependent on what the other does or does not do. That is, if the other person does what we say, we're satisfied; if they don't, we aren't satisfied, and that's it!

In short, failing to be acquainted with our needs and expressing them in some negotiable way, we often use fear, guilt, or shame in an effort to get what we want.

Becoming aware of our needs helps us understand that they exist, whatever the situation or whomever we may be with. Situations serve to activate an awareness of our needs and give us opportunities to meet them. Indeed, our needs exist ahead of any situation. Thus, we always have needed recognition or understanding, even when we were walking alone along a mountainside or on the seashore. The need is not necessarily activated at that time, although such a moment of solitude might be an opportunity, in consciousness or not, to give ourselves the recognition or the understanding we need. However, needs are part and parcel of ourselves and become more tangible when we join a group, are with our family, or are in society.

When I was a child, my need for affection was doubtless met chiefly by my mother's and father's attentions. As I grew up, I was able to meet this need for affection in my relationships with my brothers and sisters too, then with classmates, and later with my first girlfriend and other friends. During several years of emotional solitude, I was able to verify the fact that a need for affection exists for me, even if it isn't met. Today, I'm aware that the selfsame need is doubtless met especially and primarily in my relationship with my wife and children. However, at the same time, I'm aware that the need also is met in other relationships: family, friends, coworkers, people I support. Further, I'm aware that I can nurture this need by listening to music I love, by walking through a forest with rustling leaves, gazing at the evening sky, or marveling at the arrival of spring.

Neither do I expect my wife and children to meet my full need for affection.

There are two advantages to such an attitude. On the one hand, I open up to the extraordinary potential for love offered by the world, what German poet Rainer Maria Rilke describes no doubt with this verse, "A goodness ready to wing off watches over everything."[6] I deeply believe that if we were ready to taste of all the love that is continuously offered us in the thousand facets of the world, we would be so much more at peace. Unfortunately, as French writer Michèle Delaunay states, our "pessimism leads us to seeing only what we see and our distraction to not seeing much."[7]

On the other hand, I allow another, in this instance my wife, the liberty to give me what she wishes freely to give me. She is not the agent of my need for affection; she is not the half that consoles me for only being half myself; she is not the projection of the unconditional motherly love I missed out on. She is fully herself—human being, woman, spouse, and mother. Together, we do not want a role-play, albeit perfectly conducted. Rather, we want a genuine relationship with people who are both free and responsible.

This, therefore, is what I observe: Expressing our needs as distinct from expectations that are not so clear and that we have one toward another opens up for us, on the one hand, a whole range of solutions where the other person may find their place, but not only the other person. On the other hand, expression of needs practically guarantees the other individual their own free space. That is, the chance to say to us: "I hear your need, and at the same time I have a need of my own. What shall we do to take care of both in such a way that meeting yours is not at the expense of mine nor meeting mine is at the expense of yours?"

This is the freedom that makes for connection.

It is the freedom we give each other that connects us

In order to illustrate the fact that others are not present in our lives to meet our needs (even though they may contribute in that regard), I referred to the relationship with my wife for two reasons. The first is that for a long time I was a bachelor, panicking at the idea of emotional commitment and particularly fearing having to meet all the needs of my partner while ignoring my own. In my amorous relationships, as soon as the notion of "couple" threatened to materialize, I managed to sabotage the relationship, "courageously" relinquishing the decision to the woman I was seeing. Systematically, I would take neither the decision to go on and commit nor the decision to end the relationship and disengage. I now know that my fear was a sign of the following needs:

- The need to be reassured that I could be myself while being with another: not one or the other, but one and the other.
- The need to be able to continue my journey toward myself while going toward another: not only one or the other, but one and the other.
- The need to be able to exchange affection, understanding, and support, without having to assume responsibility for another or risk being taken charge of ("mothered") by another.

In a word, the need to be in a relationship with a person with sufficient inner strength and self-esteem to be autonomous and responsible, who would love me for who I am and not for what she might wish me to be and whom I would love for who she is and not for who I might dream she would be.

I did not want to spend the rest of my life responsible for meeting another's needs for affection, security, or recognition, nor having another to be there to make good my deficiencies. I therefore had a deep need for both of us to identify and experience those needs (affection, security, recognition) in order to be sure that if the other person could naturally contribute to meeting them (doubtless more than any other person), she was not the only one able to do so. This space for freedom, breathing, and trust was indispensable in order for me to be able to commit. Today, I deeply enjoy the blessing of sharing this mutual understanding with my wife. I now know that it is this freedom that we mutually offer that brings us so close to each other.

The second reason I wanted to talk about my relationship with my wife is that I have observed during my individual consultations so many people, both alone or together, who experience difficulties relating to such issues:

- "I stopped myself from existing so that they could exist, so they wouldn't be afraid, feel abandoned."
- "I haven't allowed myself to be myself (and besides, I didn't even know that one could be oneself) so as not to upset and worry them."
- "I've forced myself to do the housework and keep my job because I was so fearful of their reaction, insecurity, need for recognition, or social and family integration."
- "I did everything for them; I was stifling myself for them."[8]
- "I dare not be myself when I'm in a relationship; I become what the other person expects of me (or what I think the other person expects of me), or I stay apart, alone."

These difficulties in our relationships could be summed up in one question, which to a greater and greater extent seems to account for a fundamental challenge of our human reality: *How can I stay myself while being with another; how can I be with another without ceasing to be myself?*

How can I stay myself while being with others?

This is an issue that is often settled through violence, either externalized violence (I force the other person to do or be what I want) or internalized violence (I compel myself to do or be what the other person wants). And why? Because I get trapped in *binary thinking.* Do you remember the four mechanisms quoted in Chapter 1 that I see as generating violence?

- Judgments, labels, categories
- Prejudices, *a prioris,* rote beliefs, automatic reflexes
- Binary system or duality (either/or thinking)
- Language of diminished responsibility

In my view, this is the most widespread illustration of the violence of binary thinking: the sad, even tragic, belief that in order to take care of another, one has to be alienated from oneself. Consequences of this outlook include the following:

1. If we take care of ourselves, that means we are alienated from others. This results in the contamination of hearts with guilt because we feel that we never do enough for others, even though we may be exhausted; and as soon as we take a moment's respite (a few minutes of lying down for a nap, a few hours for ourselves in the week, a few days of holiday to do nothing), our guilty conscience begins gnawing away at us.

> **ASIDE:** As if we could take care of others properly while we ourselves are incapable of taking proper care of ourselves . . . as if we could listen properly to the needs of others while we never for a moment listen and understand our own . . . as if we could bring our respect and compassion to others in all their diversity, including their contradictions, while we don't give ourselves respect and compassion and are unable to tolerate our own contradictions . . .

2. If, despite our guilt, we wish to succeed in taking care of ourselves, we believe that it has to be by alienating others. Many a breakup, separation, divorce, flight, and withdrawal result from this because we think, "I don't manage to stay with myself when I'm with another person, and therefore I split."

Again, as I travel the path toward another, I cannot afford *not* to travel the path toward myself.

Leaving binary thinking behind

The invitation to us, therefore, is to leave binary thinking behind, represented as it is by the use of *either/or* so as to move toward complementary thinking expressed by *both/and*: I need to be *both* connected to another *and* connected to myself. Not a relationship with *either* the one or the other, but a relationship with *both* the one and the other.

> **As I travel the path toward another, I cannot afford *not* to travel the path toward myself.**

Thus, to avoid the violence of binary thinking that keeps us in alienation, separation, and division, it is truly in our interest to become aware of our needs, identify them in relation to others, and prioritize them so as to become increasingly able to understand others' needs, accept their priorities, and little by little acquire greater ease in flexibly processing the issues with them. As long as we aren't conscious of our own needs, we find it difficult to talk about them and even trickier to negotiate them with another person. We very quickly start imposing our solutions, surrendering to the solutions of others—or again adopting all manner of compromise between the two extremes of domination and submission.

For example, we can maintain the following relationships:
- A relationship of seduction—half power over the other person, half dependency on their appreciation.
- A relationship of argument—who is wrong, who is right . . . being a "right" addict.
- A relationship of comparison or competitiveness—who is or does better, who is or does less well. I delegate to

another the power to determine what is good and what is bad. I decide and subject the other person to my way of being or doing, or I submit to the way of being or doing of the other person.

- A calculating relationship—they have more or less than I have. I obtain. I earn more or less. I or you do more or less than you or I, and so forth.

In all of these types of relationships, we are not yet free and responsible. We are still dependent. We do not act out of a *taste* for giving, contributing, or sharing, but out of a fear of lacking, losing, or being lost.

I believe ever more strongly that freedom and responsibility in human relations, beginning with the relationship to ourselves, presuppose a proper understanding of our mutual needs.

A need is not a wish

Here a further key differentiation comes into play. A need is not a desire or a momentary impulse. We can fall into the trap of mistaking a wish or a desire for a fundamental need. The differentiation is important for two reasons, which the Andrea and Terry couple illustrates (see Chapter 1).

First reason: to get out of the trap. As long as Terry mistakes his wish to go out to dinner for a basic need, he (not Andrea) is placing himself in a trap. Similarly, as long as Andrea mistakes her wish to stay at home and watch a movie for one of her basic needs, she is placing herself (not Terry) in a trap. As long as Terry says to Andrea, "You don't understand my needs at all," it is in fact a reproach that he is making to himself. As long as Andrea is saying to Terry, "But you are the one who doesn't understand a thing about my needs," it is to herself that she addresses this rebuke.

Only if both of them decide to go half the distance they expect the other to go, might the evening in question and the overall functioning of this couple improve. At that point the following exchange might ensue:

- Terry expresses his need to Andrea without requiring her to meet it (negotiable request).
- Andrea listens to Terry's need without feeling obligated to go along with it.
- Andrea expresses her need to Terry without requiring him to meet it (negotiable request).
- Terry listens to Andrea's need without feeling obligated to go along with it.

> **It is the collaboration, the consultation, that makes it possible to come up with all kinds of solutions.**

It is this freedom in expressing the message *and* in receiving it that allows both individuals to move forward freely and without resistance toward a satisfactory solution for each.

Second reason: to be more creative. As long as Andrea and Terry stubbornly stick to their guns without checking the need that lies upstream, the solution found (dinner out or home video) is neither as creative nor as fully satisfying as the one the couple came up with after having had a dialogue in Nonviolent Communication. The solution by consensus to have a picnic at the end of the lake proves more novel and more pleasing than the other two proposals.

It is the collaboration, the consultation, that makes it possible to come up with all kinds of solutions.

No utopianism though! Let's be realistic: Often the solution obviously does not fulfill the needs of both persons 100 percent. Sensitivities, characters, expectations, priorities, and senses of humor (especially being able to laugh at oneself), as well as a desire for things to have meaning, vary each day. So I truly don't think we should dream of coming up with solutions that always and completely meet the needs of both parties. Experience tells me, however, that the quality of listening and respect that comes from seeking such a solution in a climate of compassion is such that the actual solution becomes secondary to the relationship itself!

First the relationship: logistics will follow!

So often in our relationships, the quality of the relationship appears to play second fiddle to actual problems. In other words, we first deal with the logistics or physical organization, and then we worry about getting along—if there's enough time.

Without knowing it, I suffered like many children from the importance given by adults to logistics, on the pretext that my parents (in particular) were overloaded with responsibilities: "Yes, dear, in a moment; I still have to put the wash away . . . No, not now. I'm cleaning up . . . You can see how busy I am, can't you? . . . I really have a lot of work to do . . . We'll talk about it later . . . Come on, quickly, quickly. I'm in a hurry . . . We don't have time."

I have no memories of having seen my mother sitting in an armchair for more than three minutes a week. That was on Sundays, before lunch. She would sit on a corner of the armchair (no time to sit comfortably in it), swallow a tiny cocktail, saying: "Oh, what a great thing it is to sit down for a little while." Then whoosh! Less than five minutes later, she was back in the kitchen to get the meal ready. Immediately after the meal, everything had to be tidied up quickly so she could get on with a thousand other things. If I wanted to have a few moments with her on my own, I had to use cunning: help her fold the linen, clean up the kitchen, put things in their place in a room, or take advantage of a trip in the car. Then, on a secondary basis, the relationship was allowed to exist.

When I think back, I realize how much more effectively I learned to *do* than to *be,* to do things rather than to be in a relationship. And, very naturally, I reproduced the hyperactivity. Diaries bursting at the seams is something I know all about!

The degree to which I gave precedence to organizational busyness rather than relationships blew up in my face when Valérie and I were getting ready for our wedding day in Holland. I was in Belgium a few days before the event. She called me from Holland to settle a few urgent matters, questions of logistics to be precise, and she reached me in my car as I was driving between two appointments. I got a bit upset because I was not there with her. I got the impression that we had not understood each other, and I feared that one part of the festivities that I was very keen on would not be possible. I answered her more curtly than I would have wished and, with considerable anxiety and stress in my voice, brought the conversation to a close. I instantly realized that I was reproducing my old pattern: I was allowing logistics to take precedence over the relationship. Suddenly the priority had become organizing the wedding rather than the quality of my relationship with the bride!

I called Valérie back immediately to say I was feeling both surprised and sorry at my reaction (F); that I really did wish, on the one hand, to be more receptive to her concerns (first N); and, on the other hand, to give precedence to the quality of our mutual understanding rather than to logistics (second N). In practical terms, I suggested taking more time that evening to sort out with her the items still pending (concrete R). She told me later the second phone call was an important one to her.

Let's come back to the situation I was referring to when, as a boy, I wanted my mother to listen to me. If my mother and I had known some of the rudiments of conscious and nonviolent communication, we could, for example, have had the following exchange[9]:

"Mother, I'd like someone to listen to me and give me some attention (N). Would you be willing to sit down with me for five minutes (R)?"

"I'm touched that you want to talk to me (F) because I need to listen to each of my children (N), and at the same time I'm concerned (F) because there are so many things I'd like to finish before the end of the day (N). Would you like to talk to me while helping me?"

"I'm really glad (F) to hear you say that you need to listen to each of your children. That reassures me (N, for emotional security). At the same time, when I hear your proposal (O), I'm not so sure (F) that you will really be able to listen to me if you're working at something else at the same time (need for availability). Would you like to be sure that if I'm asking for five minutes, it will really be only five or ten minutes and not half an hour? And then you would still have the time you need to do what you want to do?"

"Yes, I need to have a good sense how I use my time in order to make sure I finish what I have to finish (N). I feel grateful (F) when I see that my time matters to you, and now I suggest we take five minutes together as soon as I finish what I'm doing here. Is that OK with you?"

"Yes, thanks."

Remarks

1. It was the trap of the binary system that made my mother say, "I don't have time" or, to be more precise, "There are five of you children, and I don't have time (i.e., to listen to all of you)." I am convinced that she would have loved to have said, as in the example: "I have both a need to listen to each of my five children and a need for the household to function properly, and I don't know how to go about taking account of both of those needs." However, as it is difficult to identify our various needs when several of them are concerned—and particularly the ones we don't see how to meet *or even see*—she referred only to the need that appeared to her to be the most urgent or the most obvious, without naming the others.

2. Taking care to identify and name the various needs is enlightening even if no solution appears possible in the immediate future. Why?

First, because this brings us back to the helm consciously rather than allowing ourselves to be remote-controlled by our subconscious mind. It makes it possible for us to redefine our priorities in order to be open to any changes that may become necessary. As long as I'm not clear as to the status of my various needs, I might well plunge ahead into a behavior that could meet one of them but disregards all the others. The danger is a kind of rigidity that, in the end, isn't all that far from *rigor mortis!*

Second, it is clarifying to identify our needs because this process opens up our mind to the possibility of envisioning solutions. There was practically no chance of seeing solutions appear as long as a need had not been identified. This is the invitation to creativity I referred to earlier.

In the example, my mother fails to identify her needs—let us say in the logistics area (order, efficacy, harmonious operating of the household)—without mentioning her need to offer fair listening time to each of her children. As long as this remains her pattern, the chances of finding time to listen to each of them are lower than if she is aware that she is caught between two needs: logistics and listening. In the latter case, even if she cannot see any wholly satisfying solution immediately, she gives the need a chance. She and the child might at least speak about it and, for example, realize that it isn't particularly hours of listening that are necessary but a few minutes of personal time, granted specifically to one child at a time, reassuring each in turn about their identity. Another creative solution could be for the children to offer to help the mother for a while in a task, then have quality time together after that.

Third, it is important to clarify our needs because, even if there is no possible immediate solution, the awareness of the dilemma at least makes it possible for the need to exist, for part of ourselves to come alive, even though this may remain in the background for a time.

> ## This brings back to life a part of us that is in the background and helps us mourn it so that we may move on freely.

I notice, for example, how many parents repress their artistic or creative side: "I don't have time for that; the children, the spouse, the family come first." And naturally, priorities like that can lead us to postpone the exercise of a talent until later. What is urgent is to allow this need to exist in and of itself, to welcome it and, at the same time, recognize the impossibility of meeting it just now.

Thus, rather than allow the need to be stifled by the behavior referred to above ("I don't have time"), it is of value to welcome it, both to give it life and to grieve it: "I would have so loved to find time to develop my artistic talent or follow my bent to be creative. Yet, for now, I truly want to give my time and energy first and foremost to my children, my spouse, my family." This brings back to life a part of us that is in the background and helps us mourn it so that we may move on freely.

Allowing all the parts of our self to exist rather than repressing any one of them is to bring oneself to life. If we suppress one part of our self, failing to welcome it, we drag along within us a part of our self left for dead, which we necessarily haven't mourned since we haven't even allowed it to live. The part of ourselves left for dead then falls with its full weight on the living parts and compromises our life momentum as a whole.

Two key expressions

1. "For now . . ."

In the above sentence ("Yet, for now, I truly want to give my time and energy first and foremost to my children, my spouse, my family") it is the notion of time that provides the space to breathe. We keep alive an awareness that everything is evolving all the time. We maintain an open door to our talent, for which, later, we'll be able to provide space.

Think, for example, of something that, at the present time, you can't do, then say to yourself something like this: "I don't understand a thing about data processing, I can't sing, and I'm not very good at speaking in public." Then ask yourself how things are inside. Now, simply add, *for now*: "For now, I don't understand a thing about data processing. For now, I can't sing. For now, I'm not very good at speaking in public." What has become alive in you now?

You see, we can choose between language and consciousness that either enclose us or open us up to new possibilities.

2. **"And at the same time . . ." rather than "But . . ."**

There is no opposition; there are just two parallel needs—the one that can be met now and the other that cannot. Any use of *but* causes us to split in our awareness by canceling out or diminishing the first proposition. Using *and at the same time* puts both propositions into perspective. Take any sentence you might tend to say, for example, "I agree with you because . . . *but* . . ." Replace the word *but* with *and at the same time* and then look inside to see if you just might get a different picture.

Our needs require recognition more than satisfaction

A banker friend who had taken part in a training course I led told me a few weeks later how difficult it was for him to make himself available for his children when he came back from the office around eight o'clock in the evening. "I just feel like doing nothing, opening a paper, or watching television. I don't have the energy to be 'assaulted' by my three children. Yet I also want to see them a little each day, so I force myself to play with them. But I frequently feel that I'm not truly available, and I quickly get annoyed."

I reformulated the scene to check that I had understood properly and to enable us to identify the needs concerned: "Do you feel frustrated because you'd like to be more available in support of your children when you get home?"

"Maybe in a perfect world, but mostly I just feel exhausted and can't cope with their level of energy."

This is important feedback in my quest to make sure I've understood properly. It helps me refine and reformulate my guess: "Do you feel divided between a part of you that is exhausted and that has a need for relaxation and calm at that time of the day—and another part of you that feels touched by the enthusiasm of your children? And you would like to find the energy to respond to it?"

"Yes, I need time for myself, but I usually don't manage to get it. And every evening when I get out of the car in front of the house, I feel the same tension, and that exhausts me."

"If you're open to it, I would like to suggest that even before you get home, you pull over and simply take a few minutes for yourself to listen to your needs and get connected to the various parts of yourself. On the one hand, you have a need for peace, relaxation, and time for yourself and, on the other hand, you need and want to be available and welcoming to your children. Simply take the time to say to yourself inside, or even aloud, so things will be clearer in your heart: 'I really feel a need now to put my feet up, sit on the sofa with my paper, and watch TV and nothing else. After this stressful day, I need to land. I need to settle and rest.' Take the time to taste the simple well-being that goes with this way of seeing things. Let it come alive in you so you are more open to the other part of you that is saying inside: 'And at the same time I also need and want to be available to my children and devote time and attention to them.' Only then take the last leg of your journey, pull into the driveway, and go into your house.

When you walk in, stay present to these different needs and allow yourself to negotiate them openly with your children."

A few days later, this man phoned to thank me: "I had found it difficult to believe that your proposal would help me. So I'm surprised to observe how peaceful I have been feeling, becoming aware of what's alive in me without forcing one part of me or repressing another part. Previously, it was as if I was leaving a part of myself in the car. These last few evenings, I've felt that I've gone back home whole and able to express all my needs."

In the course of a workshop, taking place over a few spread-out days, a child-care worker in a center for children said how tired he was of always being the "sucker" or "flunky" who would stand in at a moment's notice when colleagues were not able to come to work. "I'm always the one to get called in at the last minute, especially when it comes to taking groups to the swimming pool in the evening, because they know I never say no. I go along, of course, because someone has to be with these youngsters, and if I don't go, the outing they are so excited about may be canceled. But what happens is that I'm not very available to the children. I fume the whole evening and quickly lose my cool with them. As a matter of fact, they're the ones who pay the price for my bad humor."

"Do you feel upset because there's a part of you that is fed up (F) with regularly getting called in to substitute for others' absences? And that part of you would like to be able to say no? You'd like to spend an evening on your own, and you'd like other colleagues to make themselves available (N)? But another part of you is really concerned (F) at the idea of these young people not getting the outing they are so looking forward to (N)?"

"Yes, I feel divided, and that keeps me from really being present with the children."

"If you listen to these various needs—the need to share tasks among colleagues, the need to respect your free time and your private life, and the need to contribute as much as possible to the well-being of the young people you take care of—how do you feel?"

"Touched, because I'm aware that by accepting to stand in for others, I'm choosing a priority need: helping the young people. One day, I might well make a different choice."

"I suggest that the next time you receive such a request, you take time to listen to your various needs, so that you're really available for what you choose to do."

A week later, he told me he had once again accepted to serve as a replacement for an evening at the swimming pool with the young people. "I took time to listen to myself as you had suggested," he began. "The need around the young people was clearly the top priority in my mind, and I went along joyfully. Although I was counting on doing several things at home that evening, I was able to accept postponing them, and I felt fully available to the youngsters."

I have on so many occasions worked on understanding what is at stake here. Most of the time, what appears is that we have not really taken stock of our needs. We do things out of habit or duty "because it has to be done; I have no choice" or because the other person or the thing we are attending to is quickly perceived as the factor preventing us from being ourselves or from living our life. We end up making other people pay openly or more subtly, or we pay for it ourselves. Violence is triggered openly or subtly. If we take the time to take stock of the situation on our own, we give ourselves the opportunity of being fully available and present to what we're doing and those we're doing it with.

> ## We wish to become aware so we don't deny or disown what is alive in us.

Identifying our need for rest, to have some time for ourselves, to do what we want with our evening, etc., doesn't necessarily mean we'll meet the need. We simply wish to become aware of it so we don't deny or disown anything that is alive in us. Through awareness, living choices can be made that involve us in all of our aliveness and not just 10 or 15 percent of ourselves.

Regarding our needs

At the end of this book, you will find a list of needs. This list, like the list of feelings, makes no claims to be exhaustive. It is the result of observing the needs commonly worked on in NVC seminars or during consultations. The way it is presented is merely a proposal. We refer to:

- Physiological needs (eating, drinking, sleeping)
- Individual or personal needs (space, identity, autonomy, evolution)
- Social or interpersonal needs (sharing, recognition, giving, welcoming)
- Spiritual needs (love, confidence, meaning, kindness, joy)
- Needs to celebrate life (gratitude, communion, mourning)

Formulating a Concrete, Realistic, Positive, Negotiable Request

Even though, as we have seen, some of our needs have a greater impetus to be recognized than to be met, nonetheless we would like to meet a fair number of them. Contenting ourselves with awareness of our needs without knowing what to do in practical terms might well leave us in an unsatisfactory virtual world, a sort of insatiable quest: "I need love, I need recognition, understanding; but I never take action myself to meet them. I wait for 'someone' to take care of me."

Bringing the need into the here and now

Here are the benefits that result from making a request or a concrete, realistic, positive, negotiable proposal for action:

A concrete request

We can float through life amid ideas, ideals, and magnificent concepts. If we do so, we might never encounter reality, never bring ourselves fully into the here and now. I personally was quite stuck in the Peter Pan complex, summarized as follows: "Reality through a windowpane is all right, but I'm afraid of really getting into reality, fear of failure, fear of imperfection, fear of shadows and incompleteness. I will make choices later." Immersed in an apparently conventional legal career, I pursued my dream that all was possible. For a long time, I tried to keep all doors open in front of me without going through any of them. Eventually, though, I became aware that while in one life many extremely varied things are indeed possible one after the other, there is only "a single possible" at a time.

It is the request that provides the need with "a possible" and prevents it from being stuck behind the windowpane. It gives it an opportunity to take on reality. In my support work, I observe that the difficulty of moving into the request or concrete action is strongly linked to the difficulty of entitling oneself to exist and deciding on true practical action independent of others' expectations and values.

My thoughts turn to a man, some sixty years old, who came to a consultation, preoccupied by the sharing of his inheritance with his two sisters, who had made a proposal that didn't suit him. Fairly quickly, he clarified his need for fairness, but when I asked him how, in concrete terms, he envisioned meeting his need for fairness in the breakdown of the inheritance, he was unable to propose any practical division of the estate. He constantly came back to his strategy and his need: "It's got to be just. What's being proposed is not right." But he was making no proposal his sisters could respond to, such that finally they had acquired an aversion to him, and that did nothing to facilitate understanding!

It was truly difficult for him to define his request in concrete terms because defining means finishing, and finishing means accepting finiteness. This notion was a blow to his heart. The idea of providing a concrete boundary, a precise measure of his quest for equity, repelled him. For various reasons, his need for justice was never met. Regarding any proposal, he went into comparisons and saw only a limitation unacceptable in the light of his insatiable quest. In fact, underlying his need for fairness were unmet needs for recognition, identity, and esteem. By working on the concrete and highly pragmatic nature of a request, we are working on getting into reality and accepting our finiteness.

A realistic request

A realistic request takes reality into account—such as it is and not such as I fear it may be or such as I dream it may be. People who have, for example, a need for change, are often imagining a change objective so radical that in it they have the best reason never to change: "It's too hard . . . It's too great a burden . . . It involves too many things . . . It concerns too many people or aspects of my life . . . So I'm changing nothing!"

> **Seek first the smallest thing we might do, and change will follow.**

That is why it is so invaluable to invite another or to invite oneself to say: "What is the littlest thing or the most pleasant thing, however small, I could say or do in the direction of the change I wish for, in the direction of the change I've identified?" In short, seek first the smallest thing we might do, and change will follow.

We're talking here about not the biggest thing, but the smallest—not the most painful, but the most pleasant. This often comes as a surprise to people because our mind, accustomed to performance and bent on results, seeks a trial of force, a significant challenge, as if reality were not made up of many little things woven with other little things . . . and yet more little things that together make up very big things.

This modest and *realistic* side of the request often gives rise to misgivings at a time governed by automatic trigger mechanisms: telephones, TVs, electrical household equipment, cars, computers. One click and we zap from show to show, program to program, one person to the next. Serenely accepting the slowness of a living process is so uncommon that many have trouble trusting nature's slow but steady way. But there are exceptions. Case in point . . .

A woman much afflicted by the death of her husband came to me for support. After several consultations, she identified the principal feeling alive in her—fear. It indicated her need to trust herself. She was surprised to learn this because, she said, "I never thought about trusting myself. Such words didn't even exist in my head. I always trusted first my parents, then my husband and my family. Now I believe that I really do have a need for self-confidence, but at my age I'll never make it."

I urged her to take practical action: to put the self-sabotage producing the negative beliefs and cloudy mental pictures to one side ("At my age, I'll never make it") and simply state her need aloud to give herself the right to exist.

She repeated it hesitatingly: "I need to trust myself. I need to believe that I can trust myself."

I stayed silent for a while and then said to her: "I suggest you simply stay aware of this need in the days to come, without being concerned about any result. Simply bring your attention to this need, and don't look for a solution. Let the need resonate in your heart."

At the next session, a week later, she began by saying: "I'm grateful you urged me simply to allow myself to be aware of the need to trust myself. It's amazing how I had the impression of not having to 'do' anything or look for anything, but simply to allow what was alive in me to well up, allowing myself to feel the confidence taking root. It's still very fragile, but something is already different, and it's reassuring for me to rely more on myself."

A few weeks later, she truly began to reorganize her life in very practical terms. In this case, the principle of reality was elementary: First of all, simply accept the notion of need itself. The solutions will come later.

A positive request

Imagine you are listening to music while your husband is working in his office. He says to you: "I'm working. Will you please turn off the music?" How do you feel?

Now imagine he has just said to you: "I need some quiet to do my work for another hour. Would you agree to listen to your music in an hour or to go on listening to it in another room in the house?" How do you feel now?

When I do this exercise in a group, I often hear:

"I prefer the second version."

"Why?"

"Because I don't like being prevented from doing what I'm doing. In the second version, I hear a proposal to continue what I'm doing later or elsewhere. It's more pleasant than having to stop."

Indeed, we do not like having to stop. Certainly, we have heard more than often enough, "Will you stop moving around, making so much noise, playing, etc.?" We do not like being prevented *from doing*. We much prefer being invited *to do*.

It is subtle, you might say. Doubtless. And that is precisely it, as far as I'm concerned, the subtle essence of the form of communication I am proposing: avoiding both in our language and in our consciousness whatever divides, compares, separates, hampers, encloses, resists, sticks, embarrasses—and preferring language that opens, conjugates, connects, allows, invites, stimulates, facilitates. Worthy of note are my own old reflexes. The title of this book gives food for thought: "Being genuine," not just nice!

A negotiable request

It would have served no purpose to carefully make factual observations such that another person will not perceive any judgment or criticism (compare the mother/child example quoted above: "When I see your shoes on the staircase and your backpack on the sofa . . ."), or to express feelings to avoid any interpretations or judgments ("I feel sad and disheartened . . ."), or to check having properly identified a need that does not involve the other person ("I have a need for order and respect for the work I do . . ."), *if* at the request stage one gets caught up in totally nonnegotiable requirements: "And now go clean up your things immediately!"

It is the negotiable nature of the request that creates the space for connection. This is more or less how it happens: If we don't make a request, it's as if we weren't allowing ourselves the right to exist. We remain with a virtual, disembodied need. We aren't truly taking our place in the relationship. Furthermore, if we issue orders or make requirements, it's as if the other person doesn't have the right to exist either.

The ability to formulate a negotiable request—and thus to truly create the space for a connection—is a direct function of our own security and inner strength: in short, our confidence in ourselves.

CHAPTER 3

Becoming Aware of What Others Are Truly Experiencing

If you only half say it, only half of it
will be understood.

ANONYMOUS

Communicating Is Expressing and Receiving Messages

Saying it all, listening to it all

Every day I see that, for a host of people, communicating means managing to express oneself and allowing others to express themselves. And after both sides have had opportunity for expression, the belief is that there has been communication. How many of these people, however, complain about relational difficulties and say: "But my husband and I, or my children and I, communicate so much. We tell each other everything; I don't understand why we don't get along better"?

They say *everything!* Yes, but do they listen to everything?

The key often lies here: We fail to hear because we fail to listen. The title of a book by Jacques Salomé, *If Only I'd Listen to Myself,*[10] is eloquent in this respect. Although we may often have learned to express ourselves, if only a little, at school or by observing others, seldom has anyone learned to listen, to listen without doing anything, without saying anything.

It is no easy matter. People come to me and say, "I communicate quite well with my husband, my children . . ." But they don't easily accept that they're very much at ease when it comes to *saying* everything—for saying what is in their hearts, preaching to other people, or giving them advice—but less at ease, or even incapable, of hearing things, simply *listening* to what another holds in their heart. They are less capable of examining the feelings and needs underlying the words, and then, in their turn, expressing the feelings and needs (without judgments) that are alive in them.

Talking true, listening true

Just listen to typical table, society, work, or reception conversations. Seldom do we *listen* truly. Rather, we politely wait for our turn to take the floor while preparing our own bit—at best focusing only haphazardly on what the others are saying and at worst using their comments essentially as a springboard for our own opinions. Sadly, most of these "conversations" are little more than sequences of monologues. There is precious little encounter, and that explains why there are so few nourishing, stimulating, energizing conversations. We don't talk true, nor do we listen true. We pass each other by. We miss each other.

More and more, I'm of the belief that in this "passing by" lies the basic emptiness from which most of us suffer so acutely. We're missing out on the nurturing presence that is born of true connection. And we're missing out on the connection both to ourselves and others.

> **As long as we don't know what we're looking for, we try to fill the void with all sorts of tricks.**

As long as we don't know what we're looking for, we try to fill the void with all sorts of tricks: We get a high out of work, amorous conquests, hyperactivity; we get giddy with consuming, possessing, seducing; we drive ourselves silly with alcohol, drugs (whether prescription or otherwise), sex, or gambling; we hide behind a screen called responsibility, duty, concepts, and ideas. Sometimes we desperately wait for a miracle breakthrough from a therapy workshop, a trip to the other end of the world, or a spiritual experience, before discovering, like Paulo Coelho's alchemist, that we are sitting on our treasure, that our treasure is at the heart of the connection to ourselves, in ourselves, and with others.[11] U.S. essayist and philosopher Ralph Waldo Emerson put it this way: "What lies behind us and what lies ahead of us are tiny matters compared to what lies within us." Indeed, there is no other form of possession, no other power to hold, no inebriation to enjoy, no marvel to contemplate other than connection. Connection brings us to ourselves, to others, and to the world, so that we are neither excluded nor separated from anything unless by our own divisive thoughts.

The entire universe is moving and connecting—creative force itself.

As long as we live a polarizing binary consciousness (I leave you to be with me; I leave me to be with you), we shall experience separation, division, and therefore emptiness. It is by working the extra consciousness, unified consciousness, that we shall be more and more able to get a taste of unity through diversity, joining universality out of individuality.

Let us come back to feelings. In the way you use feelings, I urge you to be especially alert to your intentions, your motives. What is my intention, my motivation? To cleverly induce another person to do what I want or to move compassionately toward another? Beware of emotional manipulation!

Indeed, another old and unfortunate habit has gotten us into the habit of frequently using feelings to control others or exercise power over them. For example: "I'm sad when you get bad marks at school . . . I'm angry when you don't keep your room clean . . . I'm disappointed when I see your report card." Or, "better" yet: "You disappoint me greatly . . . You make me completely give up . . . You exhaust me."

This way of acting provides minimal information about our needs and brings the full weight of our feelings onto the shoulders of another; another person becomes responsible for our state, and we make them pay the price. We allow our well-being to become virtually dependent on them, and we intend to make them aware of their responsibility for our well-being, also expecting them to feel guilty for our misery.

Acting this way, we assume less responsibility for what we are experiencing and give away to another disproportionate power to determine our happiness or our unhappiness. We give others the remote control for our well-being. They zap, and we skip from mood to mood at their whim.

An exchange between mother and child

Conventional version
"I am sad when you don't clean up your things." For the mother, that means:

- "If the child tidies things up, I'm happy."
- "If the child doesn't clean up, I stay sad."

I therefore give another the *power* to keep me sad or keep me happy but not the *freedom* to do something else or to do something differently. In other words, I maintain an emotional power game, a trial by strength, where there isn't real freedom.

As for the child, unless she understands and at that time shares the same need for order as her mother, she can only say to herself: "Oh, Lord! Mother is sad, so I'm going to be in for a rough ride if this goes on. I want her to be happy, so I'll do as she says even if I don't understand the reasons, even if I don't agree with the reasons, even if it is done unwillingly." At the end of this repeated conditioning, the child learns to adapt, even over-adapt, to the desire of others, ignoring herself.

Or the child may say to herself: "It has nothing to do with me. I do what I want to do, and I will never clean things up if I'm *ordered* to do so." And at the end of this repeated conditioning, the child learns systematic rebellion, automatically contesting everything she is asked to do.

Nonviolent version

"When I see your exercise books on the table and your clothes on the floor (neutral observation to show the other person, without any judging, what I'm talking about), I feel upset (F) because I need help in setting the table for the meal (N). I would like to know if you would agree to put them away (concrete, negotiable R)."

The mother is annoyed *because she has a need that isn't being met; she isn't annoyed because of her child.* She expresses this need to her daughter and thus gives her a sense of her annoyance without accusing the girl, then she makes a negotiable request that allows her daughter complete freedom.

As for the child, she has the opportunity or the freedom to position herself in relation to the need expressed and may say:
- "Yes, I agree to put them away."
- "No, I don't agree because I don't want to put them away—or maybe I'll do it later. Why don't you talk to my brother? He's a lot messier than I am."

Perhaps you have doubts about the efficacy of such an exchange, and you say to yourself for example: "Oh, my goodness! With my child that would be impossible. If I don't demand something, I get nothing." If that is so, check inside regarding:

- *Your feeling.* Are you not tired with this situation?
- *Your need.* Is it not a pleasure for you to share your values (order, for example) and your needs without systematically stirring up resistance or having to compel the other person?

If you can identify with the fatigue or the need, rejoice! You are reading the right book. Sharing, transmitting, and exchanging our values without submitting or making another submit is one of the advantages of practicing the method I am presenting to you here.

> **Obeying and taking responsibility are not the same thing.**

By naming the need, on the one hand, we shed light on our own clarity and assume full responsibility for what we are experiencing; on the other hand, we inform others of what is alive in us and, at the same time, respect their freedom and their responsibility. *We invite them to take responsibility and not simply to obey.* We invite them to get connected to themselves while staying connected to us.

When noticing how carefully I had stressed the importance of expressing true feelings, identifying our own needs, and expressing them to others in the form of a non-compelling request, a workshop participant once told me the following story . . .

"In fact, I used to believe that I had trained myself through my readings and discussions in nondirective language and the 'I' form. I believed, therefore, that I had learned to speak about myself simply because I said 'I' rather than 'you.' However, the 'I' allowed me, with no compunction, to chuck my rubbish bin of frustrations in the face of others. I would scream at my husband: 'I'm exhausted because you don't do anything for the children . . . I'm at the end of my rope because you give me no help . . . I'm fed up because you're away so often.'

"And he would reply (because he had read the same books as I), 'But honey, use the 'I' form, talk to me about you, about what you feel, about what you want.'

"Then I would answer, 'Well, that's what I am doing; I'm telling you that I think you are away too often, that you should help me more, and that it's time things changed.'

"And he would answer: 'But I do help you sometimes, and then with my work I don't have any choice. You just keep complaining.'

"In this exchange (one could hardly call it a dialogue because I was complaining; he was arguing and contradicting me) we were not trying to get closer to each other. We were both trying very hard to bring our spouse around to our point of view. I can now see the importance of expressing the feeling and the need together because that clarifies things and increases personal responsibility."

An exchange between father and child

Conventional version

"I am very disappointed with you when I see the school results you got this month. If you go on like that, your year is going to be charming indeed! And then you won't be ready to find a job later. Look at your sister; she is much more conscientious."

I use the feeling here to make the other person react out of fear, guilt, or shame. Now reread this version as if you were the child, and check for yourself the state of mind you are in, the taste for life you have after what you heard your father speak that way.

Nonviolent version

"When I see your school results this month, and especially a D in math and an F in statistics (an observation that is both neutral and detailed, to express to the other person what I am reacting to), I feel worried and concerned (F). I need to be reassured about two things, namely that you:

Understand the significance of these subjects and know how they will be useful in the future.

Feel OK and welcome in your classroom with your teacher, so that if you do run into difficulties, you will feel at ease about saying so (F). Would you agree to tell me how you feel in relation to all that (R)?"

Once again, ask yourself how, if you were a child, you would feel if your father spoke to you that way. What energy, what taste for life would be alive in you?

When I do this exercise with children, the reaction is immediate. In the first version they have the impression of being judged, misunderstood, rejected. To get out of the discomfort caused by these feelings, either they sulk and argue ("It's the teacher's and the school's fault . . . I'm hopeless . . . A buddy took my notes") or they feign indifference ("I don't care; it's not important—just a minor test, no problem at all") or they clearly demonstrate their distress over the meaning of things ("In any case, school is a waste of time since we're going to wind up unemployed in the end").

In the second version, the children feel considered and realize their feelings and thoughts count. They are made to feel welcome with their difficulties and the progress they may have made. The desire of the parents to understand without judging touches them. The proposal to speak freely (without fear of any compulsion, any expectation to face up to, any result to achieve) allows the leeway to express themselves freely. In the next two sections, "Communicating is also to give meaning" and "Listening without judging," I will suggest observing and analyzing the reactions of two young people, John and Isabel, after hearing the second version of the parent/child exchange.

Communicating is also to give meaning

Here is the reaction of John, a fourteen-year-old student:

"Well, I'd like to say to my parents that I don't give a hoot about math. I'd like them to tell me why I have to study that subject. They always say back to me, 'Because it's in the curriculum' or 'Because that's the way it is' or maybe 'You don't always do what you want to do in life.' But I need to talk about it and find out why."

"Are you saying you have a need to understand the meaning of what you're doing, and if you don't understand the meaning of it, then you don't want to do it, or you do it badly?"

"Well, yeah . . . right. If I don't see the meaning of it, I need someone to explain."

Remarks

For me, this is the number-one property of communication: *providing meaning* for what I do or what I want. In previous generations—and certainly in mine—one might have heard: "That's the way it is because that's the way it is . . . Stop asking questions . . . Do it because I said so . . . You'll understand later . . . There are things you have to do in life whether you like it or not."

Not to mention, of course, the tragic "It's for your own good," which has done so much damage and to which psychoanalyst Alice Miller devoted a well-known book.[12] The book *For Your Own Good: Hidden Cruelty in Child-Rearing and the Roots of Violence* taught me a great deal about the subtle mechanisms that generate violence from infancy, in a way that is all the more insidious as it is dressed up in good intentions. Fortunately, this attitude is on the wane. Many in today's young generations are calling for meaning and are refusing things that don't have meaning in their eyes.

> **Sooner or later each of us will be called upon to review how we define our life and our priorities—and deal with issues surrounding meaning.**

The situation is relatively new, at least on a broad scale. Millions of young people are taking on the previous generation about meaning and are refusing to obey and blindly follow instructions, habits, automatic reflexes. It could be argued that this phenomenon already took place in much of the world in the 1960s and 1970s, but the trend appears to be even stronger today, enhanced in no small measure by global mass communications. I see here a fabulous opportunity for human beings to become more responsible for their acts because they're more aware of why they are acting. Naturally, this is a transformation that cannot occur without conflict and without pain. Imagine yourself a parent or merely an adult (whether or not you fit one or both descriptions). Are you generally clear about the meaning of what you are doing? Can you usually name and explain the value or the need that is guiding you in your behaviors overall? Sooner or later each of us will be called upon to review how we define our life and our priorities—and deal with issues surrounding meaning. The present cause of discomfort among many parents and school staff has much to do with their being urged by young people, directly or indirectly, to reassess their priorities and redefine the meaning of their acts and their life. The following story illustrates this:

A father, a businessman, told me how his twelve-year-old son asked him why he worked ten hours a day and why he never seemed to be at home.

"To earn a living," replied the father.

"Yes, but why?" continued the child.

"For our security and comfort," said the father.

"If it's for my security and my comfort, I'd rather you came to get me from school at four o'clock and we go and do sports together."

Here is a father who reassessed his priorities and, after consulting with his son, agreed that once a week they would go and be involved in sports after school.

So you see how life invites us to change and renew ourselves.

Listening Without Judging

Here is the reaction of Isabel, a fifteen-year-old schoolgirl:

"Uh, there's something I'd like to talk to my parents about, and if they would bring it up with me, I'd feel more comfortable talking about it."

"Can you tell what it's about?"

"Well, I feel awful in my class. Because of my schedule, I'm the only one to go to math class with a bunch of kids who know one another already. It's hard for me to fit in and feel comfortable when it comes to asking questions that are bothering me. As soon as I say I don't understand, everyone laughs and makes fun of me. So I don't say anything anymore and don't ask any more questions."

"Do you feel alone (F) in this situation, and you would like to be made welcome and understood by the other pupils (N)?"

"Yes, that's right."

"And would you like to talk about that with your parents as well so they can understand and perhaps support you (N)?"

"Yes, but they don't believe me. They think I'm not studying, that this is just an excuse. They tell me just to try harder."

"So do you feel disappointed and perhaps annoyed (F) because you really have a need for them to understand that it's not so much a question of studying but of atmosphere in the class (N)?"

"Right."

"You perhaps also feel tired after all the efforts you've made (F), and maybe you just want to have consideration for the effort you're making."

"Yes (tears in her eyes). In fact, I'm just asking them to listen to me, for me to be able to express what I'm experiencing. I don't

115

really want them to help or do anything. I want them to listen to me without judging me."

I very often hear a simple need like that: to be listened to without being judged. Why is it so difficult for parents to listen to their teenagers? Mostly I observe that it's because the parents believe they have to *do something*, act, perform, get a result, a solution and, if possible, immediately. Yet a solution may elude them, and they may feel helpless, or perhaps they're fed up with trying to come up with solutions. *Consequently*, to escape the tension brought about by the helplessness, the fear, or the fatigue, they'll go for flight, denying the problem ("Oh, but it's not so serious . . . What a drama you're making of it all . . . You could at least try . . . Life isn't always easy")—or for aggression ("It's your fault; you don't study enough . . . If only you'd look over your lessons more") rather than simply taking the time to connect with their children and listen to them genuinely.

It is worth noting that a young person can take on similar attitudes: aggression ("My parents just don't get it . . . They're such numbskulls . . . I'm so fed up") or flight ("I don't tell them anything anymore . . . I just secretly leave"), failing to make a true connection. Fortunately, listening can be learned.

Communicating means expressing and listening.

Indeed, communicating means expressing *and* listening; it means expressing oneself and allowing another to express also, listening to oneself, listening to the other person, and often checking to make sure the reciprocal listening is of good quality. Many relational difficulties stem from the fact that we don't take the trouble to ensure that we have properly heard another person and that the other person has heard us correctly. Repeating or reformulating, if need be, what the person has said will make it possible for us to check if we have properly understood. Similarly, inviting another person to repeat or reformulate what we have said will often enable us to check whether we have been accurately understood.

If we were to represent communication between human beings on a diagram, we could draw one like this:

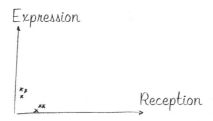

The exchange of a message, therefore, comprises two aspects: expression and reception. We have learned to be good boys and good girls—not to make too much noise, not to bother people, not to occupy too great a space, not to "bother others with our little problems." So we do of course express ourselves a little, but not too much, so as not to be subject to criticism, so as not to make ourselves vulnerable, so as not to show to what extent we are sensitive, even delicate. On the diagram, we are down on the left.

Since we have learned to listen properly to everybody else's needs except our own—and to act as a St. Bernard dog and meet everyone's needs except our own—when it comes to listening to another and receiving their messages, our tendency will be to think "I don't mind listening to you a little, but not too much because it's going to start getting on my nerves if I keep on listening to other people all the time. I have other more important things to do." On the diagram, our ability to receive another's message will often be located in the bottom left as well.

There also are extremes. From time to time, we get fed up with trying to listen to others, and we try to impose upon them our vision. We express ourselves completely, but we switch off the "receive" button. We start acting like tyrants, despots. We impose our need without listening to the other person's need. We adopt an attitude of authority, power *over* others, control.

On the diagram, it will look like this:

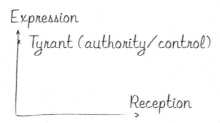

At other times, we are perhaps so exhausted at having attempted in vain to get our needs recognized, to have expressed them without getting any form of recognition or consideration, we give up. We submit to the behavior of the other person and no longer react. We just give up.

In extreme cases, we act like slaves, victims. Our attitude is one of submission, resignation.

On the graph, it looks like this:

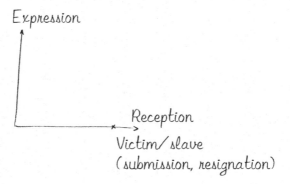

NOTE: We can be one thing at one time, another thing at other times—a tyrant at home, a slave at work, or the reverse (or a little of both, tyrant and victim, depending on the time of day and the circumstances). Within a single moment, within a single sentence, we can be both tyrannical and victimized: "Go and clean up your room immediately—and no discussion about it. Oh, my God! What have I done to deserve children like that?"

Tyrant, victim—or both?!

We can, therefore, go from one extreme to the other at regular intervals, and most of the time we wallow in an area of mistrust, which may be represented as follows:

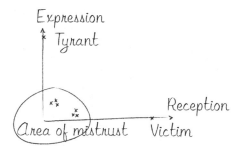

As long as we operate in this area, we're afraid to express ourselves, to reveal ourselves, to show others who we are, with our fortunes and misfortunes, our contradictions, our weaknesses, our vulnerabilities, our fear of developing our talents, our identity, our creativity, our fantasies, our multiplicity. We wear a mask to conceal most of that, to protect ourselves from others' eyes.

Similarly, we are afraid to listen to another person, to hear their stories and their difficulties. We shut ourselves off or reduce to a minimum our ability to listen and take in because another's difference or suffering makes us feel insecure or fragile and gives us the impression that we're going to have to stop being ourselves or we'll have to meet some outside expectations, a design someone else may have for us.

Relinquishing fear and moving to trust

Personally, I'm struck to see to what extent fear has for so long been at the heart of most of my relationships with human beings:
- Fear of what others may think or not think
- Fear of what they may say or not say
- Fear of too many words, fear of too long a silence
- Fear of lacking love, fear of being overwhelmed by love
- Fear to speak, fear not to speak

- Fear of being alone, fear of being in a relationship
- Fear of having nothing to do, fear of being overloaded
- Fear of pleasing, fear of displeasing
- Fear of seducing or being seduced . . .

My word! What a bunch of fears. And think of the energy that goes into fighting those fears!

It took me a long time to realize that all of this energy "eaten up" by fear was then no longer available to act, to create, to quite simply be. Paralyzed to a greater or lesser extent by fear, I pretty much stopped evolving and, consequently, I stopped being. It was as if I was coagulated in the slough of my fear—stuck, identifying with my fears most of the time, having only momentary flights of confidence and creativity.

I remember very precisely the analysis session during which this way of "functioning" (if one can use a word like that for such a *dys*functional way of living!) exploded in my face. All of these little fears, side by side, heaped up one atop the other over the years, suddenly appeared to me like a crawling cancer. I had explored them one by one, nicely, for years of analysis: "I'm afraid of this. I'm worried about that. I'm concerned by such and such." Examined separately, they looked benign, harmless, coincidental.

In a flash, though, with a breakthrough of consciousness into the fog of the subconscious, through therapy, I was able suddenly to see them as a single whole, like a teeming entity, a web-like network. I appreciated in an instant the extent to which they were neither coincidental nor occasional but structural, that is, representing the way I truly operated. At that moment, I became aware that I was in danger of dying. Perhaps not dying an immediate physical death, but in danger of psychic death, in danger of becoming what Marshall Rosenberg calls "a nice dead person, smiling and polite but dead inside, dead scared." This awareness awakened my instinct for survival; it was a matter of urgency to change. It was essential to *relinquish fear and swing over to trust.*

Tired of fear, I wanted to try trust. It was new. Trust was unknown and therefore produced . . . fear. Too bad, I had had enough! I put my money on trust; I was *counting* on it. I calmed my myriad inner voices, which were kicking up a fuss and protesting: "Watch out! Things will go wrong! Be careful!" I repeated to myself: "Trust. What do you have to lose? Fear, the main alternative, certainly wasn't satisfactory. At worst, trust won't be satisfactory either. But, hey, there's nothing to lose." In my present paralyzed way of life, I would die of boredom anyway.

This is one of the challenges of life: either staying in the known—which weighs upon us or even tortures us, but which is reassuring because it is known, as familiar as an old coat or an old pair of jeans—or swinging over into the unknown, which can be infinitely more joyful, infinitely richer, but (and here's the kicker) it involves a *passage*, a *change*.

Ah, changing! Stopping doing the same thing, saying the same thing, thinking the same thing . . . in order to do something new, say something new, think in a new way, pray in a new way!

If I don't change, I die; if I don't renew myself, I die. French author Christian Bobin expresses this fear of the unknown thus: "Two words give you a fever. Two words nail you to your bed: change life. That is the aim. It is clear, simple. But we can't see the path leading to the goal. Disease is the absence of a path, the uncertainty of routes. We are not faced with a question. We are inside. We are the question. A new life, that is what we would like, but willpower, part of the old life, has no strength. We are like these children, holding a marble in their left hand and not letting it go until they are sure that the swap is in their right hand: we would like to have a new life but without losing the former life. We refuse the moment of passage, the moment of the empty hand."[13]

As soon as I decided to quiet my fears and swing over to trust, my entire energy field changed. More precisely, the energy I had previously been devoting to fighting my fears and attempting to manage them could now be engaged in change, in openness to novelty. And, within a few years, my professional life and my emotional life changed radically in ways that were fulfilling beyond all my hopes and expectations. In two or three years, my life evolved more than in the previous thirty-five.

I often get the feeling that one sometimes has when sailing. After a long time of sluggishness, with the water lapping against the boat and the boat turning around on itself, its sails flapping, there's a stomach-churning moment, then the wind picks up and fills the sails, the boat heels over, finds its heading, and sets off toward the open water. It is that euphoric feeling of being carried away, joyfully forward, that is most often alive in me these days.

Although I have observed and experienced my own mistrust, I observe it just as much in people I work with. Whether at workshops with groups or in individual sessions, my observation is that the feeling dominating much of human experience is an uncomfortable mixture of fear and mistrust.

> ## Do I act out of the joy of loving or out of the fear of not being loved?

Even for couples, where the dream might be all trust, emotional security, a letting-go in love, oh, what fears! What doubts! "If I do this, what will he believe or say? If I undertake to do this, what will she think? I must do this or that; otherwise they will be sad, angry, disappointed, etc." So many behaviors are guided not by the joy of loving but by the fear of no longer being loved, not out of the joy of giving but out of the fear of not receiving in return. I buy love, I buy belonging. It isn't a generous exchange of love in a spirit of abundance; it's more in the spirit of a subsistence economy.

Many live in relationships governed by projection and dependence: "I cannot live alone; you cannot live alone. If you go, I die; you die if I go. I lean on you; you are the father (or mother) I didn't have. I am the child you need to smother with all the care you yourself did not receive. I expect you to protect me and reassure me eternally; you expect to be able to comfort me eternally. Together, we attempt to fill up our gaps and voids, insatiably."

It seems to me that very few people living as couples are truly in a person-to-person relationship, a relationship of responsibility, autonomy, and freedom where each party feels the strength and confidence to say, "I am capable of living and finding joy without you; you are capable of living and finding joy without me. We, you and I, both have this strength and autonomy, and at the same time we love being together because it's even more joyful to share, to exchange, and be together. We don't strive to fill up the gaps, but to exchange plenitude!" Sometimes this state of being is called synergism—where the whole is greater than the sum of its parts.

Also evoked here are "pearls" of wisdom from Gestalt co-founder Fritz Perls of Germany who wrote:

> *I do my thing, and you do your thing.*
> *I am not in this world to live up to your expectations,*
> *And you are not in this world to live up to mine.*
> *You are you, and I am I.*
> *And if perchance we find each other,*
> *It's beautiful.*
> *If not, it can't be helped.*

The practice of Nonviolent Communication also is an invitation to live confidently and to enter confidently into relationships. It urges us to find sufficient inner security and solidity, confidence and self-esteem to dare to take our place without fear of trespassing onto someone else's space, confident that there's room for everyone—to dare to say what we want to say, to be who we want to be, without fear of being criticized, made fun of, rejected, or abandoned. It therefore makes it possible for us to dare to maximize self-expression and self-actualization.

In the same way, by helping us find greater inner security and solidity, in better nurturing our self-confidence and our self-esteem, Nonviolent Communication encourages us to listen to others as completely as possible, to dare to welcome them in their complexity or their distress, without assuming we are responsible for what is happening to them. Nor must we "do something" other than listen and attempt to understand. Nonviolent Communication urges us to love others' taking their place without fearing that they're trespassing on ours, confident that we can set our own boundaries and that there is room for everyone.

On our diagram, this quality of presence—with oneself and presence with others, with oneself listening and expressing, and with others listening and expressing—may be represented like this: maximization of expression and reception shown by a cross in the top right-hand corner of the diagram, the area of trust.

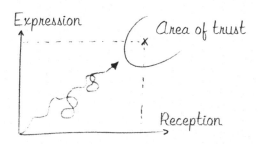

We strive, therefore, to maximize our ability to express what we feel, what needs we have, *and* to maximize our ability to receive the feelings and needs of others.

We thus live increasingly in a climate of trust, trust that we can be in the world without fearing "bothering" other people and that others can be in the world without fearing our being "bothered" by them.

You can see that I have marked an arrow between the mistrust area and the trust area. This arrow does not go in a straight line. It represents the path we are invited to set out on—as long as we really want to—to evolve from the mistrust area to the trust area.

Walking quietly toward a fountain

An image that for me is an illustration of this path is one I found in *The Little Prince* by Saint-Exupéry, a book that has never lost any of its freshness. Remember, the Little Prince travels from planet to planet. One time, he meets a tradesman who has found a pill to make it possible never ever to be thirsty again. And the merchant is so proud that he boasts the qualities of his pill, saying, "Thanks to this pill, you will no longer have to go and draw water from a well or drink at a fountain. I have calculated that it will be possible to save fifty-three minutes a week!" When the Little Prince hears that, he is dismayed and answers, "If it were me, if I had fifty-three minutes, I would walk very slowly toward a fountain."[14]

In other words, I would take the time to go very slowly toward anything that quenches my thirst, that which revitalizes me. I would rejoice at the freshness of the water even before tasting it. I would refresh myself with its melody even before having wet my hands. I would take the time to be wherever life nurtures me, truly quenching my thirst.

We live in an era, however, when *we are communicating ever more quickly and ever more poorly.* We have cell phones, answering machines, e-mail, information highways, and so on. We exchange huge volumes of information. Yes indeed, but do we connect? Do we have nurturing connections, satisfying ones?

We often use pills so as not to be thirsty. I worked for a business where a woman, a mother in an executive job, telephoned her son regularly around seven in the evening: "Darling, Mommy has a lot of work to do, and tonight she has another meeting. She'll come back later. There's a great pizza for you in the freezer. Put it in the microwave for five minutes, and you'll have a good meal." Pill! In other words: "I don't have time for you, sweetie, so the pizza will be a substitute for a family dinner."

Or: "Darling, Daddy has to leave this afternoon for an important meeting. There are two DVDs in the TV cabinet.

Have a good time. Kisses, and see you tonight." Pill! I don't have time for you, darling. My golf game, my tennis match, or my meeting is more important. Watch the movies. That will be a substitute for a family evening together!

Or, more subtle yet: "Darling, I understand how very unhappy you are. Sleep well tonight, and all will be better tomorrow." Pill! You know, listening to you tires me and bothers me. I have other things to do, and in any case it's late and I'm tired. This piece of advice will be a substitute for understanding.

And we race on and on, from thing to do to thing to do, from pill to pill, and then we are surprised to be insatiably thirsty on our way, on a quest, ever dissatisfied, our throats and hearts dry! Not to mention our children and spouse . . . Without knowing it, we're sitting next to the only well that could truly quench our thirst. It's called presence with self, presence with others, presence with the world, presence with divinity.

Taking the time to understand one another

During a training session, a mother screamed at me: "That's all well and good, but we don't have *time* to listen to one another like that. You just don't know, for example, the race it is in the morning for everyone to be on time to school and for me to get to work! Look, every morning for weeks, around 7:45, just when the two oldest children already have gotten into the car, with their backpacks on their laps, to be at school by 8:15, and I still have to drop off my smallest daughter so I can be at work by 8:30 . . . do you know what the little one is doing? She's combing her hair in leisurely fashion, looking at herself in the bathroom mirror! Do you think I have time to say to her how I feel and what my needs are? I just explode and call her a selfish airhead and drag her off to the car."

"And how do you feel then?"

"Furious. We waste time every day. The boys nearly always arrive late at school, and I'm late too. And besides, everyone grumbles for the whole journey."

"And you say this has been going on for weeks?"

"Yes, every morning. So surely you can see that we don't have time to discuss things as you're suggesting!"

I proposed that she herself play the role of her daughter, and I would take her own role. Experience has shown that when we put ourselves into another's shoes, that often allows "pennies to drop" and awareness to be enhanced. She threw herself into the part of her daughter, who was doing her hair in carefree style in front of the bathroom mirror.

"Daughter, when I see you doing your hair now (O), I really feel worried (F) because I'd like the boys to be on time to school, and I'd like to get to the office on time too (N). Would you be willing to come with us now (R)?"

(Silence.) The mother, playing her daughter, continued to do her hair, unperturbed.

As for me, in the role of the mother, realizing that talking about myself would be of no use at that time, I chose to speak about her and to attempt to connect with her. I then voiced the feeling and the need I imagined she may have had, because they were the ones apparent in me if I put myself in the shoes of the daughter who was choosing calmly to do her hair at this time of the day when everyone in the household was getting hot and bothered: "Daughter, are you sad (F) about something? Is there something you would like me to understand (N) that I don't always understand?"

"You're mean!"

"Are you sad (F) because you aren't reassured about my loving you as much as you would like (N)?"

"You don't wake me up in the morning anymore!"

As soon as those words came out, the mother stopped the role-play and blurted: "That's it! I've got it! For several weeks now I haven't been going up to give my daughter a special hug in her bedroom to wake her up in the morning. I always used to do that before waking up the boys with a 'Morning, boys. It's time.' Waking up was different for the boys and for her. Now I go along the passage and ring out a single 'Morning, children.

127

It's time.' And I no longer give her a hug. In fact, she's perhaps sad to be put on an equal footing with the older children and to lose her special status as the youngest child."

The workshop was spread over two days at a week's interval. So the woman had an opportunity to practice at home. She came back the next week and said, "That *was* it! The next morning when my daughter was once again taking her time to do her hair at 7:45, I decided we would perhaps all be late today, but that we were going to settle this matter once and for all. I sat beside her calmly in the bathroom and said to her: 'Tell me, are you sad because I no longer come and give you a big hug every morning?'

'Yes, you don't love me anymore. You love the boys more than me.'

'Are you disappointed because you'd like to be sure that you're still my darling little girl and that I won't force you to do the same things as the boys just because you're growing up?'

'Yes.'

'What can I do to reassure you that I love you very specially and that you can grow up at your own pace?'

'You can give me hugs again in the morning!'"

Thus, the mother resumed the ritual of the morning hug. Naturally, that day everyone arrived a few minutes late, but the younger daughter no longer had any need to hold everyone up every day to remind them that she existed and mattered.

Curiously, we often have time to argue every day for weeks but not the time to connect for just a few minutes! What are we truly focusing on? Logistics (being on time) *or* the quality of our connections (being on time willingly)?

When I see to what extent our misunderstandings can often be clarified in short order through reciprocal listening, I'm more and more surprised to observe the tragic old habit of considering that "arguing is normal" and that devoting a great deal of time and energy to arguments is "part of life." But sitting down, listening to one another, and taking time together are often considered a waste of time or are quite simply not considered at all. Are we so allergic to well-being, the pleasure of being together, peace itself? Or is it difficult for us to believe that well-being, the pleasure of being together, and peace can actually be built up?

> **Each of us has the power to make war or to make peace.**

For me, it's a matter of urgency to revise our old patterns; each of us has the power to make war or to make peace. Faced with any situation, we choose our behavior: Constrain the younger daughter and repeat the scenario every morning or understand the younger daughter and connect with one another more deeply every day. We have that power in our hands.

Empathy: Being Present With Oneself and Others

Karim—swinging over to trust

I give the following example to illustrate the fact that the here and now takes root in our inner security, born of our self-knowledge and our confidence in our ability to listen, our ability to receive another's message and take it in.

Karim is a twenty-year-old who suffers from a serious drug addiction and has been unable to break free. He joined the association for young people I belonged to. He was unemployed and had no plans. He lived alone in a small one-room apartment. I had just bought a house I wanted to refurbish, so I suggested paying him to paint and renovate the house. In the end, he settled in one of the rooms in my house and stayed for four or five months. He enjoyed the work because he saw his efforts producing results, day after day, and even hour after hour. As he was satisfied and tired in the evening, his consumption of drugs dropped dramatically. At the same time, a relationship developed between us, based on friendship and trust.

129

One day he said to me, "I'm deeply grateful to you. Not only have you given me work and an opportunity to earn my living, you give me shelter, and I'm no longer all alone. But most of all, you trusted me when I no longer trusted myself."

Sometime later, he fell in love and left to live with his partner, two hours by car from Brussels. We kept in touch for some time. Then he moved again and did not give me his address, so nearly two years went by without any news from him. One weekend when I was at my father's place in the country, he called. I was completely taken by surprise—two years without a word and then this call to a number he did not know before he left. That was strange. Here is a summary of the conversation we had, which in reality lasted nearly an hour.

"Thomas, this is Karim. You'll be surprised to hear from me, but things are not working out at all with my partner. I'm alone again. I'm going crazy. I'm going to shoot myself or throw myself into the canal. She's crazy. I'm crazy. Life has no meaning. We beat each other up. It's not possible! You're the last person I'm speaking to before I kill myself!"

To say Karim was in a state of panic would be an understatement. His words came tumbling out as if he had held them in for such a long time that only a torrent of words could relieve him of the pressure that had built up, as water behind a dam that is finally released. I first of all listened to him at length without interrupting. When he slowed down a bit, showing that the pressure was decreasing, I tried to connect with him by expressing my empathy for his feeling and needs:

"Karim, it sounds like you are feeling completely desperate (F), and I can see that it's difficult for you to believe that your relationship can improve (N)."

"I tell you, it's over," he screamed again. "What a mess! I can't believe in anything anymore. All I need is a bullet in the head."

"It does look as if you're at the bottom of a hole (F), and life has no meaning anymore (N: that life has meaning) and you prefer to get it over with (R or A—action). Is that how you're feeling?"

"That's right."

"It must be very painful (F) for you to see that your relationship isn't working out as you had wished (N: that the relationship should evolve satisfactorily), and there's such a fear of being alone again (F) that you would rather cut yourself off from this suffering or protect yourself from it (N: protecting oneself from suffering), and you've come out with no other solution than putting a bullet in your head (R or A)."

"Well, yes . . . I can't think of anything else."

"You must be in such pain (F), and you can see everything collapsing. Nothing is worthwhile anymore (N: that things should stay in place and have meaning). Is that right?"

"Yes, that's right."

(Silence, a long silence.) I can hear him breathing more calmly. I go "Hmm, hmm" for a while, listening, alert to what he is experiencing and what I myself am experiencing (also to show him that my silence is presence). Then, I resume:

"Is it OK for you if I tell you how I feel in relation to all that?"

"Well, you can try."

"Well, first of all I'm deeply touched that you would call me (F), that you would have gone to the trouble of finding me here this weekend."

"You're surprised, aren't you?"

"Well, yes. How did you find the number?"

"I called the association's secretary, who said that perhaps you'd be there. And it worked."

"Well, I'm really grateful (F) for your confidence (N) and that you wished to speak to me from the depths of your distress."

"Grateful?"

"Yes, I receive your trust as a gift of friendship, a friendship of the heart that isn't burned out just because two years have gone by, but that is alive between us. And that trust and friendship, you see, is what I cherish more than anything." (Silence.) "Perhaps that surprises you?"

"Yes, somewhat. I see myself as so useless and hopeless that I don't see what I could contribute to you."

"Do you feel surprised (F) because it's difficult for you to believe (N: need to believe that sharing one's pain is useful) that sharing your pain could actually be a source of joy?"

"Well, yes."

"For me, it's the joy of being together, of looking at things together, of seeking together how to go forward. The joy of counting on each other. You give me the joy of being with you, even if it is in suffering. How do you feel when I say that to you?"

"Better. That's nice for me to hear. It even helps me relax a little."

"Now, I know from experience that in a relationship one can stub one's toe on the same stone, and one doesn't see it because of being too close to the situation. Would it suit you to talk about it one evening so we can better understand together what's going on?"

We went on chatting a bit more. He regained confidence, seeing doors ajar here and there, which a half hour earlier had seemed to him to be bolted shut. He was betting on life again. We both ended the conversation with warmer hearts and an agreement to meet again within a couple of weeks. (Karim isn't out of the woods yet, but at this writing he's doing much better again.)

Remarks

1. What is dangerous is not going through a suicidal phase; what is dangerous is not listening to what is happening during that phase. Underlying the desire to die is a desire to live that has been disappointed, perhaps bitterly so.

2. I witnessed similar cases when I started working with young people. I had never been trained to listen, and often I used such clumsy tools as the following:
   - Denial or reduction: "Oh, it's not so serious; you'll get over it; life is wonderful, come on."
   - Moralizing/advice: "Such-and-such relationship isn't good for you. Get out of it."
   - Advice: "Come and play some games. That will be a change for you."

- Returning to self: "You know, I too have been through difficult times . . ."

In those sincere but largely misguided efforts I was denying the others' suffering or was seeking to deflect their attention from it, too afraid myself of the idea of suicide, fearful of the small suicidal part of myself that I had never taken the time to listen to or domesticate. I was, therefore, not available to listen to the distress of others, to move into their pain with them on an equal footing. I was trying to skirt the issue. Finding that looking at a festering wound was intolerable, I was attempting to distract the injured person by drawing their attention elsewhere, or I simply covered the thing over with a layer of ointment and a big bandage.

It is well known that to tend a wound, you need to clean it, that is, *look at it closely to see what is hurting and why*, get into it, get right inside again and again, and only then let it air, rest, heal. It hurts, yes, but it ends up hurting even more if real attention isn't given as soon as possible. And the hurt of dressing a wound seldom harms it. In short, what hurts does not necessarily harm . . . and often helps.

What hurts does not necessarily harm . . . and often helps.

When it came to reflecting Karim's pain back to him in the way I did, previously I would not have had the inner security or the trust in myself, in the other person, and in life to live through a long silence, to welcome Karim, and to offer him my presence after saying, "Nothing is worthwhile anymore?" I would immediately have attempted to supply him with all manner of solutions and good advice to reassure myself that I was doing everything that could be

133

done. That's because what I had learned best was to *do* things rather than to *be* and be *with*.

3. If today I manage to support people at the bottom of their pit in a more satisfactory way, it's because I have understood that what they need most is presence, to not be alone. Karim saw himself (and he said so) all alone again, that is, abandoned and rejected, which was the essential drama of his life.

   If I display for him all my solutions, my good reassuring advice, *I am not taking care of him but of me*, of *my* anxiety. I am not with him, but with me, with my panic or my guilt at the idea of failing in "my duty to do good." So then he is more and more alone, more and more convinced that no one can understand the extent of his distress. And then the only solution for such a person is suicide, the ultimate anesthesia. Whereas, if through empathy I reach him, if I accompany him in his distress with my fully compassionate presence, he has a greater chance of feeling less lonely. Doubtless he is experiencing great pain, but at the same time we are together. And we converge on the need that lies at the very heart of Karim's drama, as well as many others' suffering: to count for someone, to have a place among other people, to connect, to exist in someone's heart.

4. If today I'm more successful in the practice of this type of support, it's because I have explored my own distress and continue to do so when it surfaces. I no longer discard it as I did before by running off "to do something"—see people, flirt with someone, get into activity (and then hyperactivity) in what French philosopher, mathematician, and epigrammatist Blaise Pascal called "entertainment." I took a look at it, close up. I went in there often and observed that *the only way of getting out of pain is to go into it fully*. If, on the other hand, I'm pussyfooting around trying to minimize things ("It's not serious . . . It will be better tomorrow") or by going into my concrete bunker

("No, you don't cry . . . Snap out of it . . . Think of something else"), believing that I can elbow my pain off to one side, I end up placing it right in the center and cannot get out of it.

It's because I have gotten in touch with my own pain (some might even say "domesticated" it, though such is never completely possible) that I can hear Karim's tale without having to immediately protect myself. Yet I don't have to dwell on my story as I listen to another's. It's important that the pain of someone else is not simply a springboard or a bridge to mine, no matter how profound or fascinating my experience seems to me. If my attention is largely on how another person's story compares with mine, I am not empathizing. The key to compassionate listening is staying present with the other's pain—as long as it takes.

5. I would go a step farther by suggesting not only to be open to our emotional or psychic suffering, as well as the suffering of someone else, but to actually welcome it as an opportunity for further growth. If we want to see what this suffering means, it can be a chance to grow, to learn something about oneself, about another, even about the meaning of our life. In my experience, welcoming suffering always heralds (always—as long as we accept *going in* in order to *get out!*) profound joy, both renewed and unexpected.

Not that I would wish anyone to suffer. Let me make something clear: If we can spare ourselves pain, so much the better. Far be it from me to suggest seeking suffering, as some religious schools of thought have done in not granting individuals well-being and life in every respect. Since at least a certain degree of emotional or psychic suffering tends to be the lot of humanity, however, I suggest experiencing it as an incentive to get to a new level of consciousness, to change one's plane of existence.

Indeed, my belief is that most often our suffering is

out of ignorance. I am ignorant of a dimension of life in myself, a dimension of meaning that is walled up in a room lost inside my inner palace, a forgotten chamber. Suffering produces cracks in the wall, opens a breach, or turns the key of a secret door so I can gain access to a new space within myself, a profound and unexpected space, a place where I will get a better taste of ease and inner well-being, greater solidity, and more inner security. From that place I will be able to look upon myself, others, and the world with greater compassion and tenderness. And then the forgotten chamber opens like a balcony upon the world.

Listening at the right place

Empathy or compassion is presence directed to what I am experiencing or to what another is experiencing. Empathy for self or empathy for another means bringing our attention to what is being experienced at the present moment. We connect to feelings and needs in four ways: *the stages of empathy.*

Stage 1: Doing nothing

When we were young, we would often hear, "Don't just stand there, do something," so we dance around in a hundred and one different ways, and we're truly incapable of just contenting ourselves to listen and be there doing nothing. Buddha suggests the following (just the reverse): *Don't just do something, stand there.*

How difficult it is if we are too encumbered with our own pain, anger, and sadness to open up to the suffering of others—their anger, their sadness—and to accept just *being there.* Succeeding in listening to another while doing nothing presupposes that we have integrated what all human beings have within themselves: the resources necessary to heal, to awaken, and to know fulfillment. What alienates people from their inner resources, what conceals them behind a veil, is their inability to listen to themselves in the right place and in the right proportions. The inner resources are there. What is lacking is our ability to perceive them in a balanced way.

> **The inner resources are there. What is lacking is our ability to perceive them in a balanced way.**

I've lost count of how many young, soul-searching people say to me something like this: "I would just like my father (or mother) to listen to me for a while when I want to talk to them about my difficulties. But as soon as I start to talk about what is not going right, they bore me to tears with all their advice. They bring out heaps of solutions that are *their* solutions. They tell me everything I should do or everything they did in their day. They don't really listen."

And this is typical. Doubtless the father or the mother, overwhelmed with a concern to "get it right," is not available to deeply listen to the young person's needs. They are virtually overcome by the fear of not measuring up to the perfectionistic and paralyzing image of the good father and mother, fearing that their child will get bogged down in untold difficulties. They panic at the idea that their child will be a school dropout or get into drugs, sexual excess, and/or manipulation by peers. The whole of the parents' energy is being mobilized—most often unconsciously—in taking care of their own need for security, attending to their own need to provide help, or by the image of the good father/good mother, that is, their need for self-esteem. They are therefore not willing or able to listen in silence to another person. Being empathic with another, particularly if that other is someone close to us with whom we have significant emotional ties, requires considerable inner strength and security.

Stage 2: Focusing our attention on the other's feelings and needs

The life within us manifests itself through feelings and needs. It would, therefore, be wise to listen carefully with the ears of the heart to another's feelings and needs, listening beyond the words being said to the tone of voice, the attitude. To do so, we need to take time to resonate with the other person: "I wonder what they may be feeling—sadness, solitude, anger, some of each? When I feel things like that, what are the needs in me that those feelings may be pointing to?"

We set ourselves up as an echo chamber; we resonate or vibrate with the other person. You know how tambourines vibrate with one another: If you place several tambourines side by side, with the fabric parallel, and if you strike the first one, the vibration is transmitted down the line, by sympathy, to the last. Empathy invites us to vibrate out of sympathy.

Beware! This does not mean assuming responsibility for what the other individual is experiencing. That is their business. However, we do offer our presence.

Stage 3: Reflecting another's feelings and needs

This is not a question of interpreting, but rather of paraphrasing in order to attempt to gain awareness of feelings and needs. It is of vital importance to realize that repeating or reformulating another's needs doesn't mean approving them, agreeing with them, or even being willing to meet them. Here is an example:

"My wife never appreciates how hard I work to earn the money she spends. She's such a typical, demanding woman."

"I see. You are angry, and you need respect as a man."

Here we have not a reflection but an interpretation that maintains the "macho man/demanding woman" conflict. Yet what we really want is to check if we have truly understood the needs involved by avoiding any language that maintains division, separation, and opposition. We will hook a need onto the feeling. If we only reflect the feeling, the risk we run is of getting into complaining and aggressing.

"Are you angry (reflecting a feeling without a need)?"

"Yeah! You said it. She's just unbearable. Now the other day . . ."

The person in pain continues accusing without getting any nearer to himself, without getting into his own pit. If we hook a need onto the feeling, we invite the other person to go deeper within himself to do the inner work that makes it possible to enhance both consciousness and the power to act.

"Are you angry (F) because you have a need for recognition and respect for the work you do (N)?"

The answer may be:

- "That's absolutely right. I need both recognition and respect" or . . .
- "Not at all. I *do* feel recognized and respected. And I'm not angry. What I feel is sad and disheartened, and I need encouragement and cooperation."

The reason I'm giving both responses is to show that it isn't necessary to guess another's feelings and needs accurately. Reflecting feelings and needs is like throwing the other person a lifeline. A response of this nature, on the one hand, is an incentive for the other person to look inside, to go deep down and ascertain an inner state. On the other hand, it demonstrates to the other person compassionate listening, which is needed to become aware of inner resources. It is, therefore, *active* listening. We are present and are displaying our presence by accompanying the individual in their exploration of their feelings and needs. The listening will be all the more active since the other person will tend to go back into their head, into a mental space, possibly needing help to come back to their feelings and needs.

If the man says, "In any event, all women are demanding, and nothing will change that," we won't pass by a "mental" sentence such as that because it is both a judgment and a category. On the contrary, we're offered an opportunity to look at an invaluable need. Marshall Rosenberg rightly observes that "judgments are tragic expressions of unmet needs."[15]

> ## "Judgments are tragic expressions of unmet needs."

We might, for example, go on as follows:

"When you say that, are you disheartened (F) because you would like human beings, and particularly women, to be more understanding and cooperative (N)?"

"With my woman, that is not about to happen!"

"Are you sad (F) because you would love to be able to trust her, believe that she can change, believe that she has the resources in her to change (N)?"

"Oh, of course. Naturally, she has amazing qualities. But she cuts herself off from most of her qualities. She is armor-plated."

"As you say that, are you perhaps feeling divided (F) between one part of you that feels quite touched (F) by the qualities (N) your wife displays and another part of you that is disappointed (F) that she makes so little use of them (N)?"

"Yes, that's right. I'm very touched by this woman and feel so close to her caring, compassionate side. At times she shows such sensitivity! But she's so afraid of showing this side because she says she has been hurt in the past. And I'm sad when she doesn't offer me the gift of her sensitivity." (Silence.) "Isn't that funny? Just now I was judging her as demanding, and now I see her as a sensitive and attentive woman who has gotten caught up in this game."

"How do you feel when you notice that?"

"Moved, at peace (F) because I understand better (N) the game we're both playing."

"Do you mean you also see yourself included in this insight in relation to her?"

"Quite so. And as both of us are playing our games, we're not always in a genuine relationship." (Silence) "I need to change, to take off the mask, to show her who I really am and not who I would like her to see me as."

"Specifically, what can you do along those lines?"

(Silence) "Ask her if she would agree to listen to me for a while and dare to say to her what I've just shared with you."

Remarks

1. Empathy literally means "staying glued" to another's feelings and needs. It also means putting yourself in the other person's shoes. This means, on the one hand, you invent nothing, no feeling or need, and you attempt to get as close as possible to what the other is feeling by putting their feelings and needs into words; on the other hand, the other is urged to listen carefully and explore their feelings and needs rather than going up into their head, their intellect, into cultural, psychological, or philosophical considerations. The other person guides us, shows us the way.

   Thus, in the "All women are demanding" example I don't argue back, saying, "Not at all, not all of them, I know some men (including yours truly) who . . ." or "You're right, they are unbelievable . . ." This would simply result in our going 'round and 'round, strengthening either the separation or the confusion. On the contrary, I keep up with the proposal, I accompany it by staying "glued" to what the other person is feeling and experiencing behind the words being said. For example, "Do you feel disheartened because you would like other human beings and especially women to become more understanding and cooperative with each other?" By doing that I'm inviting the other person to leave the world of images, ready-made categories, and prejudices propounded automatically by generations of people over the centuries—*to connect with what is alive in them* and bring them to life *at that precise moment*. I suggest that the

141

other person direct their awareness toward what they truly want, a genuine need, concealed behind the catchphrase, habits of language, and particularly complaints.

> **I'm often aware of what I don't want, and I complain about that to someone who does not have the skills to help me. I can work on my consciousness of what I want and address my request to someone who has the relevant skills.**

2. When we complain, we often tend to identify with what we don't want or no longer want. Then we talk about that to someone who isn't able to help us. This is a recipe for spending a hundred years of one's life complaining, while changing nothing. Our conscience and Nonviolent Communication help us identify and become aware of the need underlying the lack and to share that with a person able to help us—that person often being oneself. Thus, in the recent example of the man who acknowledged that "both of us are playing our games" and expressed a readiness to change and open up to his wife, here is a person who has left complaining and moved into assuming responsibility for himself.

3. Empathy is the key to a quality relationship with both ourselves and others. It is empathy that heals, relieves, nourishes. Look carefully at your sadness, your distress, your loneliness when these emotions get hold of you. Do they not stem from *not* having been made welcome, listened to, understood, and loved as you would have liked? Look at the suffering occasioned by grieving, a separation, the failure of a project. If you're alone to endure the pain, it is hell. If you're connected empathically to one or more caring individuals, to a family, then the situation is very different because you can share what

you're experiencing in an atmosphere of understanding and mutual esteem. It may even be an opportunity for renewed communion and a transformed well-being, as profound as it is unexpected, if you can seize this opportunity to move to another level of consciousness.

4. In the example, I showed that it wasn't necessary to guess another's feelings and needs accurately. But it was useful to propose a feeling and a need to the other person, to help them reach that level themselves. I recently had an opportunity to illustrate this point with a group of students. We were working in a poorly heated classroom in the middle of winter, and the end of the morning was approaching. At one stage, I asked a girl the usual two-part question: "How are you? How are you feeling?"

She replied, "Hmm . . . I'm all right."

Then I continued, "Are you thirsty?"

She said, "Yes."

"Are you cold?"

"Yes."

"Are you hungry?"

She answered, "Yes," laughing.

"You see that if I ask you more precise questions, you observe that you aren't all that well after all. I didn't force you to be hungry, cold, or thirsty. What I did do, though, was to invite you to check if you were in touch with those needs. You might well have answered no to my three questions or have added, 'But I do feel tired' if that had been the case. I threw a line to invite you to pay greater attention to yourself rather than answer in some automatic way. That is what empathy proposes—listening to oneself in the right place."

Stage 4: Noticing a release of tension, a physical relaxation in the other person

Our nonverbal language often shows when we're feeling understood, joined. Waiting for this sign is invaluable in checking whether the other person feels understood or is ready to listen to us.

In the exchange with Karim, that moment came clearly. Karim was in no way open to listening to me as long as he had not been listened to himself. With Kathy it took a little longer.

Kathy—allergic to empathy

I observe that most people have a huge hunger for empathy and feel deep well-being when they're listened to in the realm of their feelings and needs, rather than in excessive talking or chitchat. At the same time, I also see people who have so lacked understanding, compassionate listening (free of judgments), and a nondirective openness to who they are that they're even allergic to empathy. It's as if being joined and understood by another person would dispossess them of the most precious thing they have built up: their rebellious, misunderstood identity; their shy and dark loneliness; their pervasive, inconsolable sense of ill-being.

Once again, there is fear of the unknown, but here it takes the form of existential angst: "I've always fought, always protected myself, always kept on armor. Will I survive if I open up, if I speak, if I give up any of my weapons?" Human beings as wounded as that need a great deal of silent empathy, for often they categorically reject words. This ranges from "F--- off . . . shut your trap . . . none of your damn business" among street kids to "I can't stand the psychobabble and the wishy-washy concepts; I like things clear and logical!" from educated adults who see themselves as prim, proper, and all business. By dint of thinking and "thinking right," they no longer dare to feel anything. Going a step farther, they no longer dare to exist.

The vigor of the rejection often reflects the depth of the need, as the example of Kathy illustrates.

A few years ago, I was canoeing down a river for a few days with about twenty young street people, or people living in group homes, in a very sunny, lovely region. Kathy had been abandoned by her mother at birth and was put into a home. For a fourteen-year-old kid, she had vocabulary that would have staggered a veteran prison guard. It was impossible to talk to her without getting back a whole truckload of swearwords, indecent images, and other expressions of her energy and vitality.

From the first few days, as we went down the river under a remorseless sun, I had suggested she put a long-sleeved shirt over her T-shirt to avoid getting sunburn. Able for once to be in the sun, she didn't want to lose a second of it. That was understandable, but . . .

Come evening, when we set up camp, her arms were stiff with sunburn.

"Kathy, I have after-sun cream if you want some. I'm afraid your sunburn may hurt tonight."

"I don't give a rat's a--. Go f--- your mother . . ."

"OK, Kathy, no problem. I'll leave it there. If you want some, help yourself. Nonetheless, I do recommend you put on a shirt tomorrow, otherwise you'll burn even more. The sun is much stronger here than back home."

"Do I have to tell you again? Shut your face! Leave me alone."

The next day, she again spent the whole day getting as much sun as possible without covering herself. In the evening, she was all red and stiff with burns. This time there was some blistering.

"Kathy, I think that must be hurting quite a lot. My cream is on the stone behind my bag. If you want, I can help you for your neck and back . . ."

"F--- you! Hands off, voyeur."

"OK, Kathy."

She left to put up her tent. I was looking and saw that she couldn't do it. She saw that I was looking and called me.

"Hey, you bloody idiot! Can't you help me put up my tent instead of sitting there messin' with yourself?"

Playing it down the middle, I said, "Sure, Kathy." I think I managed to suppress any "tone of voice."

Then with a wink, I added, "You also may call me Thomas rather than 'bloody idiot' if you like."

At that she giggled. I helped her put up her tent. We chatted a while. In our conversation the gentleness of the little girl peeked out from under the mask of the rebel. I went back to what I was doing and put after-sun cream all over myself. I then heard Kathy call me by my first name, showing me her red forearms, fluorescent with sunburn: "Hey, Thomas, why don't you put some on me too?"

For that evening, the forearms were enough. The following day, she also accepted the nape of her neck and her shoulders. After that, it became our little ritual. Every evening of the journey, she would come to me and ask for this little refreshing massage, which was also an opportunity to casually receive tenderness and talk. We had come to terms with each other. Several contented sighs were further evidence of this.

Recall the fox in *The Little Prince:* "I would like you to tame me," said the fox. "But what does *tame* mean?" asked the Little Prince. "You see, I'm a fox like any other fox for you, and you are a little fellow like so many others for me. However, once we have tamed each other, we shall become unique, one for the other."

Becoming unique for another, being unique in another's eyes, is doubtless what Kathy had been awaiting for fourteen years—being grounded, identified, welcomed as unique. Having missed out on all that to such an extent was a suffering so great that she couldn't accept my first overtures, which she interpreted as intrusions.

When we got back, she was picking up her luggage to load it onto the bus to go back to her home in a large French city when she dropped her two bags, looked at me, smiled, and said: "I don't want to go back home. Will you adopt me?"

An opposition toward empathy occurs in many marital and family relationships. Some people have accumulated so much suffering in relationships that they can't take even one word, even a loving one, from this other person. For both the people concerned, a situation like that is extremely painful. The one who keeps the relationship closed suffers from shutting themselves off (without being aware of it, of course) in their distress. They are trapped and don't want to believe that they hold the key to the trap. They have almost overwhelming feelings of powerlessness and loneliness.

The individual in the boat who's trying to throw a line to the other person soon starts to suffer from not having their good intentions and efforts recognized or welcomed. Often, out of despair, this person in turn essentially gives up and gets aggressive in return. That only confirms to the first party that they were right to keep the barriers up. The vicious circle—even the spiral of violence—has begun. And it can last for centuries. Just look at the tribal or family hatreds that have lived on from generation to generation!

What can be done?

When we're desiring to open a closed door

For the person who wants to keep the lines of communication open: First, avoid any aggression. That only begets aggression. However, if the situation has existed for some time, a healthy outburst of anger expressed in Nonviolent Communication will often make it possible to clearly express frustration without committing acts of aggression against the other party. We'll see later how to express our anger forcefully without being aggressive toward anyone.

What frequently happens, though, is that the person who would rather sink than swim (with someone else's help) takes everything personally. In this case, even an outburst of anger expressing needs with no aggressiveness can be taken as an act of aggression.

> **What remains is silent empathy—
> empathy from the heart.**

What remains is silent empathy—empathy from the heart. This calls for inner-empathy work so that one doesn't in turn get caught up (or bogged down) in the spiral of aggression.

In my view, the only way to refrain from getting into the vicious circle or spiral of violence is to maintain compassion, receiving within oneself both the suffering of the other party and the suffering that their behavior engenders in oneself, and work to get to a place of inner peace whatever the circumstances. Each of us is responsible for the war or the peace maintained in our own heart.

This work can require help if we don't feel we have the strength to stand up alone to the spiral of violence. Personally, I have been able, on occasion, to sense a need for outside support and have asked colleagues to listen to me or give me empathy at times when I believed I was on the verge of switching into aggression, whereas I wanted to stay compassionate.

Naturally, I might have been able to obtain certain results by exploding aggressively. For example, throwing an alarm clock on the floor may get it going again, but it also might smash it to smithereens. Or I might lose an eye if a spring pops out the wrong way! I no longer have a taste for attempts to "resolve" conflicts in this way. I have too great a concern about such strategies backfiring. Now what I seek is not so much a result as a climate where the two of us can connect. Maintaining a climate of empathy, even unilaterally, is more pleasant for me than nursing resentment.

"All very fine," you may say, "but what happens next?" Well, here is what may often happen in this kind of situation. We know full well that we can't force other people to change. The only person I can change is me. I also can change how I see another individual. What happens is that if I change, the other person changes too or, in any event, there's a greater chance they will change if we accept changing. But if I harden my stance, there is every likelihood that the other person will harden theirs. Just as it takes two to play aggression Ping-Pong (I aggress you, you respond, I up the ante . . . unless I decide to put down my paddle and tell you I don't want to play anymore), I believe it takes two, not only to tango but also to sulk for the duration.

To alter the metaphor, I have witnessed relationships mending because one party persistently kept the doors open, even though the other was bent on keeping them shut. In fact, what is the petulant person seeking by closing the doors and shutting themselves away? They basically want the other person to understand how much they're suffering, perhaps to do something for their distress. However, since they don't have the words or the drive to say it, they "shut up" and cut themselves off. What can be done by the party who wishes to open the doors despite the behavior of the other person? Show in words or even in silence their compassion for the suffering in the other person and show them by their behavior that they're accepting them with neither judgment nor blame.

Empathy is like water that cuts its own path through the hardest of rocks, because it is called there by that part of the heart that has the greatest need to quench its thirst. But be forewarned. Empathy often requires much, much, much patience; many may wish to choose to use their time and energy in a more gratifying way.

When we're with those who want to keep the door closed

For the person who wants to keep the door closed—unless the situation appears to them in the end so uncomfortable that they will want to get out—I must recommend taking the risk of delving into the pain in order to let it out, to abandon the comfort of complaining ("It's Father's, other's, the husband's, the wife's, the mistress's, the children's fault"), to stop haggling with oneself and with reality ("Things will be better later . . . I'm going to start over, move, or go away . . . Everything will be different with my new spouse"), and to get into the wound to tend it.

This work will often require help too if we wish to avoid going 'round in circles forever. Unfortunately, there are few people who, in situations like these, can accept the idea of outside help.

They tend rather to dwell on their "proud inconsolability" as French poet Gérard de Nerval expresses it in his poem:

> *I am the widower, gloomy, inconsolable,*
> *The Prince of Aquitaine in the Abolished Tower.*
> *My only star is dead, and my star-studded lute*
> *Bears the black sun of my melancholy.*[16]

To ask for help is to offer one's indigence, one's frailty. And it's already a steep step deep into our wound, and therefore into self-knowledge, simply to acknowledge our fragility. However, this affords us an opportunity to show our true strength, the strength of the heart, while our indigence is a chance to show our true wealth, the wealth of the soul.

What I refer to as "proud inconsolability" is coming to a stop on a step upward in our awareness: I am stuck there, draped in my pain, persuaded that I never will be understood. Nonetheless, I wait, with greater or lesser consciousness, for "someone" to rescue me, lift me up, and take care of me. Doubtless just staying there is what is best for the person at that particular time—in those particular circumstances. And doubtless that person no longer has the energy to ask for help or simply look at things differently. In this respect, I have no judgment to make. I am simply filled with enormous sadness at the idea of human beings allowing themselves to get bogged down to such an extent in their suffering that it prevents them from taking advantage of the situation and growing. I also fear that a person who has stiffened into a stance of inconsolability and become petrified in a particular mood will be able to move and live again only under the influence of a shock produced by an accident, a separation, sickness, or mourning.

Our needs must be recognized more than met

A woman, the head of a preschool, took part in a weekend training course and on Monday morning was back at work. Upon arrival, she noticed the behavior of a young assistant who was trying to calm a little girl who had just been dropped off there for the first time by her mother. The toddler was in tears, and the young assistant was trying all the conventional means of "solving" the problem.

First response: "No, no, sweetie, you're not sad. It's fun to be here; you'll see." Denial of the other's feeling; her feeling is experienced as a bother because we feel powerless to "do something," and we go into denial.

Second response: "But you shouldn't be sad; there are so many little girls out there in the world who are much less lucky than you in this beautiful nursery with so many wonderful toys . . ." Guilt induction! We're censuring her for experiencing what she is experiencing, for being what she is at that time. We get her to hear that her feeling is a mistake and that she is wrong to be sad. Therefore, we invite her to have doubts about what she's feeling or to repress her feeling in order to fit in!

Third response: "I'm fed up with your crying. You're really a mess. I'm going to leave you here, and I'll come back when you're a good girl." Judgment and manipulative anger.

Watching this scenario unfold, the head of the preschool told the young assistant that she would take care of the little girl, who by now was sitting on the floor crying even harder. She came up to the little girl, knelt beside her, and said, "Sweetie, you are really, really sad, aren't you (F)?"

"Yes," answered the little girl, sobbing.

"Are you sad and also angry (F)?"

"Yes," said the girl, sniffing.

"Would you really have liked to stay with Mommy this morning (N)?"

"Yes," said the girl, sighing.

And the preschool head sighed too as she looked compassionately at the little girl. Then she suggested to her, "Do you want to come and play with me now?"

"All right," said the child.

What happened? The girl, who had felt so alone and so abandoned, now felt rejoined and understood: "Ah! Finally there

151

is an adult here who understands me and who isn't just giving me a lot of rubbish! Finally, I exist here. So, yes, I do want to go and play."

The woman knew that listening to another's need relieves the other person of frustration without the listener becoming in any way responsible for relieving it. This consciousness made it possible for her to come up with a need—"Would you really have liked to stay with Mommy this morning?"—fearing neither to make things worse by twisting a knife in the wound nor to have to respond by phoning the mother.

This example stresses again the fact that often nothing in particular needs to be "done." And just being there doesn't necessarily take a long time.

The conditioning influence of judgments

The little girl who sometimes hears that she is "difficult" will have many a reason to hold on to this identity and caper about under her new banner: "I am the preschool's difficult little girl, and you will just see how right you were in having labeled me this way! I can't exist in my anger, so I'll exist in yours. My distress isn't allowed, so I'll do everything I can to create distress in you."

I have so often noticed the conditioning power—and self-fulfilling prophecy—of judgments and labels. How many young people in difficulty, deemed to be "dangerous second offenders, incurable addicts, aggression specialists, holdup experts," have found in these judgments an opportune identity to fill a void and have thereby reinforced their behaviors, which for them at that time had become the only way of being somebody rather than nobody?

Parents who continually tell their children that they're "no good"—or unfavorably compare them with siblings—shouldn't be too shocked when those kids live "down" to the expectations imposed upon them.

I remember Tony, an eighteen-year-old who already had been in prison several times and who, between crimes, had regularly taken part in our youth programs and activities. Tony had been beaten by his father and hadn't been given much of an opportunity to love himself, so he sometimes lacerated his body with a penknife to punish himself when he wasn't happy with himself. One day I learned, before I had had time to see him again, that he had been out of prison for only forty-eight hours when he was back in again for another three months.

After that sentence I asked Tony what had happened, and he answered: "Well, you know, the judge said to me, 'You'll wind up spending your life in jail' and, y'know, I've become a jailbird. When I'm in prison, everybody knows me. I have buddies, and I'm the boss. When I'm in the street, y'know, nobody knows me. I'm a nobody; I'm pathetic! What a mess! So I attacked an old lady in front of a cop, and jail was in the bag! That very same day I was back with my buddies in jail."

I draw two conclusions from this example:

1. There was conditioning power in "I'm a jailbird; I'll wind up spending my life in jail." For want of something better, Tony did his best to meet the "goal" set for him. The judge's statement was a self-fulfilling prophecy.

2. Ah, the irrelevance of principles to encompass a reality like that! I was still a lawyer at the time. Thanks to Tony and a bunch of others, I was beginning to understand that the principles of law (It's legal; it isn't legal), moral principles (It's right; it's wrong), social principles (That's done, that's normal; that isn't done, that isn't normal), psychological principles (destructive personality, an outlaw) simply aren't relevant when it comes to apprehending Tony's reality such as it is. In other words, Tony was dragging behind him eighteen years of a lack of love, a lack of identity, emotional insecurity, and so on. Saying to him, "It's wrong . . . it's not legal . . . you have a psychological problem" was like speaking Martian to him and further widening the gap between him and society.

153

I know now, through experience, that virtually the only way of allowing a heart torn like Tony's to endeavor to seek reconciliation with itself and with society is to listen empathically, in the right place, taking all the time necessary. Doubtless the necessary security measures must be taken to protect people—but not shutting him away behind bars and hoping for a miracle conversion. I am, therefore, disappointed to observe that, with few exceptions, societies and countries do not yet know this—or do not yet believe this. So they continue to allocate considerable resources in money and staff to shutting away and isolating people who often have such a great need for belonging, listening, connection, and a possibility to give meaning to their lives. I'm not saying that the principles of law, moral principles, and social principles don't have any justification. They are certainly sometimes necessary. They are, however, seldom sufficient when it comes to finding sustainable and truly satisfactory solutions to myriad and complex human problems, such as delinquency, the true causes of which lie mainly in the emotional realm.

CHAPTER 4

Creating a Space to Connect

We are all united. The fate of the whole of humankind depends on our relationships with each other. Never have we been dependent one on the other to this extent. But we fail to understand it. Human beings have proved unable to become compassionate, to help each other. If we persist with this mind-set, which requires that we consider our neighbor as our number-one enemy, if we continue to incite revenge and hatred to pollute our world and our thinking, this will mean that we have learned nothing from the great masters, not from Jesus, not from Buddha, not from Moses. And if we do nothing to correct these Pavlovian reflexes, we shall be helpless when it comes to taking on the era when human beings will be striving ever more furiously to exploit, conquer, tyrannize. Grabbing as much as possible, with no concern for the aftermath. Living at the expense of those who have no way out, no resources . . . We must share with those who do not resemble us, for their difference is a source of enrichment. We must respect the uniqueness of others.

YEHUDI MENUHIN

Heads Together

As noted late in Chapter 2, the ability to formulate negotiable requests—and thus to create the space for connections between people—is directly related to our self-confidence. If we are sure inside ourselves that we can hear the other person's disagreement, we don't have to fear that we'll have to sacrifice ourselves. I say "sure inside ourselves" because often we know this intellectually, but we haven't integrated the fact into the emotional knowledge that we have of ourselves. We are then very fragile when it comes to differences of opinion and disinclined to welcome them with open arms.

With practice of this method, through intimate experience with it, we begin to trust that it's not because we take an opportunity to express a need and a request that another person will simply give up their own need. We also begin to trust that it's not because we allow another person to express their need, perhaps different from our own, that we'll have to give up ours in order to meet theirs. We know that we're going to strive to seek together a solution to meet the needs of both parties . . . or at least agree that we disagree.

We also know—and this is of paramount importance—that deep down our well-being will derive not so much from the solution to a problem as from the quality of the connection made possible by seeking that solution.

When we are operating on the mental or intellectual plane only, having no awareness of our needs, we tend to live our relationships in the following mode:

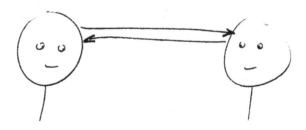

We exchange information or preconceived ideas: "Pass me the salt. Come get me at the station. What are we going to do over the weekend? Don't forget the garbage cans . . ." In disputes, we argue about "who is wrong, who is right," and often that settles matters. Not in any very nurturing way, but we manage. In a manner of speaking.

Unfortunately, we often happen to communicate as follows:

We miss each other; we overshoot each other! "In vain do I repeat myself a hundred times . . . He just doesn't hear . . . I just don't know what language to speak to him in." We have the impression that we are being clear, emitting a message, but the message is not received. It's as if the other person didn't have the right antenna or was capturing other wavelengths. Conversely, we also often have the feeling that a message has been emitted by another (absence, silence, sulking, fits of anger, scoldings), but we don't really have the right antennae to decipher it. Finally, we sometimes communicate like this:

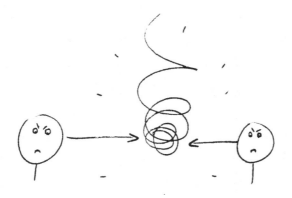

Instead of meeting, we crash into each other. This is what leads us to the use of razor-sharp words—or even to aggression.

Facing the Façade

Looking at these drawings I included for your perusal, I was saying to myself that we stay so much on the surface of things—face to face, mask to mask. Then there came to mind an image that Anne Bourrit, one of the original NVC trainers I had the privilege of assisting regularly while I was training, utilized to get people to understand how to connect with their needs. The image is of a man being like a well; he can go down inside to seek what is alive in himself. Combining the image of the masks and the image of the well, another drawing came to my mind. Here I show three façades on the surface of the earth: one very modest, the tent; the other more elaborate, a small house; and the third highly elaborate, a tower, solid and imposing.

Remember the first chapter? When we judge, we see only a small part of another. We take the small part that we see, and we believe that we see the other person fully, then lock them up in that image. If we come back to the example of the boy with his orange hair in a crest and his piercings or the woman in her flashy car, we could symbolize the boy with the tepee, the woman with the tower, and caricature the exchange between them as red bullets being fired at each other in the form of criticism and prejudices:

"You filthy snob, give me your dough and your ride . . ."

"You dirty little punk, go and get dressed properly . . ."

Often, to avoid going overboard in this way, we keep a low profile, and we go for the harmless façade—the little house in the middle—not too small so as not to be crushed, nor too big so as not to be the target of projectiles, but we certainly don't show ourselves to be exactly as we are. That would be scary. Here is the drawing that results from that:

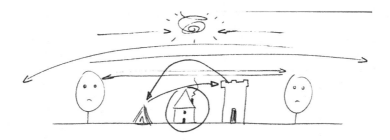

Thus is the relationship when we stay in the mental mode, alienated from our feelings and needs, as well as from the feelings and needs of others.

All Wells End Well

I suggest continuing the drawing as follows, aware that every dwelling on this planet has to be in some proximity to water. So I dig a well under the façade of each one, and what do I observe? However different the façades may be, they are connected to the same water table through their wells.

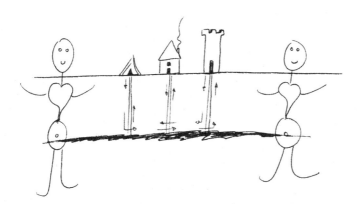

Human beings are like the wells; if they go down inside themselves, they get connected to each other via the same water table. The same water keeps all human beings alive. The same needs are their lifelines. Indeed, whether we're desert nomad or CEO of a multinational corporation, street sweeper in a forgotten district or famous politician, peasant farmer or show business icon, basically we have the same needs for identity, emotional and physical safety and security, and community, whether in a group, a tribe, or a family. We all have a need for sharing and connecting, for freedom and autonomy, for recognition and achievement. We all need to love and be loved, and so on.

As long as we remain on the surface, face to face, mask to mask, there is every probability we'll maintain a language that separates and divides. If we wish to go down into our well and accompany another person in theirs, there is a great likelihood that we'll find a language (water!) that unites us.

Taking the directions followed by the arrows in the well, when you look at the drawing on page 159, you'll see that in order to connect effectively with another person, we have to go by way of ourselves. In order to meet another person in their well, we first of all have to go down into our own. This truly illustrates for me the fact that the path toward another necessarily goes through myself.

Dancing Gently Toward Each Other

Meeting is a movement, often slow and interior, from me to me and from me to another. The movement takes place in a space of freedom that we give ourselves, which is a fundamental criterion for connection: I now know, through my own personal experience, that without this space of liberty, there is no breathing, no movement, no "creative friction."[17]

Here is a sketch that attempts to represent the movement of connection, which in Nonviolent Communication is like a dance. That is, we dance with ourselves and with the other person in order to connect. Remember, for example, the exchange between Terry and Andrea (see Chapter 1) regarding the restaurant versus the video.

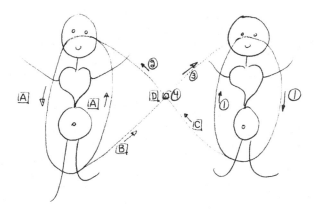

Terry	Andrea
A. I'm connected to myself. I'm taking stock of my needs.	1. I'm connected to myself. I'm taking stock of my needs.
B. I'm connecting with Andrea; with her I'm taking stock of her needs without ceasing to be connected to myself, until such time as we either agree—or agree to disagree.	2. I'm connecting with Terry; with him I'm taking stock of his needs without ceasing to be connected to myself, until such time as we either agree—or agree to disagree.

This is a four-step dance, a thousand-step dance. Although taming is done through constraint and coercion, domestication is achieved through trust and freedom. In domestication, you dance the approach.

Cherishing a Relationship

Each of us regularly gives ourselves body care. We tend our hair, our beards, our clothes, our homes, as well as the whole range of machines and apparatuses that we use, from the coffee machine to the computer, not forgetting the lawnmower or the car. We do maintenance on all of these things for our own well-being and that of our families. And all the logistics are perfectly well-mastered and built into our routines. This is true to such an extent that we can with no difficulty postpone an appointment by claiming that the car is at the garage or that the computer has broken down. Also, without the slightest embarrassment, we can rearrange our entire schedule around a medical appointment ("Let's postpone the meeting until next week because this week I'm having medical examinations") or even an appointment with the hairdresser ("Oh, honey, we can't meet this afternoon; I forgot my appointment with the hairdresser"). But how about this? "I'll be absent next week; I'm doing the annual checkup on my relationship with myself" or "We have to postpone tomorrow's meeting because I'm looking after a relationship that is precious to me" or "Sweetheart, we won't be able to see each other this afternoon; I need to do some inner beauty work."

What's strange is that relationships, whether with ourselves or with other people, are expected to operate unassisted, without any fuel, with scarcely any maintenance! It's hardly surprising, therefore, that they so often wear out, burn out, or break down. We don't take care of them. We get more wrapped up with logistics than with closeness, as if closeness were taken for granted. We don't go and look, we don't want to know, for intimacy instills fear. It's true that if we don't know each other well, if we aren't fully grounded, intimacy both with ourselves and others can instill fear—the fear of losing oneself, the fear of dissolving like a drop of water in the sea. Then we run off to do things, while *connection* is frequently consigned to the scrap heap.

I have an architect friend[18] who did intensive training in Nonviolent Communication in order to better understand his clients and, more particularly, help them to understand themselves better. Many of his clients are young couples building their houses or refurbishing them. Very often, quarrels occur while the work is going on. When the house at last is built, the couple is undone. So many young couples' houses are up for sale almost as soon as they are completed. What happens? Logistics takes precedence over the relationship, organization over connection. Each party is so obsessed with their study, kitchen, carpet, or pastel colors that there's no longer any study, kitchen, pastel colors . . . In fact, these couples might have seized on the opportunity to build their house in order to build their relationship, an opportunity to refurbish the house *and* refresh or renovate their togetherness. They tended to stick with their house, study, kitchen . . . project rather than with the other person. The project is empty and results in a "For Sale" sign in the front yard.

Here's a true story that took place in Africa; a participant at a training session told it to me a few years ago. This man had worked for a European organization that did development project management in Africa. One of these projects was to install water pumps in a remote village. The organization had observed that the inhabitants had to walk a whole day to the river to wash their clothes and get their water supplies, then walk back a whole day to the village, of course on a regular basis. Indignant at this situation, the officials immediately allocated the necessary budget to dig wells in the village and install pumps so the inhabitants could get water easily. And the pumps were soon to be inaugurated, with great pomp and ceremony! A few months after the pumps came into operation, however, the organizers realized that the inhabitants had deliberately made the pumps unserviceable by pelting them with large rocks.

An inquiry was held. The inhabitants stated that they had deliberately chosen to do away with the comfort of the water pumps to regain the well-being of their unity. They had in fact observed that people were no longer talking to one another. They came out just to take a few jars of water at the pump and soon went home. Then, in the isolation of enclosures and walls, they developed the practice of gossiping about others rather than speaking to each other directly. Bad feelings began to take root, and quarrels and misunderstandings broke out, so the elders of the village decided to do away with the pumps and to reinstate the ritual journey to the river. They were aware that this trip would make it possible not only to do the laundry physically but also to wash the "family's dirty laundry" *as* a family. The trip would make it possible not only to fetch the water necessary for the villagers' needs but also facilitate the connections necessary to the quality of life.

The village once again had its natural talking place.

Talking Places

It seems to me a matter of urgency to set up more talking places—in businesses, schools, institutions, medical and hospital units, the nonprofit sector, government departments, and even in families!

I facilitate monthly talking groups in hospitals, in families and schools, as well as in youth support institutions. The institutions and people who call me in have all chosen to give priority to relationships in their field, and they cover the costs in terms of time, human resources, and budget. All of these groups are struck when they see to what extent misunderstandings can be clarified, ambiguities cleared, cold wars settled, and "unsaids" said, because a safe framework is proposed where each person knows that they will regularly be able to express their thoughts freely, even though clumsily at times, without being either judged or rejected. It's also an opportunity for work groups or other gatherings of people to share their joys and enthusiasms. Such meetings can therefore make it possible to clean out anything that has been encumbering a relationship and stimulate what has been nurturing it.

Although I rejoice at the ever-growing numbers of initiatives that have this aim, I am still astounded to observe the impressive number of bodies, institutions, associations, government departments, and businesses that operate, often even in the area of human relations (schools, hospitals, youth aid institutions, etc.), that have no talking places or any interaction groupings. Imagine the energy and creativity lost in gossip, rumor, demotivation, and an undercurrent of rebellion! All that talent and vitality could develop so much more satisfactorily if a framework were put in place to ensure the maintenance of group relationships.

In addition to gossip, countless communities of so many kinds—administrative, commercial, religious, and family—are gnawed away from within by silences and the unspoken word, and this sometimes goes on for generations.

As "good boys and good girls," many of us have learned to shut up, putting the unspoken word to one side like putting cheese in a cupboard. The problem with cheese in the cupboard is that in the end it makes the whole house stink. It isn't "aside"; it's all over the place!

It has been a long time since we walked to the river to fetch water as a community. But will we be able much longer to go on effectively producing care, education, assistance, trade, services, and industry if we fail to take the time to get to know and love ourselves, as well as one another? Are we not running the risk— all cared for, educated, assisted, clothed, fed, waited upon as we are—of dying of thirst and shriveling up with dried-out hearts?

CHAPTER 5

Emotional Security and Meaning: Two Keys to Peace

It is obvious that a single man apparently unarmed, who dares to shout out loud a true word, who supports his word with his whole person and his whole life, and who is ready to pay for it very dearly, surprising though that may seem and although formally he may have no rights, holds a much greater power than the person who, under other conditions, has at his disposal thousands of anonymous electors.

VÁCLAV HAVEL
Czech writer, dramatist, and statesman

I Love You as Long as . . .

In this chapter, we shall be looking at the conditioning factors around conditional love and the way such love generates emotional insecurity and confusion in relation to meaning, as well as to violence.

We have learned to do, not to be

Most of us have learned very well to *do*, not to *be*. I notice the use by recent generations of people in education (parents, teachers, child-care workers, religious orders, et al.) of a feeling followed by "you" without any mention of a need ("I'm happy when you do as I say; I'm sad when you don't"). This conditional usage has generated terrible emotional insecurity, even damage. What most people with whom I work in counseling settings—and I myself for many years—have actually heard lurking behind "I'm happy when you . . ." is "I'm sad when you . . ." or "I'll love you if . . ." or "I won't love you anymore if you . . ."

I'm not saying that is what the person who was speaking intended to say. I'm saying that this is what was heard, what was taken on board by the listener. The reality of that deciphering is what interests me since it conditions the way we are in relationships, the way we are in the world.

The real message: "I love you when you clean up your room, when you work well at school, when you obey, when you're good, courteous, kind, etc. I don't love you when you are nasty, angry, absent-minded, excited, fanciful—when you don't do as I say and don't measure up to my expectations . . ."

We have been drilled to respond and measure up to others' expectations, to adapt and over-adapt to them. We know exactly what to do to please a person, but we don't really know how to be, how to simply be ourselves. We have learned to do everything to measure up to the image of good boy, good girl, listening to the good father and the good mother, and later we'll attempt to do everything we can to measure up to the image of the good husband, the good wife, the good executive, the good employee. As we work at this, we often get wound up in many activities and projects; we will be zealous at work, in the family, and for social causes, without taking care of our inner well-being, since most of us have never learned to become conscious of it. Often we'll only be able to love ourselves if we do a lot of things, and often loving ourselves is merely a function of the number of things we do. We aren't living in a consciousness of being in the world, of enjoying our identity, and of our presence to all things—and the connection we have with them. Many of us live in a state of permanent deficit when it comes to good and bad conscience. We aren't on the ship's bridge of our life, taking stock of the stars in the cool sea air, getting our heading, trimming the sails, or holding the wheel and enjoying the pleasure of sailing. No, we're down in the hold of the boat, looking over our accounts, in a state of slight, albeit constant, seasickness. Are we celebrating our consciousness—or constantly "keeping the books" on good conscience and bad?

> **Are we celebrating our consciousness— or constantly "keeping the books" on good conscience and bad?**

Consciousness or "accountancy"?

Most of us tend to feel more or less responsible—and especially more or less accountable—for others' feelings. If another person is sad or unhappy, we tend to believe it's our fault. Such accountability in reality is more like accountancy—being a "bean counter" in relationships. We should have "done something." We're prone to guilt. In return, we're keen to consider others responsible or guilty for our feelings ("I'm sad or unhappy because you . . ."). In neither case do we know "being."

In the first place, preoccupied as we are with the belief that we're responsible for others' states of mind, we don't know, for example, how to simply open our ears. Remember (in Chapter 3) the adolescent who wanted his father (or mother) to listen to him, but his father was unable to listen and could only proffer a thousand pieces of advice and ready-made solutions? Listening means trusting in the ability of another to be, which allows them to come up with their own solutions. When you accompany a sick person, a dying person, a grieving person, listening means accepting that there is nothing to "do." Just being there with compassionate presence is what matters most. Allowing a person to go down into the well of their pain—and explore the tensions around their suffering by providing them with listening and support through our behaviors—is an opportunity for them to observe that they aren't alone, that they're accompanied. Often the tension of feeling "the other person is not well; I must do something" is such that we're incapable of simply being present to another's pain.

We have a tendency to risk getting caught up in a certain pride at our own performance. We force ourselves to do "the right thing." We want to be the one who "says the right thing." By doing so, we risk missing out on the essence of an encounter—the "connection" between me and me, between "me and thee," and between the other person and themselves.

"Caring for" does not mean "assuming responsibility for"

Caring involves helping another person to live what they have to live. It means not preventing them from doing so. It means not attempting to get them to spare themselves from suffering a bump in their road by minimizing it ("It's nothing serious . . . Think no more of it . . . Come along and have some fun") or by assuming responsibility for it ("It's my fault . . . I shouldn't have . . . I'm going to do this or that in their place"). It means helping another person to get inside their difficulty, to penetrate their suffering so they'll be able to get out of it, aware that this path is their path and that only they can make themselves walk along it.

Caring means focusing our attention on a person's aptitude to heal from some suffering and to solve some difficulty they're experiencing, rather than providing a ready-made remedy. It means trusting that the other person often has all of the requisite resources to pull through, if they can succeed in listening to themselves and being listened to *in the right place*. This presupposes that we have acquired trust and self-esteem. How could we trust in another's ability to *be* if we have not gained confidence in ourselves about our own?

If we assume responsibility for another, we run the risk of not being aware that it isn't them we're concerned about but rather about ourselves: our self-image as a good St. Bernard, as a savior, and often our need for recognition and good conscience. If there's a risk, it's that our attitude may not be appropriate, not adequate, because we're looking after ourselves even though we believe we're looking after the other person. This may maintain both of us in a state of frustration, confusion, or dependence.

My thoughts turn to Vivian, a forty-eight-year-old mother who assumes responsibility for all sorts of difficulties encountered by her twenty-year-old daughter Rachel, a university student. Vivian is convinced her daughter is not mature enough to manage her life and that she always has to be "after her" about something, and Rachel is content to let her mother assume these responsibilities.

Vivian organizes Rachel's student apartment at the university, schedules her weekend activities, even ends Rachel's problematic relationship with a young man. And the more Vivian strengthens the control measures (evenings out, encounters, tutoring, weekend activities, holiday destinations), the more Rachel demands, and the more Rachel takes liberties, then the more the mother builds up the controls—a vicious circle if ever there was one!

One weekend Rachel went on vacation with a group of friends who had rented a house. When the she came back, Vivian heard from friends who were there that it was her daughter who had organized the whole household, managed the budget, organized the shopping, the meals, the daily schedule, and barred smokers from smoking in the house. In a word, she was managing things very well all on her own (reproducing to a large extent a well-known model).

Vivian and I were working on this situation, and what transpired was that she was so tied up in her image as a "good mother who does everything for my daughter" that she was incapable of trusting Rachel—of even considering the possibility she might be having difficulties, burn her fingers a bit, or be pained in her heart—that Rachel had in her all the resources she needed to manage her life. So as soon as her daughter expressed an unpleasant feeling ("I'm sad, disappointed, anxious . . ."), Vivian leaped into action to solve the problem without allowing her daughter any opportunity to wallow a bit in her difficulty and to get in there and work at things in order to get out on her own.

Vivian and I worked on:

- The need for identity: Can I be myself without exhausting myself by doing everything that has to be done in order to be a good mother, a good spouse? If I'm not a good mother, then who am I?
- The need for emotional security: Can I be loved and love myself for who I am and not for what I do?
- The need to trust others: May I trust the fact that things will work out OK even if I don't control everything?

Having had a demanding and controlling mother herself (in relation to whom she had over-adapted as a good daughter), Vivian had not given herself an opportunity to truly be what she wanted to be. Therefore, quite unconsciously, it was difficult for her to admit in turn that her daughter was becoming what she wanted her to be. In fact, the freedoms her daughter wished to take were much too threatening for Vivian; she might have to become aware that she herself had remained a prisoner of her own image as a good daughter and then a good mother, too painful an observation for her to be able to handle without help. Together, we welcomed this newfound awareness and worked both on the grieving of the years of imprisonment and the awakening to a new life.

For this mother to be truly able to meet her daughter such as she was, she first of all had to meet herself. The beauty of this path is that as she became more and more herself, Vivian implicitly allowed her daughter to become more and more herself, rather than reproducing the maternal model to a greater or lesser extent!

In the second place, when we tend to have another person assume responsibility for what we are experiencing, we're unable to listen to ourselves to understand ourselves, to assume responsibility for ourselves, and to become both autonomous and responsible. We often remain dependent, fearful of the judgments (real or imagined) of others.

We don't learn to be loved as we are, but to be loved as others would like us to be

Although we have learned to live up to the expectations of others, to apply pressure on ourselves for their sake, correspondingly we almost always expect that others should measure up to our expectations and get into action for us. Thus, we generally don't learn to love others as they are but as we would like them to be.

In addition, if we bent over backward to measure up to the image of the good daughter to please our father, there's every chance we'll expect our spouse to live up to the image of a good husband to please us as we bend over backward to live up to the image of good wife and good mother to please him. If we stop ourselves from being ourselves, there's a good chance we'll find ways (subconsciously, of course) to prevent others from being themselves.

It's only if we succeed in being truly ourselves—our masks off, our labels removed, tension-free—that we'll succeed in allowing others to be truly themselves—their masks off, their labels removed, tension-free.

True connections take place between beings, not between roles. Connecting means, first of all, being.

> ## Connecting means, first of all, being.

This doesn't mean that we may not have a taste to evolve, to grow, and more especially to grow together. Growing together— as a couple, as a family, among friends, within a work group—is

173

certainly one of the most profoundly nurturing sources of satisfaction. To love another as they are also means that we are interested in them and welcome whatever they may become. It means loving another with their potential for growth, openness, diversification. I see so many couples or families where each one has locked the others into roles, preventing or at least hampering any process of personal and interpersonal evolution. Anesthesia quickly takes root and, unfortunately, "grows." What is love without respect? Christian Bobin expresses this wear and tear, this anesthesia, thus:

> Life is worn out, it is less lovable in taste, it rubs against the soul, spoils the dream. And we cannot speak about it to anyone. We cannot confide in a person that we would like to leave this life for another and that we do not know what to do. How can one tell one's family: your love brought me alive, now it is killing me? How can one say to those who love us that they do not love us?[19]

Thus, if someone begins to change, to evolve, to review their way of being, others become resistant: "You've changed; you're not like you used to be (between the lines: 'That's not done; one has to stay what one always was'); you're not being natural; don't leave me."

"I confess that I love the plan I have for my son more than my son himself . . ."

The movie "Dead Poets Society" is a good illustration of this tragedy. The father has a single-minded goal for his son: to become an engineer. However, during his final year at secondary school, the son discovers in the school drama group that he has a flair for acting. His father (doubtless convinced that it's impossible to study to become an engineer *and* act) forbids the lad from rehearsing the end-of-the-year play. The son does so anyway and receives a standing ovation from the entire school and all the families at the end of the play, much to the fury of his father, who is in the theater.

When the play was finished, without saying a word about the talent his son showed, deaf to the applause the audience had just given the youth, the father dragged his son home, lecturing him on his future: "Your mother and I made such efforts to finance good schooling for you, and you will, therefore, become an engineer." There was no negotiating this stance. The son went up to his bedroom and, with his father's handgun, committed suicide.

The father was more attached to his (virtual) plan than to the reality of his son, with the best of intentions, believing that he was doing "his strict duty as a good father, tough but just." The father believed that listening to his son would be like failing to do his duty. The son believed that listening to his father would mean the sacrifice of his talent. The father made demands; the son took flight. Ultimately, there was no connection. They tragically passed by each other, like two ships in the night.

Among couples particularly, I note how people often have plans "for" another person. They hold to a concept or a theory of marriage or the life of a couple, and (like the tragic father-son story just preceding) they are more attached to that than the other person!

If one party (in this case, say, the husband) starts to change, to revise his plans, to alter a theory, then the other's full attention is not on listening to him, understanding him, loving him as he develops, nor on envisioning changes herself. Quite the contrary! Her full attention focuses on how to preserve her project, how to ensure that her husband fits in with the basic concept, how to maintain her theory unchanged.

Jacqueline is fifty-one years old. She comes along for a consultation on her own, completely disorientated by the departure of her husband after twenty-five years of marriage. From the outset, she told me that marriage is sacred and that there was no question of her divorcing. "When you get married, it is for life," she said. After a few sessions, seeing that she often came back to this issue and dwelt on it, I tried with her to identify the needs underlying the behavior (once again, the example is much condensed):

"Jacqueline, when you say, 'In my eyes, marriage is sacred; you do not get divorced; you are married for life (O),' are you feeling really sad and torn by your present separation (F) because you would like to experience again the gentleness of intimacy with another, the well-being that comes from accepting trust and authenticity, the joy of being together (N)? Is that what saddens you?"

She looked at me, tears in her eyes, and I left a long silence before resuming. "Are you touched by what I said there?" I was thinking she would say to me, "Yes, that is why I'm crying, and that is what I'd love to regain."

Instead of that, she said to me: "I'm so upset because in twenty-five years of marital life I never experienced the gentleness you just described to me. I'm becoming aware that I've lived all this time in a structure, and now I'm wearing myself out to get my husband to come back into the structure rather than trying to understand him."

Indeed, every time she saw her husband again, they fought. She felt too insecure with the collapse of the structure to have any real availability for understanding what was happening. The more she tried to recover her husband through argument, chastisement, anger, or moralizing, the faster he fled.

One day, I suggested to her—and she accepted—that I be put into the shoes of her husband, who "said" this to her:

"Jacqueline, I'm fed up with our role-playing. I'm at the end of my rope. After twenty-five years behind a mask, I cannot go on (F). I need to live a genuine relationship where I can be myself rather than the 'good husband who does well everything that's necessary.' I have a need for freedom and trust. I'm tired of all the controlling and programming. The problem is that I don't have the words to say it. I've just learned to hide my feelings and be nice, so for a long time I just shut up. Now I want more. I'm leaving, but that doesn't mean I don't love you."

And after the role-play:

"How do you feel when you look back at all that?"

"It's really enlightening. I can see the scene that we've both been acting in. I think I truly loved my 'life plan' for the two of us more than our life as a couple—and my plan for a husband more than my husband himself. Now I can see my part of the responsibility, whereas I used to consider that he alone was responsible for my misfortune."

Jacqueline and I worked on her need for identity, self-esteem, and safety:

- Can I be myself, even if I'm without my husband?
- Can I picture myself existing alone or with others even if our couple is undone?
- Can I love myself even though I wonder if he still loves me?
- Can I feel safe within myself even if the outside environment has changed?

The more Jacqueline began to trust herself, rather than simply trusting her role, the more she gained self-esteem as a person—and not simply as a good spouse and mother. The more she developed her inner security without being at the mercy of her husband's attitudes, as well as the attitudes and principles of her family, the fewer quarrels occurred when she saw her husband again—and the more her husband, very gradually, began to talk about himself, to remove the armor plating and get into a more genuine relationship. Naturally, the work is very long, and stripping off the layers is painful. It's a question of letting go of the old patterns made up of habits, clichés, preconceived principles, and getting beyond one's fear of change and solitude and walking on tiptoe into novelty and authenticity. There is nothing to say that a caterpillar finds it pleasant to shed its cocoon to become a butterfly.

> There is nothing to say that a caterpillar finds it pleasant to shed its cocoon to become a butterfly.

Difference experienced as a threat

Does not the following question lie like a watermark beneath so many of our relationships, tainting nearly all of them with distrust: "If I don't do what you say . . . if I don't measure up to the image of the 'good boy' or 'good girl' that you have of me . . . if I stop being good, kind, courteous . . . if I differ from your expectations, *will you love me?*"

When we perceive difference, we tend to be scared. Sometimes excited and intrigued, but usually scared. Faced with another's difference, what do we do? We avoid it, or we reject it. We tolerate another person insofar as there is "sameness" and "they love me." To achieve this, we tend to gravitate toward people who think like us, speak like us, dress like us, have the same beliefs as us, pray like us, do the same things as us . . . It is so reassuring!

We often experience another's difference as a risk, a threat. "If the other person is different, I run the risk of having to change, adapt, become what they expect of me and stop being what I believe I am." This inner insecurity can be so strong that it gets externalized in the form of racism, fundamentalism, anti-Semitism, homophobia, or xenophobia. However, more commonly, it is manifested through judgments, criticisms, rebukes, suspicion. Difference does not awaken compassionate curiosity but rather doubt and mistrust: "Those people are not like us!"

The most common feeling: fear!

If we have learned to be *pleasers*, we are never totally sure of doing "the right thing" for another person, either at the right time or to the right degree. We run the risk of living mainly in a state of fear

178

of disapproval, criticism, or indifference. We distrust the other's reactions and have misgivings about our own qualities or skills. Thus, mistrust and doubt often appear as a double-edged principle of life, even a recognized *modus operandi*.

The other individual, to a greater or lesser degree, is perceived as a judge whose approval or disapproval controls our well-being. We ourselves, therefore, live in fear of not "having done enough" to *deserve*(!) other people's consideration or to purchase their clemency. We tend to live in commercial relationships (buying recognition, selling authenticity), rather than truly human ones. Marshall Rosenberg develops this notion in *Nonviolent Communication: A Language of Life* by saying, "Used to a culture where purchasing, winning, and deserving are conventional modes of exchange, we are often ill at ease when it comes to simply giving and receiving."[20]

As I stated at the beginning of Chapter 3, when presenting the expression and reception diagram of human communication, most of the time we hang around in an area of mistrust. We're fearful of taking our place, of truly existing, of asserting our identity, because we aren't sure of being loved and welcomed as we are. Therefore, we're afraid the other person will take their place, truly exist, assert their identity because we aren't so sure of being able to continue existing alongside this person! A 1969 book by John Powell, S.J., was titled *Why Am I Afraid to Tell You Who I Am?* Inside, the answer to that question was: "If I tell you who I am, you may not like who I am, and it is all that I have." The other person, even someone as close as a spouse, is to a certain extent perceived as a potential wet blanket. I wouldn't go so far as to say an enemy, though I have often heard this comparison—someone who obstructs us from being who we are.

I'm used to hearing the following outburst: "And you believe that it's possible for me to be myself while I have a spouse, children, a boss, parents! All of that prevents me from being myself!"

Well, actually, no. "All of that" does not prevent us from being ourselves. What prevents us is the way we see "all of that," the way we live these relationships. What prevents us from being ourselves is that our needs for inner security and trust have not yet received sufficient attention to develop and allow us to experience "all of that" with greater ease. I don't think we can eradicate fear totally because it's simply part of our lives, along with trust, pain, and joy. What is liberating is to no longer fear being afraid.

Let's be genuine, not just nice!

This phrase came to me one day during a training course. At the end of a role-play, a participant had just become aware that her violence often resulted from the frustration she felt at having concealed her true feelings and needs in order to be nice. After years of being nice, she wound up exploding.

A moment after I said, somewhat in jest, "Let's be genuine, not just nice," a woman participant reacted instantly and said, "What you are saying clarifies what I often experience with my husband. I love going to the theater and the opera. I meet my girlfriends there, and I let myself get completely into the show and into the emotions of it. I always have a little cry, and I love chatting at intermission. But my husband hates that sort of thing. He gets impatient, makes loud comments about the actors' performances, is about as emotional as a dead tree, and twists and turns in his seat all the time, sighing as he does so. So I lose my cool. That spoils my evening, and we have an argument at intermission and another one in the car. The only thing is, every time I book a seat for a show, he's afraid I'll miss the last bus or I won't find a taxi. And so, to be nice, he accompanies me. And as for me, to be nice—since *he* is trying to be so nice—I accept! And both of us have a ghastly evening. It would be much better for me to be genuine next time and say to him, 'I'm very touched (F) that you are so concerned for my safe return. I love knowing that my safety and comfort are important to you (N). At the same time, it doesn't seem like (F) it's really very much fun for you to go to these events (N). As I need both of us to have a nice evening (N) and particularly to be able to enjoy the show without worrying about your well-being (N), I suggest you do something you really like and I manage to get back on my own or with my friends (R). How do you feel (F) when I say that?'"

Here was a participant who was only too happy to get herself out of the miserable trap she had gotten herself into and finally remove her mask! (Also see the next section for a definition of the kind of "niceness" I'm talking about.)

Off With the Masks!

If we wear a mask and the other person wears a mask, that isn't called a relationship, it's called a masquerade ball! And that is OK? If it's fun, and if both parties derive pleasure from the masks and the games, we can rejoice. Unfortunately, experience has shown that a regular diet of such balls (literal and figurative) eventually becomes sad and distressing. They don't unite, they isolate; they don't get us dreaming, they prevent us from sleeping; they don't conclude with a fireworks show, they shrink away!

As for *niceness*, let's come to some agreement on the term. What I'm referring to here is niceness/complacency, a niceness of attitude not borne up by any real heartfelt enthusiasm, which I would term: a profound wish to give and to contribute with joy to another's well-being. On the contrary, the niceness I'm describing is motivated out of fear of losing, the fear of rejection, the fear of criticism, the fear of asserting their identity. That sort of niceness is often a lifeless mask that stifles the sound of truth and siphons off vitality.

> ## "Politeness is organized indifference."
> ## —Paul Valéry

Behind this vacant mask of complacent niceness, we may as well get used to living anemic, bleached relationships that we could easily mistake for genuine, living, breathing human interaction and intimacy. Thus, if we never have drunk anything but water, we might spend our whole lives without ever imagining that it might be worth it to taste wine.

In my capacity as a lawyer and then a business consultant, for more than fifteen years I was well-acquainted with office courtesies practiced among business people and colleagues—smiles, warmth shown by tone or expression, perhaps even humor—masking deep indifference and a mere concern to settle a matter or just to get along without too much obvious rancor. Some people can be so nice with everyone that they have no idea who they are! Marshall Rosenberg, as I've already said, refers to these folks as "nice dead people." No identity, no presence, no life.

Indeed, it often *is* easier, in the short term, to be nice rather than genuine. After all, being genuine carries some risks. When as children we pocketed our anger or sadness in order to be able to join the family circle, unconsciously we felt it simpler (perhaps even smarter) to be nice than to truly live what was alive in us. We thereby learned unfaithfulness to ourselves. In the long run, the price for that is high! Finding oneself takes time and energy. Ah, if only we were able not to lose ourselves. Fortunately, though we may have gotten into the habit, we also can lose the habit. If we (and others) programmed ourselves this way, we can deprogram ourselves (sometimes with the help of others, such as counselors or consultants) and reclaim our true nature, our true self behind the character. Quoting French poet and philosopher Paul Valéry above, I certainly have no intention to criticize the courtesy that stems from a true movement of the heart. Good manners, courtesy, and etiquette constitute some of the pleasures of life. I'm referring to a false or phony niceness. I think we know the difference.

When I'm giving conferences or doing workshops, I often hear this reaction, "Yes, but it's not natural to speak like that, using feelings and needs." What I think, in fact, is that it isn't *habitual* to talk about feelings and needs, whereas in the final analysis it is *natural* to us.

A child will say: "I'm mad (F) because I want to go and play with my friends (N). I'm sad (F) because I want to stay here with you (N)." That's natural. But then, over time the child (and young adult) will be taught a series of social graces—and these learned behaviors will cause them to do things or not do them "because you have to . . . because it's time . . . because that's the way it is . . . because that's the rule."

If niceness in the meaning I intend here is not necessarily good, it's worth noting that true goodness is not necessarily nice. I personally have a decided preference for clear, straightforward truth rather than the uncertain masquerades of niceness. Just imagine the lies told to stay nice in couples, in families, in business relationships! Most of us have at one time or another invented fake stories—led someone "up the garden path"—in order to get out of a mess supposedly unscathed. And sometimes the lie is told to avoid hurting someone.

A lie? Yes, to be nice!

It's as if truth were adjustable, as if one could parody it to suit oneself or to suit another without any consequences.

When looking at our overall responsibility as an inhabitant of the earth, I fear that such an attitude is just as irresponsible, dangerous, and polluting in the long term as the attitude of those who claim to share the ideals of protecting nature, yet don't hesitate to throw their cigarette butt or their beer can out the car window without thinking twice about it.

My confidence in human nature doesn't go so far as to claim that all truth is good to speak at all times to all people. Far from it! Doubtless there are circumstances when saying nothing will meet a need for patience, taking one's time, a need to wait for the right moment, a need to think things over, a need for compassion or verification, and so on.

I am saying that if I choose to say something rather than to say nothing, I need to contribute to respecting truth and therefore not to distort it through complacency or "niceness." In fact, I ask myself the following question: Today, do I wish to add to the confusion in the world? Canadian and French astrophysicist

Hubert Reeves says pollution in the world is not one major problem, it is seven billion small problems. It seems to me that confusion in the world—its chaos and disorder—is not one major problem, it is seven billion small problems. We each can choose. We each have the power in our daily lives to contribute or not to clarity, transparency, peace. Amazing, isn't it?

Finally, we can become conscious of the fact that being in touch with nice people—that is, people who don't really say what they're thinking for fear of hurting or being judged or of showing their vulnerability, their fragility, and/or their strength—makes us rather insecure. To feel at ease in a relationship, we need to be at least relatively sure that if another says yes, it is yes. If they say no, it is no. No games. If we have to continually imagine what another's true reasons may be, because we don't trust them to be honest, it's exhausting and keeps us worried about things backfiring. For example, we're all acquainted with the classic example of the person who helps you and declares that it was a pleasure to do so, whereas in fact it bothered them and afterward they complain to others about everything they have done for you and the lack of recognition for it or the fact that you don't help them in return. How fatiguing such situations are!

When Valérie and I got married, we made each other this promise (doubtless an unusual variation on the traditional sweeping declarations of newlyweds, but of fundamental importance to the safety and comfort of our life as a couple): "I promise never to be nice to you but always to be genuine." Thus, whenever we have doubts about the other person's motives, and we worry they may do something unwillingly "to be nice," we remove each other's masks: "Are you being nice, or are you being genuine?!" And with a joke, this gives us an opportunity to agree on things to do, as well as on the reasons we have for doing them, so that neither of us does things out of duty or "because it has to be done . . . because there's no one else to do it," but instead out of the joy of giving and contributing to the well-being of our shared life.

"Are you being nice, or are you being genuine?!"

What I'm talking about here appears to me to be a principle of emotional ecology as well known as it is unpracticed: We can do without truth and authenticity if we're willing to live sustainable and unsatisfactory relationships or satisfactory and unsustainable relationships; but I don't believe we can establish sustainable and satisfactory relationships without taking care of these two values/needs: truth and authenticity. Naturally it isn't easy, because in the short term it's certainly a challenge to be genuine. It requires vigilance and practice to acquire the strength to express oneself and the flexibility to be receptive to another.

How can we say no?

In the course of my work, I have noticed a recurring reason to explain the widespread difficulty of saying no: We have not been invited to do so. We haven't been invited to be different and to experience difference easily. As I stated above, it's more that we have been invited to "do likewise," "reproduce the same thing," agree with Mommy, Daddy, the teacher, customs, religious practice, the social or professional circle. "When one is polite, one says yes. A good little girl, a good little boy says yes; it's not nice to say no."

Therefore, since, on the one hand, difference (of opinion, of character, of behavior, of priority, of sensitivity . . .) is experienced as a threat, and, on the other hand, obedience has for a very long time been promoted as a moral value, it's often very hard for us not only to say no, but even simply to state that we don't agree.

Contrary to an idea that has been so all-pervasive in the world of education for generations, obedience has seldom led to responsible human beings. The more likely result has been automatons. Once again, obedience is the expression both of mistrust and misgivings as to the ability of another to assume responsibilities and the *in*ability to join the other person and to understand them. As we fail to get our need recognized and fail to get the other person to respect it, we make of it a demand and impose it on the other person without any discussion. We simply expect the other to obey!

Obeying automatically, or adhering responsibly?

Consequently, we often say *yes* in order to be nice, whereas we actually think *no*. Most of the time, we do this to avoid a quarrel: "If I get into a fight, will I still be loved? Will I remain lovable if I show disagreement?" Or, on the contrary, we regularly say no out of rebelliousness, out of a fear of losing ourselves, because this is the only way we have come up with to take care of our needs for identity, safety, and recognition: "I object, therefore I exist." It works for two-year-olds, and it works sometimes for adults too!

Learning to say no is a stage in the process that I am very fond of because it invites us to work essentially on four values that are close to my heart:
- *Respect* for the feelings and needs of another as for my own.
- *Autonomy* to take the time to check out what I'm feeling and what I'm needing.
- *Responsibility* for listening to the various components at play and for attempting to take care of all the needs present—not only the needs of the other person at the expense of my own and not only my own at the expense of the other person's.
- *Strength* in expressing my disagreement and proposing a solution or a behavior that is perhaps completely different from what was asked of me.

We now know that underlying any request is a need. We also know that we very often confuse the two. So let's focus attention on the other person's need, which lies upstream of their request, in order to clarify what is truly involved. Here is a simple and easy example:

My old friend Annie has left three messages inviting me to a barbecue, and I haven't yet responded. I like Annie. I would be glad to see her again. At the same time, however, I don't want to go to the barbecue. I really have a need for rest and time to myself. Formerly, in order not to disappoint her (and to be nice), I would doubtless have said, "Yes, of course" and gone along leaden-hearted, abandoning half of myself at home and running the risk of moaning and groaning that the guests are boring, the kebab is overcooked, the rose wine lukewarm, etc. It's worth recalling that when we act counter to our needs, someone pays the bill—ourselves or others. Or perhaps I would have invented a story to wriggle out: "I'm not free; I have to work." I would have lied in order to be nice!

The fourth time Annie calls, I'm at home and pick up the telephone. She begins:

"Well? You're a fine friend! You don't even answer my messages anymore?"

"Are you disappointed (F) because you would have liked me to respond sooner (N)?"

"Well, of course! But his lordship is never there, and his lordship just drops his old buddies."

"Are you angry (F), Annie? Do you want to make sure I haven't forgotten you (N)?"

"Of course! If I don't invite you from time to time, we'd never see each other at all!"

"And you'd like to sense that I'm contributing to our friendship, that I give it some space (N)?"

"Yes, that's right! That's why I'm hoping you'll be coming to my barbecue. Are you free that evening?"

"Yes, indeed, I am free that evening, Annie, and I'm hesitant (F). I'm touched by your persistence (F), and I truly want to invest time in seeing each other again (N). At the same time I feel exhausted this week and overwhelmed with encounters and connections (F). I truly need to stay alone and get back in touch with myself this weekend. This is my first free weekend after several weekends of training (N)."

"So I see you're just dropping me!"

"Wait until I get to the end. If I come to your barbecue,

we're not going to connect as I would like. You know how things are: Everybody makes small talk with everybody and nobody. So I would really love to spend some time just with you and catch up on your life (N). How would it be if just the two of us were to see each other at lunchtime next week? We could go and have a salad together and chat (N)."

"You'd have time to do that? You're always so busy. I never would've imagined you could find the time for lunch with me. That's why I invited you to my barbecue. Of course that suits me. I also prefer to have time just to chat, the two of us."

I said that it was an easy example. In this case, coming up with the true need (looking after our friendship) underlying the request (the invitation to the barbecue), observing that we share the same need at the same time and that we can nurture it in another way (the more intimate lunch) was both simple and pleasant.

Things can be much more difficult and much less pleasant when we notice that we don't at all have the same need, that we don't share the same feelings in this respect, and that we're planning to use our time and energy in a completely different way from what is being suggested by the other person.

Beyond the No, What Are We Saying Yes to?

By practice in easy situations we develop our muscle power to be able to say no in more difficult instances. Succeeding in saying no, in setting boundaries while respecting others, is all the easier as we acquire both strength and flexibility in the way we live our needs for self-confidence, inner security, recognition, identity. By working on our own self-knowledge, we get better and better at knowing what we are saying yes to.

> **"Integrity needs no rules."**
> **—Author Unknown**

This results in more ease in saying no in a constructive and creative (and non-hurtful) way—or hearing someone else's no without taking it personally. Rather than saying merely no in opposition, we shall focus our attention and our energy on what we are saying yes to. Here are a few examples where the expression of the need shows what we are saying yes to:

- "No, I don't want you to listen to music now." *We might say:* "Yes, I need quiet, and I would like you to listen to your music later or elsewhere."
- "No, you are not going out to a nightclub at your age." *We might say:* "Yes, I need to trust that you will be able to feel at ease and safe no matter who you're with, and I would like to build up this trust little by little with you by suggesting that first of all you go out to the homes of people I know. Then we can talk about it and see how it went for you."
- "No, you will not take the car anymore." *We might say:* "Yes, I need to be reassured about your awareness of the risks, and I would like you to think about it for several days. Then we'll talk about it before planning to let you back behind the wheel."

By developing our awareness of what we're saying yes to, we also develop our awareness of what others are saying yes to when they say no. This opening of the heart is invaluable to avoid the unfortunate habit of taking any refusal from another personally. Because it's hard for us to *say* no, out of the fear of rejection (or not being seen as nice), we may, on account of that very fear of rejection, have difficulty in *hearing* a no: "I was told no; therefore, I'm not loved."

This same inner security enables us to hear a no without misgivings, without losing trust. This security therefore makes us available to listen to the feelings and needs of another behind their behavior and look for whatever they are saying yes to. The example of the little girl who did her hair in the bathroom at the moment the car was leaving for school, expresses a no: "No, I'm not going to come down with everyone else, and no, I'm not going to get into the car on my own." We saw that if the mother felt secure enough to listen to what lay behind her daughter's no, she could finally hear "Yes, I need a special sign of tenderness that reassures me that I'm truly loved as your last little child." The solution that emerges is more constructive and satisfying than having a fight every morning!

I'm scared of conflict

Behind the fear of conflict almost always lies a need for emotional security. As I've already recalled, the background question is: "Can I still be loved if I'm involved in a conflict? Am I still lovable if I say I don't agree?" I note that for people who complain of having this fear (and there are many of them) conflict has seldom been experienced as something enriching, a satisfying opportunity to get to know oneself and to strengthen mutual esteem. The result has rather been an impression of failure, mismanaged and undigested tension, and feelings of bitterness and confusion. The game "Who is right, who is wrong?" was decided by "Whose fault is it?"—and none of that has ever proved satisfactory in practice.

In systemics, the science of systems, we learn that any system tends first of all to perpetuate itself, to maintain its existence. This is the law of homeostasis. In such systems as the family, the couple, or a range of other relationships, difference and divergence produce fear because they represent a risk of compromising the system by destabilizing it. Faced with such fear, the trend is often to endeavor to reestablish unanimity as a matter of urgency, either through control or through submission. Thus, to regain equilibrium in our family, marital, or other relationships, that is, the homeostasis or stability of our system, we often impose solutions compelling everyone to agree, or we submit without a word of discussion. What you get is fight or flight, and there is no real encounter.

Yet conflict is frequently an opportunity for evolution. It makes it possible to work on our inner security, our autonomy, and our ability to listen and be empathic. Conflict is an invitation to connect more with ourselves and with others, to develop both interior strength and interior flexibility. It's an opportunity for us to grow together, and it's an invitation to creativity. I believe that in the fear of conflict lies a desperate quest for another's approval. *If we don't give ourselves measured, just appreciation, we run the risk of spending much of our life desperately seeking disproportionate appreciation from others.*

How to live anger

I see two reasons that anger is difficult to experience, whether it's a question of expressing it or hearing it.

The first reason is of the same nature as the one that made us hesitate to say no: the fear of rejection. We have often enough heard "You aren't fun to be around when you're angry" and have understood that anger is neither socially accepted nor welcome. Thus, our own anger is experienced as a threat ("Will I still be loved if I show my anger?"), and the anger in the other person is threatening ("Will I still be lovable if someone gets angry with me?").

The second reason, which urges us to stifle our anger and to prevent anger in the other person, is that every day we witness the tragic consequences of outbursts of anger when human beings let rip insults, blows, crimes . . . The world over, anger explodes in tragic ways. Because the consequences are often destructive, we tend to believe that anger itself is destructive. In fact, frequently there's confusion between the feeling of anger and what each of us does with this feeling.

Although the consequences of anger can be tragic, anger in and of itself is a healthy feeling since it's the expression of inner vitality. If our feelings are gauges on our psychic dashboard, anger is the red blinking emergency light: It shows that vital needs are not being met and that it's increasingly urgent to pay attention. Indeed, everything else may need to be put on hold because there's no longer a reliable driver behind the wheel. Saying or thinking "I'm beside myself," which can stem from anger, indicates that the first thing to be done is to come back to myself. Thus, anger invites us to have ourselves "hospitalized" in the intensive care unit for our own listening and our own empathy. It's necessary to get to the bottom of our anger, not bury it.

To bury anger is to bury a land mine

When you see in the newspaper that a killer running amok got out a riot gun and fired into a crowd or killed his wife and children before committing suicide, the neighbors often declare that this man was so nice, that he never said a thing, that he was such a quiet person, and so on. It isn't hard to imagine repressed outbursts of anger suddenly exploding because the person wasn't able to express them one by one.

In fact, if each time we have been enraged since childhood, we buried it, we masked it, and then carefully covered it over for thirty, forty years, it's a bit as if we had buried land mines one after the other, one beside the other. On the outside, a beautiful, well-kept piece of property . . . on the inside, a minefield! We're sitting on a minefield. It will explode! Often, for everything to blow up it takes only running into a minor annoyance, a normally harmless additional frustration in oneself, like a hailstone falling on the detonator of the last ill-buried mine! Forty years of repressed rage blow up in our face—the straw that breaks the camel's back!

Why will one straw do so much damage unless it's because we haven't been aware of the growing load? Why do we explode in anger, often with disproportionate consequences? Is it because we haven't taken care to regularly defuse our rage?

It isn't another who is responsible for having broken my camel's back. I'm responsible for not having taken care to keep a watchful eye on the camel's load. If I were to get my anger out regularly, would that not presuppose that I am being genuine rather than nice?

How then can we truly express our anger without aggressing others? How can we be genuine without being aggressive?

Conventional wisdom regarding anger holds that the other person is largely responsible: "I'm angry because you . . ." In such a state of mind, we tend either to repress our anger so as not to explode, or to blow up right in front of the other person, who then becomes our scapegoat for the tension generated by the anger. Often the other person gets a good dressing-down completely disproportionate to the circumstances because several nearby mines also exploded at the same time due to the reverberations from the first one.

Expressing anger in this way—by pouring it out over another person—brings up anger in return, and the game of Ping-Pong starts, generally leading to a spiral of violence. Or, it triggers flight in which the other person leaves or shuts themselves off in silence, sulking, solitary revolt, or cold war.

Most of us have often experienced that this conventional way of expressing our anger isn't satisfactory. The only satisfaction we can draw from it is to have exploded, to have released the overload of tension that the anger has given rise to, to have "let it out" and expressed it to the other person. It's "funny," isn't it? Does one have to be angry, have the alibi of anger, in order to be genuine? Why is it so difficult to exchange our truths gently, compassionately? *Are we so disabled when it comes to expressing ourselves that we must have the energy of anger in order to say what is bubbling away in us?*

Taking care of our anger

When we address anger in Nonviolent Communication, we're working on our own sense of responsibility on the one hand, and we're ensuring that the other person is listening to us on the other. To do so, we connect with ourselves and stop being "beside ourselves"!

1. The first step, therefore, is to *keep our mouths closed, to shut up* rather than *blow* up, not in order to repress our anger, to push it down, or to sublimate it, but precisely to give it its full and authentic voice. We know that if we

explode in another's face, instead of having someone in front of us who's listening to us and attempting to understand our frustration, we'll get a rebel plotting a rebellion, a victim preparing an assault, or an escape artist who has already flown the coop! Yet, what is our need if we are angry? In short, that the other person hear us, understand the extent of our frustration and our unmet needs. To be sure, in order for us to be listened to well, we know we first of all have to listen well to ourselves.

2. The second stage in dealing with our anger takes place within: *receiving the full impact of our anger, accepting the intensity of it in Technicolor and without compromise.* I observe that for many of us (and I've experienced this myself) there is such a stigma around anger that it's even difficult to imagine our being angry. We'll say we're sad, disappointed, or preoccupied—socially and "politically" correct feelings—rather than allow ourselves to have real awareness of the anger in us.

This second stage is therefore fundamental to me: recognizing that we *are* angry, even enraged, and mentally noting all the visions and fantasies that come to our minds, recognizing the violent images that surge up: throwing the other person through a window, cutting them up into small pieces, running them over with our car, getting out our old gun . . . You get the idea!

> **The inner acknowledgment of images of violence has the effect of the pile of plates that people sometimes hurl to the floor—or the chair they smash to smithereens against the wall.**

This inner acknowledgment of these images of violence has the effect of the pile of plates that people sometimes hurl to the floor—or the chair they smash to smithereens against the wall. Such overt actions provide relief and a safety valve for the excess energy that anger brings about that prevents us from listening to ourselves. Only after regaining some calmness, after the emotional catharsis these visions and projections evoked, will we be able to attempt the descent into our well. This stage is also difficult because it jeopardizes the good-boy or good-girl images we like to have of ourselves: "Me? Such a nice and polite boy, such a well-mannered girl, just imagine me wanting to smash someone's head against the wall? What nonsense! Violence like that is for other people, not for me!" However, if we want to be free from our anger and its violence, we need to look both of them straight in the eye.

3. The third stage consists of *identifying the unmet need(s)*. With some of the pressure released during the previous stage, we're more open to listening to what is happening in us rather than blaming the other person. We'll be able to name the first needs that come to mind.

4. The fourth stage consists of *identifying the new feelings* that may then surface. Indeed, if (as has been stated just now) anger is sometimes masked under more socially/politically correct feelings, we see that it also can mask other feelings in relation to which it operates much like a lid. These feelings are often fatigue with a repeated situation, along with sadness and fear. These more precise feelings will, in their turn, inform us about our needs. Then we can take stock of whatever the anger reveals. Fatigue may transpose our need for change and evolution; sadness, our need for understanding, listening, support; and fear, our need for emotional or physical security.

5. Finally we're ready for the fifth stage: *opening our mouths, speaking our anger to the other person.* Now, because we've done some inner work, we have a much greater chance of being heard by them. In reality, sometimes it's pretty hard to get into the inner listening quickly while you're still with the other person. It might be wise to say: "I'm too

angry to listen and speak to you now in any satisfactory way. I first of all need to get in touch with my anger and understand it better. I'll talk to you later. Can you give me thirty minutes?" If the pressure has become too great and you actually blow up in the other's face, there's nothing to prevent you from "taking a timeout" and working on your anger in a heart-to-heart discussion with yourself. Then later you meet with the other person, saying how much you regret having expressed your rage in such terms and in such a tone (F), that you would like to find another more amicable way of communicating to them what you don't and do want (N), and that you would like to know if they're ready/able to listen to you (R).

Don't allow anger to fester and ferment for days and turn sour, either in you or between you and the other person. Take the time to clean it out; otherwise sooner or later it may poison the whole relationship. Remember: If we want our relationships to be sustainable and satisfactory, we need to maintain them. Many human beings are inhabited by an anger they don't wish to have. Often, with most of their energy being unconsciously deployed to contain the anger, they aren't really available for intimacy and tenderness—or sustainable and satisfactory relations, inner peace, creativity. The drive of the life force is hampered, perhaps almost snuffed out. Only through working on oneself will it be possible to move ahead.

Moreover, when it's a question of listening to another's anger, we're often caught up in the following reflexes: aggression or flight. Seldom do we have enough patience and inner security to be able to listen to another's anger and be empathic with them, because we tend to think that their anger is directed against us: "He is angry right now, and therefore he doesn't love me; therefore I'm not lovable." And to spare ourselves this risk, our strong impulse is either to aggress or to flee. Reactions like that, however, prove unsatisfactory. At best, exploding in our turn would have provided relief from the tension within us; at worst, we'll both be caught in the infernal spiral. As to flight, it's superfluous to say that although we gain the impression of having extricated ourselves, flight is also unsatisfactory in the long term—and maybe in the short term as well. It merely postpones the inevitable: dealing, somehow, with the situation.

We now know that unpleasant feelings signal the presence of unmet needs. Anger in principle is an unpleasant feeling to experience. So if we observe another's anger, we'll be able to focus our attention not on their behaviors, words, tone of voice, and gestures, but on their unmet needs. We'll then endeavor to name them: "Are you angry because you would have liked more respect, consideration, listening, support, trust?" It's certainly possible that we won't accurately guess the need of the other person. In principle, however, they will note that instead of arguing to justify ourselves, fighting back, or fleeing, we stayed there and listened. Such an attitude/approach is by no means "normal" for us, but it can, with practice, become habitual. It therefore comes as a surprise to the other.

Quite regularly, from the outset of such an exchange, the tone calms down. The other person replies: "Yes, that's right. I would have liked you to . . ." or "No, that's not what it was, I wanted you to . . ." Gradually, we can enter the dance of connection. It's worth emphasizing again that recognizing another's need does not mean we accept it or wish to meet it. But at least we can seek together to connect.

More joy is derived from attempting to resolve our conflicts than from "succeeding" in escalating them.

I'm not saying it's easy; I am saying it's possible. And I'm not saying it will always work; I am saying it's worth a try! Why? Because more joy is derived from attempting to resolve our conflicts than from "succeeding" in escalating them—and because we have more joy in true connection, observing our reciprocal responsibilities, than desperately defending ourselves from being wrong (or fighting just as desperately to prove we are right). Do you realize that there are people who would rather be right whatever the price, even if it means breaking up relationships with their close family, rather than simply accepting that there are at least two sides to every story?!

I would so love it if everyone in power could call forth their strength, compassion, and insight when they speak their anger and listen to the anger of others, so that one day there would be no more mine fields for anyone to walk through. Or wars for nations to fight with one another.

CHAPTER 6

Sharing Information and Our Values

I was not told, "Come."
I was told, "Go where you will."

WILLIAM SHELLER
French singer and musician

Absolute Thinking

At my conferences, one comment is made with considerable regularity: "It's all well and good to listen to ourselves like that, but boundaries nonetheless have to be put in place!" Of course. We need reference points; we need to be able to position ourselves clearly in relation to things, people, and events. Does this mean, however, that they have to be imposed, made into an obligation?

It's required . . . You must . . . That's the way it is . . . You have no choice . . .

This is what, in the first chapter, I referred to as language of diminishing responsibility. It is one of the four functioning habits of the mind that causes violence. This language—and especially the low level of awareness that it expresses—allows no freedom and provides no information as to meaning. Worse still, this language anesthetizes awareness and responsibility.

Several years ago some folks in South Africa were campaigning for an amnesty for a number of the perpetrators of the oppressive apartheid system. In an English newspaper, I was reading the interviews of several of these torturers who had been offered amnesty in exchange for owning up to their acts. One of them, the father of two children and an amateur musician, was asked how it had been possible for him to spend the day torturing human beings in the prison where he worked and then go home in the evening to play with his two daughters or improvise on the piano. His answer: "It was my job! I was paid for it. I had to." My jaw dropped in dismay! Was it possible that the mind-numbing mantra of duty and obedience had made of this human being a torturing machine with neither conscience nor misgivings? Nazi criminals interviewed about their motives have given the same sort of replies: "Just following orders." Hearts and consciences can be deadened and robotized in the same way.

It seems to me that in our day-to-day lives, without, thank the Lord, the consequences of our acts being so tragic, we nonetheless act or expect others to act like automatons—lifeless, soul-less, senseless. "We must succeed. You must work. You have to go to school. You must take out the garbage. I have to earn my living. In this situation I have no choice."

From constraint to freedom: "I must" or "I would like to"

At my first Nonviolent Communication training session with Marshall Rosenberg, he introduced the question as follows: "Now I'm suggesting how to get out of slavery, how to get rid of *I must . . . I have no choice . . . It's compulsory . . . It's required . . .*" Then he asked if someone among us thought there were things they had to do or not do. I responded unhesitatingly:

"But of course there are things you have to do in life, whether you like it or not."

"Could you tell me one thing you believe you have to do?"

"Well, of course! I have to work. I have no choice. That's the way it is. I only get money if I work—and to earn a living as a self-employed person, you have to work hard!"

"When you say, 'I only have the money I earn through my work, and one has to work hard to live (O),' how do you feel (F)?"

"Well . . . tired and worried, if you really want to know."

"And your needs (N)?"

"I'm tired because I would like to make a more creative and generous use of my time, and I'm worried because I need physical security. Yes, I need to know that I'm safe. I need to know that I can pay for my apartment because I no longer want to live in a student room; to know that I can pay the extra pension as a self-employed person because I don't want to die of hunger at the age of sixty-five; to know that I can pay for my car because I don't want to travel only on foot or by train; to know that I can offer myself vacations from time to time, some travel, a celebration with friends, or a training session."

"When you become aware that you work because that enables you to live in a more pleasant apartment than a student room, to ensure that you get an old-age pension, to drive a car, to go on vacation, or to continue your training, how do you feel?"

"Very surprised. I had never looked at things like that. It's true that every morning I choose to put on a shirt and tie and go to work. Nobody, except me, is stopping me from going to Outer Mongolia or Tierra del Fuego for the rest of my life. I choose a certain level of comfort, a certain degree of social and family integration, a certain freedom that I could, if I wanted to, give up. It so happens that I don't sufficiently wish to be in Outer Mongolia without any resources or in Tierra del Fuego without any roots. At the same time, I realize that I have an urgent need to change professional direction, and I'm content

201

when I observe that I am contributing to that by taking this training course."

> **I could avoid the trap that was paralyzing me:**
> **Either stay safe and die of boredom,**
> **or change and die of fear.**

As soon as I was able to clarify what was at stake underlying my "I must," that is, the need for physical security on the one hand and a need for a change toward more satisfying work on the other, I understood that I could avoid the trap of the binary system that was paralyzing me: Either stay safe and die of boredom, or change and die of fear. So I made a gentle and gradual transition. Little by little, I cut back my work time as a legal consultant and developed my human-relations activities. The constraint ("I have to earn a living") had become a support: "Thanks to this job, I can change careers safely!" The energy I experienced during the transition years had shifted dramatically since the value (or the need) toward which I was working was clear.

Freedom generates more fear than does confinement

My warm recommendation, therefore, is to confront all our "I musts" and "I have no choices" with our conscious values—in order to check out which values they actually support. This makes it possible to sort things out. We very often drag along behind us dead-weight anchors, old "I musts" once voiced long ago, that haven't been updated. If behind any "I must" there isn't any real "I would really like to . . ." then it's obsolete and closer to an automatic reflex than a responsible awareness.

This prioritizing can bring about major changes. For example, I have friends, who after having combed through their own "I musts," quit everything—jobs, house, habits—to go off for a year traveling around France in a horse-drawn caravan with their children. And what about school? In the caravan, by the light of an oil lamp. And what about income? Little jobs all along the journey: Their material needs are at an all-time low. And what about the children fitting in when they come back home? We are living confidently, thank you, and in the present moment.

During a recent workshop where several families, parents, and children were together, one mother, who was also a teacher, threw a question at me:

"But, Thomas, in life there are things we have to do, whether we want to or not!"

"Could you let me hear just one of them?"

"Of course. As a mother, I have to prepare a meal every evening. I have no choice."

"How do you feel when you say that (F), and what is your need (N)?"

"Exhausted, because I would simply like to let go, perhaps just one day a week, and go up and have a nice bath as soon as I get back from school."

"So, do you feel exhausted (F) because you would like to have some time for yourself when you finish work (N)?"

"Yes. But as you can see, if I don't cook, the children will eat any old thing, and they have to eat well."

"Do you feel concerned (F) that they should have a balanced diet, and you need to be sure they eat healthily (N)?"

"Oh yes. For me, that's a real priority."

"So then do you feel divided between the need to have time for yourself, for example, to go and have a good bath and the need to be comfortable with the balance of their diet?"

"That's right. But surely you can imagine they wouldn't understand if I went up to have a bath while they were waiting for a meal."

"I see it's difficult for you to believe that they could understand that."

"Oh, I'm sure they couldn't understand."

"Since your daughters are here, I suggest we ask them how

they feel in relation to all of this rather than deciding for them that they wouldn't be able to understand." Turning toward the children, two adolescents who were taking part in the workshop, I said, "How do you feel when your mother says what she just did?"

(Practically in unison . . .) "We've been telling her for a couple of years now either to take the time to relax before she starts cooking or to let us cook. Not only do we know she needs to have a break in the evening, she also hates cooking. So that makes for a really charming atmosphere, since she isn't a happy chef! That frustration on her part often makes a real mess of the evening. She could at least trust us a bit, accept the idea that we could manage for ourselves, prepare the meal ourselves, and produce something good. We're no longer at the stage where we would eat all the cookies in the cupboard or scarf five ice cream sandwiches!"

I then turned to the mother: "How do you feel when you hear your girls saying they would like you either to trust them to produce a good meal or give yourself a little time to relax before getting the meal ready yourself?"

"Both concerned and relieved. It's true they've often told me that, and I've never really heard it. I have this image of my own mother working her fingers to the bone to do things right, exhausting herself to be a good mother, and I realize it's difficult for me to get out of that mind-set, even though my daughters have been urging me to do so. After all [sighs], the way things have been happening hasn't been very good for them or me."

This exchange demonstrates our extraordinary ability to shut ourselves up in the beliefs we have about ourselves ("A good mother must . . .") and about others ("They won't understand . . . I can't even talk to them about it . . . I know what they would say . . ."). Only a genuine connection with the other person—and some "communication coaching" in this case—make it possible to get out of the trap.

I realize how difficult it is for us to recognize our responsibility, and I see how much we tend to ascribe to others and to outside forces the responsibility, even blame, for what happens to us. It was difficult for this mother to clarify on her own what was at stake and to freely discuss the matter with her daughters. Unconsciously, we often prefer our cage and its familiar perches to the freedom of flying out through the open door. Yet the door is open, wide open, as in the poem by Hungarian poet and novelist Gyula Illyés quoted at the beginning of this book. Why do we hold back? Is it not because freedom generates in many of us greater fear than does security?

> **Why do we hold back? Is it not because freedom generates in many of us greater fear than does security?**

We're familiar with constraints, a synonym of sorts for security. Constraints are familiar—uncomfortable perhaps, but familiar. Freedom, well, whoops! Freedom is new and can generate fear of the unknown! After generations of education in duty and habit, accepting the option of acting out of choice and enthusiasm from the heart is difficult. And yet, it is vital. To ensure that the world doesn't anesthetize itself into soporific oblivion, it is urgent for each of us to reconnect with the drive and life force of our hearts.

"You must put on your slippers!"

During a training session, a mother said to me, "I cannot get my six-year-old daughter to understand that she must put on her slippers when she runs around the house in her pajamas."

I asked the mother to show me how she went about it, suggesting that she talk to me as she would talk to her daughter:

"I've already told you a dozen times to put on your slippers. I simply don't know what language to use to be understood. Go and put on your slippers at once!" she said to me (laughing as she noted the tone of her voice).

205

"If I'm your daughter and I hear that, I feel like doing just the opposite for at least two reasons. The first is that I don't understand the meaning of your request; I'm very happy to run around barefoot!"

"But I told her that at the outset: I'm afraid of her catching cold, of getting sick, and of my having to take time off to stay with her. What is true is that after I've told her something once, I believe that she has understood, then I lose my cool and don't tell her the need underlying my request."

"You may perhaps observe that she hasn't assigned to your need the same importance as you have. I think we can all easily understand that for a little girl, catching cold and staying at home with mother is less of a constraint than for the mother! So it may be useful to further clarify the need—and certainly state it again. Because you said it once, it wasn't necessarily perceived by the other person exactly as you meant it. Now I would like to ask you if, by letting her know your need and then making your request, you have respected her freedom not to agree . . ."

(Laughing.) "Oh, no! Certainly not!"

"There we have the second reason why, if I'm your daughter, I don't want to put on my slippers: I have a need for my freedom to be respected, even if I am just a little girl!"

"That is really difficult—accepting that the other person might not agree!"

"Of course it isn't easy. But if we turn our requests into demands, we get either submission or rebellion, but not connection. Now, when you say it's difficult, are you not reassured that you'll be able to hear disagreement from your daughter without giving up your own needs?"

"Well, yes. Basically, I would like her to be in good health, and I'd like her to be able to begin to assume responsibility for herself through such little things as putting on her slippers when it's cold."

"Would you like to succeed in trusting her, in accepting that she can, little by little, decide for herself if and when she puts on her slippers?"

(Long sigh and silence.) "That's it: 'succeed in trusting.' I have to admit that it's very hard for me to trust, so I try to control everything! I must say, it's exhausting!"

As the workshop progressed, this mother became increasingly aware of her difficulty in trusting other people. She also understood that it was up to her to work on herself in order to improve her relationships with her children and her husband. The workshop took place over several days. She came back one morning, very happy, saying, "I still haven't succeeded in expressing my need to my daughter clearly, but yesterday evening, instead of getting annoyed, I did ask her if she knew why I wanted her to put on her slippers. She answered me clearly: 'So I don't catch cold.' I at last succeeded in letting go of things without imposing anything. A few minutes later, I noticed that she had put on her slippers herself!"

So we see that accepting and deciphering a "You must" gives us an opportunity to go back inside ourselves and do some work on our own responsibility.

I have no choice; I don't have the time!

I of course know that circumstances exist where the range of choices can be both considerably reduced or even annihilated. I'm thinking, for example, of physical violence or coercion. These do away with freedom of action. However, I've always appreciated the courage of those who recognized that they didn't have the strength to decide, to refuse, or to change. Consequently, they chose to accept the situation, which doubtless didn't fully suit them but which nonetheless met certain needs—among them the needs for physical safety and emotional security. I believe it's courageous to acknowledge one's responsibility and limitations rather than accuse other people or even circumstances.

I think it's a language habit that causes us to say, "I have no choice," just as we say, "I don't have the time." If we had greater awareness of our needs, we would see more clearly that we choose our priorities—and that the use of our time reflects that in a very obvious way. Our schedules are indicators of our priorities. A person who works ten to twelve hours a day and who says, "I don't have time, with the job I have; I don't have any choices" might reformulate that to say, for example: "My present priority is my safety and that of my family. I haven't yet had an opportunity to find a job that is better paid and that allows me to be freer" or "I'm really interested in assuming major responsibilities and to devote myself to them because that nurtures my need to feel useful, stimulated, and happy in my work, and it provides for my material comfort. For now, I'm therefore choosing to devote most of my time accordingly." The "not yet" and the "for now" open up possibilities to change freely.

> **If we had greater awareness of our needs, we would see more clearly that we choose our priorities—and that the use of our time reflects that in a very obvious way.**

In fact, it's enough for us to examine what we're doing, what we're devoting our time and energy to, the people we're seeing. These components are an excellent barometer of our priorities and thus our choices. Beware, though! It isn't necessarily what at first sight we do, but rather the needs that are satisfied in us by what we do—and how we do them.

Once again, we can observe that it's only if we assume responsibility for our choices and the use to which we put our time that we give ourselves power of action to change what we'd like to change. A British saying states this point humorously: "If you don't like it, change it; and if you can't change it, like it!"

Breakwater or Beacon, Barbed Wire or Shepherd?

> *If a choice absolutely had to be made between violence and cowardice, I would advocate violence . . . but I believe that non-violence is infinitely superior to violence.*
>
> MAHATMA GANDHI
Indian philosopher and social activist

As I was driving one day through a small village, I was stopped by a policeman just after a bend in the road where I had absentmindedly driven slightly across the center line. In a flash, seeing the policeman made me aware that I had been distracted and reactivated in me a longstanding rebelliousness against the stereotype of the blankety-blank, cocky small-town cop. And, clinging to this preconceived idea, I was expecting to be given the usual lecture ("You've just broken rule number XYZ of the traffic code. The fine is fifteen hundred francs. That's the way it is; you have no choice") or some similar moralizing discourse ("Are you out of your mind, driving like that in a village? Have you no sense?!"). I parked my car at the side of the road and waited with a rising sense of dread about what I *knew* would soon ensue. The policeman came up to me and greeted me . . . very courteously: "Sir, I'm worried (F) because I'm in charge of safety (N) in this village when the children come out of school. When I see you driving across the center line, I'm not sure (F) that you're aware of the risks (N) for the children who might be walking along this road or crossing it. How do you respond when I say that to you?"

I almost asked him to repeat what he had said because I simply couldn't believe what I had just heard. This officer had observed a scenario without judging me. He was conveying to me his feeling, indicating to me his need, and requesting me to tell him how I felt! I marveled at the awareness of this man; he wasn't there to punish, reprimand, or constrain but to point out and remind me of a value and a need: safety. He wasn't acting threateningly or punitively; he was inviting me to be responsible. Though I wanted to jump out of the car and give him a hug, I quietly answered him that I was embarrassed at my absentmindedness, that the safety of people and particularly the safety of children was very close to my heart, and that his conscientious and responsible attitude was an invitation to me to be more aware and more responsible at the wheel. He wished me a good journey, and I drove off quite contented.

I can assure you that this story still keeps me alert when I'm driving, much more so than if I had been required to pay a fine to buy judiciary peace. This policeman, who might well have adopted a "breakwater" attitude (saying, for example, "You are in the wrong; you must pay"), still comes to my mind like a compassionate beacon—a marker I reflect on with respect and warm feelings—and that continues to urge me to greater watchfulness on the road.

To respect rules, we have to understand them

"If young people don't abide by the rules, it's usually because they don't understand them." It was Pierre-Bernard Velge, the founder of Cops and Hoods, who taught me that. I say "taught" because, for the lawyer that I am, this was true learning. It isn't because a rule exists that it has meaning or, more importantly, that it's "meaningful" for all people in the same way.

In addition, as I have already said, understanding empowers us. Instead of seeking to abide by the rule blindly, we give ourselves the possibility of seeing if the meaning of the rule, the value that the rule expresses, is perceived in the same way by all. As long as we fail to recognize that a rule is an attempt to express or illustrate a value in daily life, there is a much greater chance that we'll experience it merely as an annoying constraint.

During one of the expeditions we organized to the Sahara Desert with troubled young people, an atmosphere of tension and animosity had started to creep in. We heard that personal belongings had been stolen, and some were complaining about doing all the chores while others were idle, but we allowed the youngsters to "stew in their own juice" for a while, letting the tensions simmer. Then one evening after the meal, sitting around the fire, we suggested they talk about it, each person in turn having the time to speak, using the ritual of the speaking stick. Here is a summary of the exchange among three young people and the facilitators who started the dialogue:

"Terry, do you want to take the stick (floor)?"

"Yeah. Someone has ripped off some of my stuff. They're a-------. I'm going to smash their faces in!"

"Are you angry because you need respect for your things and for yourself?"

"Yes, I need to be respected, plus I have a need for honesty."

"Jeanine, do you want to speak now?"

(She takes the stick from Terry.)

"Yes, I'm fed up. I'm alone with two or three others, helping unload the trucks and set up camp. There are some people on this trip who do as f------ little as possible and just hang out!"

"It sounds like you're disgusted because you'd like some sense of solidarity and a fair distribution of chores?"

"Yes, it would be a lot more fun if we actually *helped* one another. Things would get done so much faster. And we'd all have more time to get our personal stuff together later."

"And how about you, Jean-Luc, would you like to say something?"

(He takes the stick.)

"Yes, I'm sick and tired with people talking about me behind my back. Corinne and Angela never stop gossiping about me, and what they say isn't true."

"Are you angry and disappointed, Jean-Luc? Would you like them to tell you up front if they have something to say to you?"

"Like I said, *not behind my back*. I'm tired of having to hear through the grapevine the lying s--- they're saying about me."

Thus, one after the other, they all spoke. We listened to each of them, reflecting their feelings and needs back to them without judgment. We heard clearly from their own lips many of the values that make for well-being in society: respect, honesty, solidarity, cooperation, fair play, candor, truth, etc. Most of these young people had lengthy rap sheets because they had committed serious crimes. Some had even been entrusted to us by court officials subject to our signing a discharge because the teens already had been categorized as hardened habitual offenders. However, isolated and in the starkness of the desert, far from their familiar turf, they shared with us the beauty of their intentions. They showed us how in their hearts they cherished such values, even if they gave the impression of trampling them underfoot in a society where people like themselves had no place. Suddenly, these values took on self-evident meaning. That is, the young people themselves were able to observe that without values, life is just resentment and misery.

Imagine if we had played prison warden, of the "breakwater" type, saying to them: "You have to respect one another; you have to help one another. If you don't, you'll be punished or sent back on the next camel." The kids would have snickered, shrugged their shoulders mockingly, or moaned, giving us the finger to top off the whole thing! Worse, we as leaders would've strengthened their belief that they were different, that they were misfits, that they were, in effect, nonexistent. They would very probably have raised the ante, simply because fighting or resentment, in the same way as mistrust or ill-being, at least produces a sensation of existing. Ill-being is nevertheless being—just as it's better for such kids to be rejected than ignored. That evening and the rest of the trip provided them with many further opportunities to become aware that one also can enjoy life when there's well-being, mutual respect, trust.

This story made it possible to realize anew that if we've been raised from little on up in an atmosphere of tension, quarreling, and emotional discomfort—if since infancy we've believed that aggressing someone else is the only way for us to have our place, unless we give up altogether—there settles in us a kind of resistance to well-being because this may prove less intense than ill-being and less safe because it's unknown. There is then the risk of our unconsciously (or consciously; recall Tony in Chapter 3 who quickly returned to jail) re-creating the circumstances that we're familiar with in order to experience again the known.

I once knew a very polite, nice, and elegant businessman who, as a child, had suffered greatly from the attitudes and treatment of his highly authoritarian father. Among other things, his father had inflicted upon him outrageous trials of endurance in order (so the father claimed) to get the child used to not feeling pain. What was painful to him in his present life were his reactions toward authority. He had come to realize that he got himself into scrapes with authority figures in order to get them into a fight! He constantly questioned all legal and administrative constraints he came up against at work, using huge amounts of energy to counter the officials in government departments who were simply asking him to clean things up administratively. He had become aware of this after being taken to a police station for insulting an officer who was carrying out a mere roadside check.

By working on his needs, he became aware that, at those times when he was fighting the authorities, he was in touch with a degree of intensity and confidence that he existed and had a place, which in other circumstances were lacking. Together we then explored all of the repressed anger and feelings of revolt linked to the behaviors of his father. Then, when he was ready for it, we explored the needs his dad had for behaving as he did, in order to try to understand the father. Finally, we highlighted the following needs: "Today, I need to feel intensely alive in ways other than through rebellion or aggression. I need to give myself all the room and respect I didn't get from my father."

> **Whether we're from the upper classes, a street-gang member, or a straitlaced businessperson, we all need meaning and intensity.**

Whether we're from the upper classes, a street-gang member, or a straitlaced businessperson, we all need meaning and intensity. And, more than anything else, we observe that if we don't attempt to understand ourselves and the mechanisms of our violence (thus becoming more aware of our ways of functioning), we run the risk of continuing for a long time to put up barbed wire and iron curtains to protect ourselves.

Hurry up, hurry up! Quick, quick!

The subtitle "Barbed Wire or Shepherd?" came to me two years ago when I was going through a region in France that I had known twenty-five years before. At that time it was so remote, so desolate, and so unfrequented that for many people it represented their dream of a return to nature. I was then an adolescent fascinated by the work of the shepherds who lived there. I loved seeing them as contemplative poets bathing in the pool of the universe. They walked freely with resolute good-naturedness among their flocks through the harsh shrubland, down ravines and up hillsides, through the stony places and plowed fields. A few light-hearted orders and many a word of encouragement showed the individual knowledge the shepherd had of each of his sheep. Making an even bigger impression on me, though, about the shepherd's life were silence and time. The shepherd would take care to adjust his pace and his route to the well-being of his flock. Returning to the region twenty-five years later, I was struck and, yes, disappointed to see fences and enclosures keeping the sheep in. No more time to roam the fields and lead the flock with personal attention; a few strands of barbed wire saw to that! The sheep marked time, and the shepherd, sadly, had been reduced to the largely ceremonial role of gatekeeper.

My thoughts often turn to schools and education, to families and homes for young people, to boarding schools or prisons, to all of those places meant to educate and regarding which everyone complains about the "lack of time." I have caught myself dreaming of quality connections between human beings. Obviously, I don't wish anyone to be a sheep, neither literally nor figuratively, with everything that metaphor entails! I've also caught myself dreaming that all the people working for welfare and education would be able to feel free, like a shepherd, and take the time and choose the route best suited to each of their charges. I've even caught myself dreaming that anyone in a learning relationship would be able to ask for help and be listened to; to express their fears or the fact that they weren't well and also wanted to be listened to; to be aware that they weren't succeeding in something and then receive encouragement; to show their distress and receive understanding, without being compelled to mark time in an enclosure.

I regularly work in the school environment, and frequently I hear the same complaint, "But we don't have time!" After a conference where I had talked about the image of the shepherd, the head of a large school in Brussels told me: "You are so right. Neither the parents nor the pupils any longer know what it means to take their time. There are two things the pupils hear continuously: 'Hurry up, hurry up!' and 'Quick, quick!'"

But do we truly lack time, or is it because we no longer want to look at certain priorities? Often it's the race for organization at home, logistics. One couple realized that they were claiming "never to have time" to see their children except at the evening meal because they were refurbishing their house. They had chosen new kitchen furnishings and a new living room, plus they were redesigning the flower garden. In addition, they "had to" change cars since the first one was getting old. So they had just bought a new turbo-diesel family car! The children complained about the parents' lack of availability and were beginning to show their distress: fits of anger, minor school problems, exam failures, sulking. The parents, who had begun to accuse their children of poor discipline and lack of respect, were willing to admit that they had, for some while, reversed their priorities by putting the house and material comfort to the fore—hence the overload of work and their concerns with money. Having gained this awareness, they reorganized their priorities, and therefore their time, differently.

In fact, what is the use of a refurbished kitchen if we're to eat there alone, or if we're to give each other the cold shoulder? What's the use of a new living room if one hardly ever has the time to sit down there? What's the use of a new car if there is quarreling on virtually every journey and if, in any event, there's precious little time to travel, go for walks in the woods, or go on vacation?

Number-one priority: chairs or listening?

A few years ago, Francois, who had been a participant at several NVC training sessions, called me to ask for help. He had just been appointed head of a home for young people in an underprivileged district of Brussels, and people had described for him a disastrous picture of the atmosphere there. Young people in the home were apparently in a state of revolt and had smashed up everything in the living room of the home that was supposed to be a gathering place and recreation workshop for them. Francois had a long career in welfare and humanitarian activities, but he had never yet been in charge of so-called street children. I met him and some of the members of his team who were familiar with the district. I learned some of the background to this revolt and took time to talk it over with some of the young people. It turned out that the previous head had promised activities and programs, but the promises had not been kept. The young people had entertained great expectations, and they felt let down. One day, hearing one final cancellation of a program, they freaked out and broke all the chairs and armchairs in the central meeting room.

Francois told me that his superiors had insisted on his repairing the home immediately and purchasing the necessary furniture again. He asked for my advice. I answered him: "Why rebuild the home if the bomb hasn't been defused? It's almost a provocation. The young people are going to see that there is money to replace things but not to look after people! It seems to me that that's the best way of pressing the detonator again. They get the impression—rightly or wrongly—of being considered worthless, considered like things that can be dragged from one program to another. It's a matter of urgency to show them human consideration, to listen to them, and attempt to understand their frustrations."

At his request, I accepted the proposal to listen to the young people and take the time to try to help reestablish peace. Francois wanted me to make a proposal with a budgeted quote that he could present to his hierarchy. Without being very sure of the number of hours of work this would take, I proposed four modules of four hours' duration each so as to have meetings with some fifteen young people in all. The price I quoted, at the time, for this work was about twenty thousand Belgian francs (approximately six hundred fifty dollars).

Francois called me a week later to let me know that my proposal had been turned down because the management had already used up all the budget for the current year by allocating eight times my quoted budget to fixing up the living room and buying chairs. In addition, he also pointed out to me that the management was of the view that it was a matter of priority; for the young people to feel at home, the rooms had to look welcoming. At the same time, management was envisaging reinforcing surveillance measures to ensure that the furniture would be respected.

Naturally, the setting is important, but what is the use of having a welcoming setting if there is revolt or hatred in people's hearts? It's all very nice, but does it really make a useful contribution to the relationships between people? Naturally, it's important to attempt to see to it that material things are respected, but does a reinforcement of surveillance really provide the most effective and satisfactory answer for all concerned?

This true story shows us to what extent our institutions resemble ourselves in that they have not yet put humanness at the center of their concerns but allow themselves to be distracted by the organization that is supporting the human beings.

Violence is the time bomb of thwarted dreams exploding

When expressing ourselves, words fail us, and when listening, patience fails us. After that we start putting up barbed-wire fences.

One time we took some twenty troubled young people for two days of climbing and risky-looking exercises on cables and rope bridges at a commando training camp, which was in the middle of nowhere and not enclosed. We had been given a litany of warnings from the young people's supervisors: "They're dangerous . . . Supervise them properly, and don't let them escape . . . You're crazy . . . They'll go drinking and cause trouble in the first pub they find . . . Bring them back in the evening."

We left trusting. And rightly so. Usually these kids lived inside the four walls of a group home or in the street. With us, they spent a whole day in the open air, swinging from the end of a rappelling rope above a three-hundred-foot drop or crossing rope bridges suspended over gorges far above the tips of the fir trees. They were hot, hungry, and scared—and then argued, moaned and groaned, and laughed with adults ready to listen to them. In the evening around the campfire, when the tents were up and the meal was on the fire, not one of them wanted to be anywhere else. And what kept them there? Well-being, the ingredients of which were the meaningfulness of what they were doing and the feelings they were experiencing.

> We're *all* dangerous if our vitality has no opportunity to express itself.

Let me put it to you straight: We're *all* dangerous if our vitality has no opportunity to express itself, if our ill-being has no opportunity to be shared, explored, and understood. Violence is a bomb of thwarted dreams exploding.

Meaningfulness and Freedom
We need meaning the way we need bread

With young people I work a lot on issues of meaning and freedom. I observe that they would like to have both but usually don't know how to go about it, realizing for themselves that doing what they want doesn't necessarily have meaning. Conversely, choosing meaningfulness can be a constraint when it involves giving up things. To illustrate the fact that being free doesn't mean being able to do just anything—but is rather a question of doing what one has chosen to do— I suggest to them the following metaphor:

> **"The bank is the river's good fortune"**
> I cannot remember who produced this punchy aphorism. Indeed, it's true that without banks a river becomes a marsh and goes no farther. We need meaning the same way we need bread. We need meaning in the sense of both direction and significance. The trick is to understand and get others to understand that the bank is the river's ally, its friend, its faithful partner. The river does not endure the bank but leans on it and gathers strength from it.

"Just imagine there are a dozen of you on some wasteland, in the sun, in the middle of the afternoon. What do you do?"

"Well, we just hang out, sleep, or we wander around the district and just get bored."

"Just imagine that I suggest a few restrictions: Draw a large, white rectangle on the ground with chalk and divide the big rectangle into two. Form two teams. Only use one ball for both teams and only for a specific time, observing a few rules for passing the ball. Then what happens?"

(A look of surprise.) "Ah, clever. We'd be playing soccer!"

"So you can see that the rules and the restrictions form a framework for the game. That's what gives you the opportunity to exercise your freedom to play in a truly satisfying way, just as traffic lights and traffic laws are opportunities to exercise our freedom to travel in a more satisfying and safe way. As long as we're unaware of the meaning of the rule, we might well prefer going off to play alone outside the frame. If we're aware of the meaning of the rule, there's a greater chance we'll find pleasure in participating in the game."

Describing meaningfulness is difficult if one hasn't pondered the question oneself. I note the helplessness of many parents and teachers in this respect. The questions adolescents and even younger children have about the meaning of what they are doing sometimes leave them stunned! Personally, I truly rejoice when young people ask themselves questions about meaningfulness and don't accept "That's the way it is because that's the way it is . . . You go to school because it's required . . . We go to work because one has to earn a living" and so on.

Through their questioning, young people are inviting adults to think over their priorities, to reformulate them even, as well as redefine what "makes sense" for them as teenagers. I see in that a sign of evolution toward greater meaningfulness, responsibility, and truth. Naturally, this shakes up our old principles and habits! And it's certainly no small task to call oneself into question and begin reevaluating long-held assumptions.

What About the Use of Force and Punishment?

If I see my young son running into the road where cars are going by, I'm going to waste no time in catching him and bringing him back onto the pavement, no messing around. This is neither the time for telling him how I feel nor what my needs are; this is an emergency! Once the child is safe, rather than telling him off and being reproachful, or worse, punishing him, I will explain to him that I felt very scared (F), that I wasn't sure he was aware of the danger, and that it was to protect him from a possible accident (N) that I grabbed him. Then I will ask him *if he agrees* to be more careful in the future (R). This is the protective use of force.

If I get attacked on the street by a mugger and have no other means to avoid being hit than by striking out myself, I will do so. Not for the purpose of attacking, but to protect my life. It's life and life alone that enables us to assess the legitimacy of physical defense. What is our intention? To subject, reduce, or suppress life? Or protect, allow, and encourage life?

Regarding the use of force "to educate," whether it be through a slap, a beating, or confinement to a room—means that are still very commonly used—I am simply stunned when I hear that parents, who say they love their children, are capable of hitting them when there is a disagreement. Do they show their disagreement in the same way with their friends or close family? As a parent, I can fully understand how one can feel exasperated and occasionally driven to the breaking point by the behavior of children and be unable to know how to react. However, I am convinced that hitting a child, even lightly, is to perpetuate the old belief that violence is a legitimate way of solving conflicts. It means legitimizing in the hearts of tomorrow's next generation the use of force to oblige another to submit. It means getting a child to accept that "if we don't reach an understanding, we hit each other." It means maintaining the old illusion that evil can bring good.

Acting out is an admission of defeat—the powerlessness to make oneself understood, to understand another. You can see how urgent it is to learn a new language, to understand one another, and to make ourselves understood. I'm not saying it isn't important for acts to be approved or disapproved, depending on whether or not they're in the service of a significant value. This very clear benchmark seems to me indispensable, not only in education but also for the well-being of a community.

Punishment and reward?

But should we use punishment? Are there not ways of showing that an act has compromised a value—ways that enhance the assumption of responsibility? I believe that punishment often reveals a lack of imagination, creativity, and trust in the efficacy of consultation to come up with a restorative-justice solution in the service of life. Judges are beginning to understand this and are issuing sentences involving work in the public arena. I'm not saying this is easy, and I'm not judging parents who are exhausted and at the end of their rope. I'm simply noting that we're all complicit in the perpetuation of an educational paradigm that approves violence.

> **Punishment often reveals a lack of imagination, creativity, and trust.**

Almost every day, I see to what extent the fear of punishment and the quest for reward, which are but the two sides of the same tragic coin, keep so many people in a state of dependency with respect to one another, in a state of paralyzing guilt and deep-seated mistrust in relation to initiatives, novelty, difference, and responsibility. So many situations trigger the fear of "being mistaken" and punished or not receiving the reward stemming from approval. The system of punishment and reward does not create inner safety and self-confidence. Often unconsciously, but durably, this system produces a somewhat desperate quest for good marks or anguished apprehension over bad marks. I have so frequently seen the mechanics of this at work, particularly within businesses, and I have been saddened to witness the damage done by an educational system that, in the final analysis, transmits its values by recourse to fear and guilt rather than enthusiasm and agreement.

Let us be clear about our intentions. What do we want from others? Do we want automatic obedience, stripped of awareness, and based on fear or shame where the main concern is to "please in order to buy peace"? Or do we want responsible adherence to values that are close to our hearts, a taste for doing things in full awareness of the common good and moral commitment?

When I was twenty-five years old, there was still compulsory military service in Belgium. At the time, I had no idea that I could do something else and, more importantly, I had no awareness of the strength and power of nonviolence. With my head filled with law books, I had a need for the open air and contact with physical reality. So I enrolled in the army in the commando regiment. After six months of extremely demanding training, both physically and psychologically, I was an inexperienced young officer in front of my platoon of twenty-seven soldiers, all of them bigger and stronger than I and most of them with several years' experience!

I soon realized it would be inadvisable to go against their wishes, even though I was their hierarchical superior. Even prior to learning the concepts of Nonviolent Communication, I didn't want these men to act out of duty or submission but out of awareness and responsibility. I realized instinctively that they needed to have the meaning of proposed activities clearly spelled out and the reasons for doing them understood. Giving orders without specifying their meaning or ensuring that the men were motivated would have deadened our relationship. I wanted our relationship to be lively and as egalitarian as possible, while clearly respecting the functionality of the roles each of us played.

I have no memory of ever having raised my voice. As a group we operated joyfully in an atmosphere of mutual trust. Although my military experience taught me a lot about myself and about how human beings function, I am certainly not singing the praises of the army. I have a dream that 10 percent of national defense budgets the world over would be allocated to:

- The organization of self-expression and intervention groups requested anywhere.
- Training in communication and mediation as early as primary school.

223

- Nonviolent conflict resolution.
- Learning respect for difference.
- Stimulating inner security and self-confidence.

Just imagine a mere 10 percent of the world investment in armament and war being reserved for tools in the service of peace! This would be a United Nations-style peacekeeping force, but with the backing and funding of national "peace" departments. When I see the amazing results that my colleagues and I obtain with ridiculously small budgets, I thrill to the thought of the extraordinary power we all have to create peace actively.

From this experience in the armed forces, I understand even more deeply in my bones that although life may have us play an authority role, it can only be authority in the service of life, a function to inspire movement and facilitate cohesion, somewhat like the role of an orchestra conductor. Will a conductor "punish" the violinist whose bow slips or the flautist who wanders off the score? Far from it! He will recall the meaning of the music and respect for the notes; he will stimulate a taste for playing together and will inspire the members of his orchestra to stay focused and leave improvisations to the jazz musicians! I maintain an awareness that one can experience strictly hierarchical relationships while deeply respecting one another, without losing either one's identity or one's dignity. Once again, it isn't so much what one does as how one does it that is so pivotal.

Finally, I'm not claiming that firmness isn't sometimes necessary. But can we not learn to be firm and assertive without being aggressive? Can we not learn to say, to shout even, "Enough is enough!" without judging, but just expressing firmly what we want and allowing the other person not to agree?

When we're exhausted, it's so easy for us to consider that another is the cause of our exhaustion. When our first daughter, Camille, was born, Valérie's and my nights were of course short and broken. One night, Camille's tears were becoming really difficult to bear; she had not yet found her rhythm between feeds. Both my wife and I got up, moaning: "She is so exhausting. This is unbearable." But quite quickly we corrected that: "No, we are the ones who are exhausted and find it difficult to put up with her crying. As for her, she is alive and is showing it. We certainly don't expect her to be nice in order to let us sleep. It's up to us to meet our need for rest in some other fashion."

French geneticist Albert Jacquart, referring to how society applies sanctions, reminds us of how important it is to fully assume our responsibilities: "The existence of a prison in a town is proof that something is awry in the whole of our society." Similarly, resorting to punishment is a sign that something is out of kilter in the way we educate, work, or live together.

Celebrating the Intensity of Life

> "What man is missing out on is intensity."
> —Carl Jung

A few years ago in a shopping area in a city in Quebec, in the middle of the freezing month of November, I was greeted by a smiling teenager, sixteen or seventeen years old, who seemed to be waiting, leaning against the corner of a wall. He came up to me and said: "Hi, how are things? Are you looking for someone?" I immediately realized what he was doing there, in the cold, looking like a schoolboy going home. It wasn't drugs he wanted to sell. He was offering himself. I replied: "No, I'm not looking for anyone. But I'll gladly get you a cup of coffee if you want one." It was bitingly cold on the street, and something about this unexpected encounter touched me. He accepted. We went into a café on the corner, and we chatted about everything and nothing.

"Tim," I said to him, "it's young people who taught me a lot of what I know and what I apply as I do my job. Would it be OK for you if I asked you a question about yourself?"

(In a cloud of cigarette smoke . . .) "No problem. Go ahead."

"What led to doing what you do on the street?"

"Drugs."

"And what led you to drugs?"

"Life."

"And what more specifically in life?"

(He gave a big sigh, dragged on his cigarette, then stubbed it out, annoyed.) "I just can't take hearing my father telling me I should go to school 'because that's the way it is.' He can't even tell me why he's working! Come on! His job can't have any meaning or purpose."

"Do you need things and life to have meaning?"

"Well, of course! And then even life is a waste, my dad is a loser, my hometown is worthless. I need to have fun, so I have a blast." (He actually giggled.)

"Would you like life to be even more intense, more alive?"

(Getting irritated.) "Yeah, well, I want things to go wild. You can imagine what things at home are like. Everything in its place, all neat and tidy, dead. Not much life there."

"Do you need to have liveliness to be alive?"

"I sure do. I need to feel that I'm fully alive. But I don't get that in my life. So I have a few lines of coke, I smoke joints, and I have sex with people I don't know. I haven't yet found any other way of living on the edge."

In a few words, Tim summarized the basic aspirations of human existence: We need to be aware of meaning in our life, the direction it is taking us and its significance—human, philosophical, spiritual. We also need to know that we're embodied in living, pulsating flesh capable of enjoying the full range of experiences and pleasures in the world. Unless we take care of these needs in some constructive fashion, we run the risk of trying to meet them in a destructive way.

Three days after we met, as I was leaving the premises where I was doing some training, I came across Tim again. He was begging on a major boulevard. I couldn't believe I was running into him again. He was looking worse than three days before, and it was clear he had come to the end of his resources. He needed twenty dollars to get a bus ticket back to his hometown.

"Twenty bucks, I tell you, that's all I need to get back to where I live. It's two hundred fifty miles away!"

"I'm willing to help you, but what is there to reassure me that you won't smoke away the twenty dollars?"

"Come and buy the ticket with me. I've got to go, I tell you!"

We were walking to the bus station, and Tim explained to me: "I'm scared of missing my bus. My parents are expecting me tomorrow, and my buddy here won't put me up anymore. So I prayed. I always pray at times like this."

"And are your prayers always heard and answered?"

"Well, *you* came by, and you're paying for my ticket!"

"Do you believe—"

"In what? In God?"

"Yes."

"Well, of course, and he always answers me."

He was confident, confident that one day he would have a wife, children, a job. He spoke of what he was experiencing as something temporary, momentary. I'm grateful to Tim for this lesson in life and faith. This encounter nourished in me a taste for digging even deeper to find the vein of truth and health, even through the mire of pain and our day-to-day existence.

As for Julian, he was a seventeen-year-old and so quiet that he was thought to be autistic. He did have drug problems, and we invited him to join us for a downriver trip we were organizing in a remote mountain region. For the first few days, he lay in the bottom of the canoe without moving a muscle the whole ride, without saying a word, whereas the others were taking turns riding in front, sitting astride the canoe floats, and enjoying jumping the river's waves.

Julian was from a very humble, even impoverished, background. His father, a foreigner, had long since returned to his native country. Julian was sad and lonely. Seeing the others have such fun, he nonetheless did become more sociable. One day he took the risk of going up front, sitting astride the canoe's floats. He was watching for the next rapids. There the wave was much larger than he thought it would be. It crashed over the whole canoe, and the eddies almost made the boat capsize. Julian was jubilant: "Did you see that wave; did you see that? And I stayed on, didn't I? Did you see? What a whopper! That was fantastic!" Then he stopped, speechless, and we were mesmerized to hear him produce so many words in such a lively way. Never had he heard himself like that or felt so good.

At that moment, the whole crew cheered him in chorus, the way one would welcome a birth! With the splash of water, Julian got a splash of life that let him into his body, let him leave the sad Peter Pan behind, let him dance, move. Gradually, Julian left his torpor and his muteness. Day after day we saw him mixing with the others, taking his place in the group, and beginning to laugh. Eight years later, I saw Julian again. He was at work and taking care of his own son.

Here is a challenge I especially like to take up: to find presence, joy, and the taste for life, even through its harshest difficulties, not denying or repressing them. The challenge is to find neither optimism nor pessimism, but simply live the experience as consciously as possible, trying to avoid the usual traps—getting set in our ways, our principles, and our old wounds. Other pitfalls include being ill cared for or not cared for, as well as flights into idealization or spiritual desolation.

Before closing this chapter, I want to celebrate life in all its many-splendored dimensions, in all of its movements and all of its moments, the life that gets us to seek what we truly want beyond the constraints that sometimes threaten to weigh us down.

I celebrate the life that leads us to dare:
- To trust our children.
- To take a bath rather than cook unwillingly.
- To pack up and set off in a horse-drawn caravan rather than accepting anomie and boredom.

> **I celebrate the life that gets us to change what we no longer like and like what we cannot change.**

I celebrate the life that:

- Gets the little girl with her slippers to stand up for herself because she is seeking to understand the meaning of what is being asked of her and seeing her freedom respected.
- Urges parents to redefine their priorities and leave their gardens, their houses, their cars to be with their children while there is yet time.
- Gets us to change what we no longer like and like what we cannot change.
- Makes us aware of possibilities in our interactions, like the policeman in the village as the children were leaving the school.
- Gets us to sit down with young people to exchange information on our values, checking their relevance and efficacy.

I celebrate sharing that:

- Lets us discover and lets us free ourselves from an old-time repressed revolt straining beneath the neatly pressed suit and polished shoes to live free.
- Gets us to jump off the runaway train in order to listen to ourselves.
- Encourages Tim to refuse to suffocate even as he wades through the mud to "resuscitate" his life.
- Joyfully slaps Julian out of his torpor and brings him into the land of the living.
- Will, finally, cause us to postpone our all-important budget for "the purchase of chairs and decorations" so that we can sit on the ground (or in the gravel if necessary) in order to start listening to our hearts.

During World War II from 1939 to 1945, my grandmother, who was a marvelously generous and a deeply devout Christian woman, hid Jews in the cellar of her house. We, who at the age of ten or twelve played there in every nook and cranny in later years, found it hard to believe that human beings could have been hidden there to protect their lives. She would tell us these stories, and we always quivered with emotion when she got to the moment when the Germans raided the house and searched it. Without so much as a tremor in her voice, Granny had dared to tell the patrol leader searching the house that only the members of the family were there and that no one else was in the house.

I was in such admiration of her dignity and courage, and yet I had misgivings. "But, Granny," I said, "you didn't tell the Germans the truth. You say that we should always tell the truth . . ."

She stopped a moment to think, her eyes closed. "You're right," she finally said. "I think we should always tell the truth. But in that case, truly, there was something more important at stake than the truth: life itself. Life had to be respected." With that, my grandmother taught me what lies beyond words, principles, and habits. Life itself.

CHAPTER 7

Method

*In recent years, we have become
increasingly aware of the profound
resemblances between all living
organisms . . . All life has similarities,
and we are much more alike than we
had imagined.*

GEORGE WALD
U.S. biologist, Nobel Prize winner

Three Minutes, Three Times a Day

German philosopher Friedrich Nietzsche once said, "Power is
in the method." To learn a new language, a new sport, or any
technique, one needs method, rigor, tenacity, and discipline.
Personally, I began to feel more or less at ease with the process
of Nonviolent Communication after two weeks of intense
practice during a training workshop. This is the equivalent of
what I would need to begin to express myself in a new language,
such as, German or Portuguese. I wish to make this clear—not,

231

of course, to discourage anyone, but to encourage everyone to become aware that, as I stated at the outset (in the Introduction), I don't believe that the mere reading of a book can transform us in depth, sustainably. Only practice and experimentation make that possible.

Having said that, not everyone is available, willing, or able to take part in such training. Without attempting to ascertain for others why they're unavailable, unwilling, or unable, I can vouch for the fact that workshops are not the only way of learning. There are many methods. The key, though, may lie in the ancient saying: "When the student is ready, the teacher appears."

I rarely give individual advice unless there is a clear and persistent request coming from a person. I trust that most of us have our toolbox at the ready given the right circumstances, but I'm aware that providing advice is often an attempt to circumvent true listening. Sometimes, however, when participants at a training session insist on having advice as to a method of regular practice, I suggest the following:

"Three minutes, three times a day! Three minutes listening to yourself without judging, without blaming, without advising, without trying to find a solution. Three presence-filled minutes for you, not for your plans or concerns. Three minutes to take stock of your inner state without trying to change anything. Three minutes to connect with yourself, check that you are truly present to yourself, and that to the question, Is there someone home? you can truly answer with all your being, 'Yes, I am there.' Do this three times a day! It is out of this quality of presence to yourself that may well be born a quality of presence to others."

Akin to a homeopathic remedy, this method is in no way like waving a magic wand. It is an invitation, with a wink, to awaken to the fact that it generally isn't helpful to set for oneself change objectives that are so huge that they entail the risk of never getting to first base. Once again I can simply bear witness to the fact that this simple and regular maintenance of my presence to myself has been essential in changing both my professional career and my personal emotional life.

When we listen to ourselves in this way, we can little by little get a sense of direction, of mission and, free from any notion of quick fixes or instant results, focus our attention and our consciousness on the life emerging within us: Where is the life force in me, what is it saying to me, what needs are being met, what needs are not being met? Once the needs have been truly shaken out and priorities clarified, solutions can begin to be perceived. This exercise is like a young music student playing the scales; the more you practice, the better you get. Two examples:

- The more aware you are of what your own anger means, the more you'll be available to listen to another's anger.
- The better you become acquainted with your own powerlessness or insecurity, the more compassionate and understanding you'll become for the insecurity in another person. Welcoming and loving our own vulnerability makes us open to welcome and love another's.

To date, I haven't seen any other way to break with our old and tragic habit of living our human relationships as tests of strength.

Healthy Consciousness

Before going any farther, let me recommend gratitude. Be aware of gratitude and express it . . . for all the needs that have been met. Be grateful—even with everything collapsing all around us—for being able to take the next breath, to have hands to feel, to have eyes to see. I fully realize how naïve such a proposal may sound. I take full responsibility for that. For me, though, gratitude is indispensable.

> **Be aware of gratitude and express it . . .**
> **for all the needs that have been met.**
> **Be grateful—even with everything collapsing**
> **around us—for being able to take the**
> **next breath, to have hands to feel,**
> **to have eyes to see.**

Once we sense the nourishment produced by everything that is going right, we find the strength to take on everything (well, at least *some* things!) going wrong. This is a principle of inner ecology. If most of our energy is consumed by the irritation we feel when a flight is delayed—and we forget all the planes that fly on schedule—we run the risk of enclosing ourselves into what might be termed narrowness of vision. Sooner or later, we're in danger of being asphyxiated in that box of our own making. Therefore, it's a matter of urgency to work on our overall vision, our overall breathing. In day-to-day life, in couples, families, and (why not?) at school or work, gratitude is the vitamin pill of relationships. Remember, it isn't a question of being nice but of being genuine!

A few questions to ponder. Do we need to:

- Wait to lose our nearest and dearest in order to express our love?
- Wait to be hospitalized to celebrate the joy of being in good health?
- Be alone in order to appreciate company?
- Wait until things "all go wrong" in order to become aware of what was going right?

If we aren't watchful, our consciousness can get filled up with all sorts of bad news, to such an extent that there is little room to take in the good news. We can keep our consciousness in good health, unclog our inner carburetor, clean our spark plugs, check the ignition, and above all make sure we have good-quality fuel. Does the engine of our life run better on good news or bad news?

Convivial Consciousness

A Bedouin guide said to me one day: "Sadness is a virus that cannot survive among our people. If someone is sad, they will immediately be listened to and comforted and will very quickly regain the pleasure of taking care of others."

In the course of the traveling workshops I facilitate in desert regions, I am struck every time by the conviviality of contacts with desert people. There is a cohesion, a sense of belonging to the camel drivers' teams or the mule drivers' teams, that I marvel at. It's as if each one had a radio receiver to pick up the needs of the others while taking account of their own. It seems to me that simply by living together in circumstances both demanding and stripped of anything superfluous, they have developed an acuity of awareness and of the heart that I call *convivial consciousness*. This consciousness combines, for example, dignity and humility, autonomy and community, integrity and integration, freedom and responsibility, presence to oneself and presence to others, awareness of the individual and awareness of the universe—as if all were complementary, which indeed they are. Each of us can develop our own radio receiver, this tuned-in consciousness. This quest lies at the "heart" of Nonviolent Communication. One of the benefits of the discussion groups I was referring to above would be the development of a common consciousness, a convivial consciousness.

In our fast-changing world, this work of cohesion and integration of our communities, at every level, to me stands out as the priority of priorities if we are to cut short the mechanics of exclusion, isolation, and violence—whether expressed or repressed.

EPILOGUE

Cultivating Peace

> *What is Evil, except Good*
> *tortured by its own thirst?*
>
> Kahlil Gibran
> Lebanese poet, philosopher, and artist

Violence Is Not Natural

I increasingly believe that in contrast to what I was always taught at school, to what I studied during my psychology lectures at university, and to what I have heard the world over, violence is not the expression of our true nature. Rather, it is the expression of the frustration of our true nature. That is my working assumption. Violence expresses our needs that are not recognized or met. If our needs are recognized, or—even better yet—met, of what use is violence? I believe less and less in the wickedness of people and more and more in the power of bitterness and fear, as well as the power that feeds on frustration. Basically, wickedness is an expression of the bitterness of people who have not taken care of—or had the opportunity to take care

237

of—their suffering. If we could speak our bitterness or our fears, even the most secret ones, the most taboo ones, and share our frustrations, even the most unavowed ones, or work on them, do you not think we could coexist without aggressing each other? So much acting out stems from the fact that our frustrations not only aren't in our consciousness, they also are neither spoken of nor shared compassionately.

Violence, an Old Habit

Most people, including all too many world leaders, have gotten into the sad, old habit of believing that the final solution for solving conflicts is violence. We have allowed ourselves to be programmed like that—to be sold a bill of goods. We now know that there are other ways of solving conflicts. So we can start deprogramming our violence. We can begin disentangling ourselves from these old patterns and start dreaming that one day, side by side with the war museum, there will be a museum for family, marital, tribal, political, ethnic, and religious violence where our great-great-great-grandchildren will learn that even in the era of e-mails and the Internet, most human beings were still unable to express themselves or listen to themselves or, of course, truly understand one another.

Nothing infuriates me more than such obsolete beliefs as "Man is a wolf for man . . . We have always beaten each other up . . . Humanity never changes." This kind of resignation, this cynicism, is what is both heralding and ushering in future violence, paving the way for the next pedophile, arming the next war. I want each of us to become aware of our own individual power to contribute to change, to deprogram ourselves out of violence, and to work toward a new shared awareness.

Like Martin Luther King Jr., I have a dream that I nurture every day, convinced as I am that it is our dreams that take us across the oceans, the deserts, or the heavens to discover new worlds. If jeans and T-shirts, Coca-Cola and multi-bladed razors in the space of just a few years have become known and used throughout the world—to such an extent that they constitute a sort of common world culture—it's because they meet needs: comfort, well-being, simplicity, identity, and belonging to a world community for clothing and Coca-Cola . . . hygiene, ease, and efficacy for razors. Although I've met many people on the various continents of the world who have taken on parts of this common culture, I've often observed the same people also are vigorously attached to their local or family traditions. Why, therefore, not contribute to a mode of communication that is also worldwide, without compromising our need for identity?

Nonviolent Communication, along with other similar approaches, fits in with the search for a mode of relationship suited to the global village for several reasons:

- It has a versatile nature, which I referred to in the Introduction.
- It suits the relationship with ourselves, interpersonal relationships in couples and families, as well as professional and social relationships.
- It respects all religious, spiritual, philosophical, political sensibilities.
- It advocates values that seem to me to be the common heritage of our human race.

Like Jacques Salomé, a writer and trainer in relational ecology, I'm hoping that communication will be included in the curriculum in schools throughout the world, like any other subject, as basic as languages or data processing. Imagine what the world would be like if all those who have been trained today in mastering a foreign language or data processing were also to learn this language of the heart?

I hope one day to meet visionary ministers of all nations—the minister of national education, the minister of public health, the minister of national security, the minister of justice, and (why not?) the minister of defense—who will be willing to invest in sustainable changes to our modes of relationships, because they will have become aware that durable change in the world is possible only when the impetus comes from the center of human beings. These leaders will accept being personally involved by starting out in developing their own awareness of themselves, then carrying the message to the citizens of their country. Just imagine more and more human beings becoming aware, once again paraphrasing Hubert Reeves, that violence and noncommunication constitute not one major problem but rather seven billion small problems. As our numbers grow, we are invited to take seriously our responsibilities regarding our day-to-day behaviors—and to take care of keeping a healthy consciousness, "What I say, what I do, the thoughts I nurture, my intentions, the plans I have . . . do they contribute to unifying or to dividing, to reconciling differences or to aggravating hostilities, to peace or to war?"

That consciousness will enable us to live in this new world, still so little known, with ease, safety, and joy. Would that not be a fine goal for the third millennium?

Cultivating Peace

I believe that each one of us, with our human dignity, receives our share of responsibility. I hope—this is the dream alive in me—that more and more men and women will become aware and joyfully recognize this responsibility and assume it in their daily lives, happy to contribute in this way, wherever they are, with whatever means they have, to the welfare of the global family of humanity. Indeed, I further believe that there won't be genuine peace in our world until growing numbers of us take care to understand our need for inner peace, then cultivate and nurture it as lovingly as gardeners tend to flowers under their care—every day.

Let us begin by cultivating peace within. It will then radiate out. Peace, my friend, is contagious!

FOOTNOTES

1. Marshall Rosenberg of Geneva, Switzerland, holds a doctorate in clinical psychology. He is a man of peace recognized throughout the world, and he is founder of the Center for Nonviolent Communication, which is based in California of the United States. I warmly recommend his book *Nonviolent Communication: A Language of Life,* PuddleDancer Press, Second Edition, 2005.

2. Guy Corneau, author and Jungian psychoanalyst, *L'amour en guerre* (Love in war), Montréal, Les Èditions de l'Homme (The Editions of Man), 1996, *N'y a-t-il pas d'amour heureux?* (Is there no happy love?), Paris, 1997.

3. Guy Corneau, ibid.

4. Guy Corneau, author of *Absent Fathers, Lost Sons, L'amour en guerre* (Love in war), *N'y a-t-il pas d'amour heureux?* (Is there no happy love?) and *La guérison du cœur* (The recovery of the heart).

5. Excerpt from the Tao of Rajneesh.

6. Rainer Maria Rilke, *The Book of Hours*, Bruxelles, Le cri (The cry), 1989.

7. Michèle Delaunay, *L'ambiguïté est le dernier plaisir* (Ambiguity is the final pleasure), Arles, Actes Sud (South Acts), 1987.

8. I recommend this book regarding the chapter that has this title in Guy Corneau's book: *N'y a-t-il pas d'amour heureux?* (Is there no happy love?), Robert Laffont.

9. This exchange has been stated in "laboratory" Nonviolent Communication to better facilitate understanding. In day-to-day life, with some practice, one can clearly formulate the various phases of feelings and needs in ordinary language.

10. Jacques Salomé, *If Only I'd Listen to Myself,* Montréal, Les Èditions de l'Homme (The Editions of Man), 1990.

11. Paulo Coelho, *The Alchemist,* Paris, Anne Carrière, 1994.

12. Alice Miller, *For Your Own Good: Hidden Cruelty in Child-Rearing and the Roots of Violence,* Vendôme, Le fil rouge (The red thread), PUF.

13. Christian Bobin, *The Very Lowly,* Paris, Folio.

14. Antoine de Saint-Exupéry, *The Little Prince,* Paris, Gallimard, 2000.

15. Marshall Rosenberg, op. cit.

16. Excerpt from Gérard de Nerval (Gerard of Nerval).

17. This expression is from Guy Corneau. Any creation is the result of a movement and therefore of friction: the violin bow on the strings, the fingers on the clay, the quill on the paper, the body in space.

18. Vincent Houba, architect, presented a conference titled *En quête de toit, en quête de soi* (In quest of the heights, in quest of oneself).

19. Christian Bobin, *La souveraineté du vide* (The sovereignty of the void), Paris, Folio.

20. Marshall Rosenberg, op. cit.

BIBLIOGRAPHY

BOBIN, Christian. *La souveraineté du vide* (The sovereignty of the void). Paris, Folio.

BOBIN, Christian. *The Very Lowly.* Paris, Folio.

COELHO, Paulo. *The Alchemist.* Paris, Anne Carrière, 1994.

CORNEAU, Guy. *L'amour en guerre* (Love in war). Montréal, Les Èditions de l'Homme (The Editions of Man), 1996, published in Paris under the title *N'y a-t-il pas d'amour heureux?* (Is there no happy love?), Robert Laffont, 1997.

DELAUNAY, Michèle. *L'ambiguïté est le dernier plaisir* (Ambiguity is the final pleasure). Arles, Actes Sud (South Acts), 1987.

MILLER, Alice, Hannum, Hildegarde, & Hannum, Hunter. *For Your Own Good: Hidden Cruelty in Child-Rearing and the Roots of Violence.* Vendôme, Le fil rouge (The red thread), Presses Universitaires de France.

RAJNEESH, *Le Tao Rajneesh* (The Rajneesh Tao). Editions of the Gange la Ferté Alais.

RILKE, Rainer Maria. *The Book of Hours.* Bruxelles, Le cri (The cry), 1989.

ROSENBERG, Marshall. *Nonviolent Communication: A Language of Life,* PuddleDancer Press, Second Edition, 2005, translated into the French under the title *Les mots sont des fenetres ou des mur* (Words are windows or walls). Jouvence & Syros, 1999.

SAINT-EXUPÉRY, Antoine de. *The Little Prince.* Paris, Gallimard, 2000.

SALOMÉ, Jacques and Sylvie Galland. *If Only I'd Listen to Myself.* Montréal, Les Èditions de l'Homme (The Editions of Man), 1990.

INDEX

The Four-Part Nonviolent Communication Process

Clearly expressing how **I am** without blaming or criticizing	Empathically receiving how **you are** without hearing blame or criticism

OBSERVATIONS

1. What I observe *(see, hear, remember, imagine, free from my evaluations)* that does or does not contribute to my well-being:

   "When I (see, hear) . . . "

1. What you observe *(see, hear, remember, imagine, free from your evaluations)* that does or does not contribute to your well-being:

   "When you see/hear . . . "

   (Sometimes unspoken when offering empathy)

FEELINGS

2. How I feel *(emotion or sensation rather than thought)* in relation to what I observe:

   "I feel . . . "

2. How you feel *(emotion or sensation rather than thought)* in relation to what you observe:

   "You feel . . ."

NEEDS

3. What I need or value *(rather than a preference, or a specific action)* that causes my feelings:

   " . . . because I need/value . . . "

3. What you need or value *(rather than a preference, or a specific action)* that causes your feelings:

   " . . . because you need/value . . ."

Clearly requesting that which would enrich **my** life without demanding	Empathically receiving that which would enrich **your** life without hearing any demand

REQUESTS

4. The concrete actions I would like taken:

   "Would you be willing to . . . ?"

4. The concrete actions you would like taken:

   "Would you like . . . ?"

   (Sometimes unspoken when offering empathy)

© Marshall B. Rosenberg. For more information about Marshall B. Rosenberg or the Center for Nonviolent Communication, please visit www.CNVC.org.

Some Basic Feelings We All Have

Feelings when needs are fulfilled

- Amazed
- Comfortable
- Confident
- Eager
- Energetic
- Fulfilled
- Glad
- Hopeful
- Inspired
- Intrigued
- Joyous
- Moved
- Optimistic
- Proud
- Relieved
- Stimulated
- Surprised
- Thankful
- Touched
- Trustful

Feelings when needs are not fulfilled

- Angry
- Annoyed
- Concerned
- Confused
- Disappointed
- Discouraged
- Distressed
- Embarrassed
- Frustrated
- Helpless
- Hopeless
- Impatient
- Irritated
- Lonely
- Nervous
- Overwhelmed
- Puzzled
- Reluctant
- Sad
- Uncomfortable

Some Basic Needs We All Have

Autonomy
- Choosing dreams/goals/values
- Choosing plans for fulfilling one's dreams, goals, values

Celebration
- Celebrating the creation of life and dreams fulfilled
- Celebrating losses: loved ones, dreams, etc. (mourning)

Integrity
- Authenticity • Creativity
- Meaning • Self-worth

Interdependence
- Acceptance • Appreciation
- Closeness • Community
- Consideration
- Contribution to the enrichment of life
- Emotional Safety • Empathy

Physical Nurturance
- Air • Food
- Movement, exercise
- Protection from life-threatening forms of life: viruses, bacteria, insects, predatory animals
- Rest • Sexual Expression
- Shelter • Touch • Water

Play
- Fun • Laughter

Spiritual Communion
- Beauty • Harmony
- Inspiration • Order • Peace
- Honesty (the empowering honesty that enables us to learn from our limitations)
- Love • Reassurance
- Respect • Support
- Trust • Understanding

About Nonviolent Communication

Nonviolent Communication has flourished for more than four decades across sixty countries selling more than 3,000,000 books in over thirty-five languages for one simple reason: it works.

From the bedroom to the boardroom, from the classroom to the war zone, Nonviolent Communication (NVC) is changing lives every day. NVC provides an easy-to-grasp, effective method to get to the root of violence and pain peacefully. By examining the unmet needs behind what we do and say, NVC helps reduce hostility, heal pain, and strengthen professional and personal relationships. NVC is now being taught in corporations, classrooms, prisons, and mediation centers worldwide. And it is affecting cultural shifts as institutions, corporations, and governments integrate NVC consciousness into their organizational structures and their approach to leadership.

Most of us are hungry for skills that can improve the quality of our relationships, to deepen our sense of personal empowerment or simply help us communicate more effectively. Unfortunately, most of us have been educated from birth to compete, judge, demand, and diagnose; to think and communicate in terms of what is "right" and "wrong" with people. At best, the habitual ways we think and speak hinder communication and create misunderstanding or frustration. And still worse, they can cause anger and pain, and may lead to violence. Without wanting to, even people with the best of intentions generate needless conflict.

NVC helps us reach beneath the surface and discover what is alive and vital within us, and how all of our actions are based on human needs that we are seeking to meet. We learn to develop a vocabulary of feelings and needs that helps us more clearly express what is going on in us at any given moment. When we understand and acknowledge our needs, we develop a shared foundation for much more satisfying relationships. Join the thousands of people worldwide who have improved their relationships and their lives with this simple yet revolutionary process.

About PuddleDancer Press

PuddleDancer Press (PDP) is the main publisher of Nonviolent Communication™ related works. Its mission is to provide high-quality materials to help people create a world in which all needs are met compassionately. By working in partnership with the Center for Nonviolent Communication and NVC trainers, teams, and local supporters, PDP has created a comprehensive promotion effort that has helped bring NVC to thousands of new people each year.

Since 1998 PDP has donated more than 60,000 NVC books to organizations, decision-makers, and individuals in need around the world.

Visit the PDP website at www.NonviolentCommunication.com to find the following resources:

- **Shop NVC**—Continue your learning. Purchase our NVC titles online safely, affordably, and conveniently. Find everyday discounts on individual titles, multiple-copies, and book packages. Learn more about our authors and read endorsements of NVC from world-renowned communication experts and peacemakers. www.NonviolentCommunication.com/store/

- **NVC Quick Connect e-Newsletter**—Sign up today to receive our monthly e-Newsletter, filled with expert articles, upcoming training opportunities with our authors, and exclusive specials on NVC learning materials. Archived e-Newsletters are also available

- **About NVC**—Learn more about these life-changing communication and conflict resolution skills including an overview of the NVC process, key facts about NVC, and more.

- **About Marshall Rosenberg**—Access press materials, biography, and more about this world-renowned peacemaker, educator, bestselling author, and founder of the Center for Nonviolent Communication.

- **Free Resources for Learning NVC**—Find free weekly tips series, NVC article archive, and other great resources to make learning these vital communication skills just a little easier.

For more information, please contact PuddleDancer Press at:

2240 Encinitas Blvd., Ste. D-911 • Encinitas, CA 92024
Phone: 760-652-5754 • Fax: 760-274-6400
Email: email@puddledancer.com • www.NonviolentCommunication.com

About the Center for Nonviolent Communication

The Center for Nonviolent Communication (CNVC) is an international nonprofit peacemaking organization whose vision is a world where everyone's needs are met peacefully. CNVC is devoted to supporting the spread of Nonviolent Communication (NVC) around the world.

Founded in 1984 by Dr. Marshall B. Rosenberg, CNVC has been contributing to a vast social transformation in thinking, speaking and acting—showing people how to connect in ways that inspire compassionate results. NVC is now being taught around the globe in communities, schools, prisons, mediation centers, churches, businesses, professional conferences, and more. Hundreds of certified trainers and hundreds more supporters teach NVC to tens of thousands of people each year in more than sixty countries.

CNVC believes that NVC training is a crucial step to continue building a compassionate, peaceful society. Your tax-deductible donation will help CNVC continue to provide training in some of the most impoverished, violent corners of the world. It will also support the development and continuation of organized projects aimed at bringing NVC training to high-need geographic regions and populations.

To make a tax-deductible donation or to learn more about the valuable resources described below, visit the CNVC website at www. CNVC.org:

- **Training and Certification**—Find local, national, and international training opportunities, access trainer certification information, connect to local NVC communities, trainers, and more.

- **CNVC Bookstore**—Find mail or phone order information for a complete selection of NVC books, booklets, audio, and video materials at the CNVC website.

- **CNVC Projects**—Participate in one of the several regional and theme-based projects that provide focus and leadership for teaching NVC in a particular application or geographic region.

- **E-Groups and List Servs**—Join one of several moderated, topic-based NVC e-groups and list servs developed to support individual learning and the continued growth of NVC worldwide.

For more information, please contact CNVC at:

9301 Indian School Rd., NE, Suite 204, Albuquerque, NM 87112-2861
Ph: 505-244-4041 • US Only: 800-255-7696 • Fax: 505-247-0414
Email: cnvc@CNVC.org • Website: www.CNVC.org

Nonviolent Communication,

3rd Edition

A Language of Life

By Marshall B. Rosenberg, PhD

$19.95 — Trade Paper 6x9, 264pp
ISBN: 978-1-892005-28-1

What is Violent Communication?

If "violent" means acting in ways that result in hurt or harm, then much of how we communicate —judging others, bullying, having racial bias, blaming, finger pointing, discriminating, speaking without listening, criticizing others or ourselves, name-calling, reacting when angry, using political rhetoric, being defensive or judging who's "good/ bad" or what's "right/wrong" with people—**could indeed be called "violent communication."**

What is Nonviolent Communication?

Nonviolent Communication is the integration of four things:

- **Consciousness:** a set of principles that support living a life of compassion, collaboration, courage, and authenticity
- **Language:** understanding how words contribute to connection or distance
- **Communication:** knowing how to ask for what we want, how to hear others even in disagreement, and how to move toward solutions that work for all
- **Means of influence:** sharing "power with others" rather than using "power over others"

Nonviolent Communication serves our desire to do three things:

- Increase our ability to live with choice, meaning, and connection
- Connect empathically with self and others to have more satisfying relationships
- Sharing of resources so everyone is able to benefit

Available from PuddleDancer Press, the Center for Nonviolent Communication, all major bookstores, and Amazon.com. Distributed by Independent Publisher's Group: 800-888-4741. For Best Pricing Visit: NonviolentCommunication.com

The Healing Power of Empathy

True Stories About Transforming Relationships

Edited by Mary Goyer, MS

$17.95 – Trade Paper 6x9, 288pp
ISBN: 978-1-934336-17-5

Empathy Is a Learnable Skill!

Empathy is the cornerstone of good relationships—but it can be hard to access when it's most needed. Luckily, empathy is also a learnable skill, with the power to move conversations out of gridlock and pain.

- You'll see how anger and blame get translated and how productive dialogues are made possible.
- You'll hear the words used to repair arguments before they cause damage.
- You'll watch how self-empathy transforms relationships—without speaking any words at all.

"Our ability to offer empathy can allow us to stay vulnerable, defuse potential violence, help us hear the word no without taking it as a rejection, revive lifeless conversation, and even hear the feelings and needs expressed through silence. The best way I can get understanding from another person is to give this person the understanding too. If I want them to hear my needs and feelings, I first need to empathize."

> —**Marshall B. Rosenberg, PhD,** Author and Creator of Nonviolent Communication, over 3,000,000 copies sold worldwide

"Each vignette provides a living example of the transformative power of this special form of listening and being. Every story, in its own way, gives a hopeful glimpse of a world where people deeply care for one another and express that caring through their language. This book inspires me to bring more empathy into my life and work to make this world a reality."

> —**David McCain,** Trainer, Coach, Consultant, and CNVC Certification Candidate

Available from PuddleDancer Press, the Center for Nonviolent Communication, all major bookstores, and Amazon.com. Distributed by Independent Publisher's Group: 800-888-4741. For Best Pricing Visit: NonviolentCommunication.com

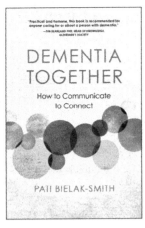

Dementia Together

How to Communicate to Connect

By Pati Bielak-Smith

$17.95 — Trade Paper 6x9, 248pp
ISBN: 978-1-934336-18-2

Build a Healthy Dementia Relationship!

If you are looking to build and sustain a healthy relationship with someone who has dementia, this book is for you.

Dementia is an illness that causes no physical pain. Yet ask anyone who cares about someone with Alzheimer's or another dementia if their heart isn't aching. The pain in dementia comes not from the illness, but from feeling hopeless, alone, or disconnected from someone you care about. And a broken relationship can be healed.

This book is for family members and friends, for spouses, caregivers, and those who simply care. It outlines a path to a life with dementia that includes more life and less illness. With imagination, compassion, empathy, and quiet humor, the real-life stories in *Dementia Together* show you how to build a healthy dementia relationship. Because there are ways to communicate that result in greater capacity to receive as well as to provide both warm connection and practical collaboration.

"Emphasises how authentic relationships are at the heart of supporting someone with dementia. Makes a compelling case for how—with a curious and empathic approach to communicating—two-way connections can be enriched over time. Practical and humane, this book is recommended for anyone caring for or about a person with dementia."

—**Tim Beanland PhD**, Head of Knowledge, Alzheimer's Society

"A book that acts as a guide in the richest sense: lucid, compassionate, and illuminating."

—**Nicci Gerrard**, award-winning journalist and author of
The Last Ocean: A Journey Through Memory and Forgetting

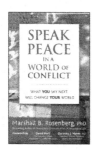

Speak Peace in a World of Conflict
What You Say Next Will Change Your World
By Marshall B. Rosenberg, PhD

$15.95 – Trade Paper 5-3/8x8-3/8, 208pp, ISBN: 978-1-892005-17-5

Create Peace in the Language You Use!

International peacemaker, mediator, and healer, Marshall Rosenberg shows you how the language you use is the key to enriching life. *Speak Peace* is filled with inspiring stories, lessons, and ideas drawn from more than forty years of mediating conflicts and healing relationships in some of the most war-torn, impoverished, and violent corners of the world. Find insight, practical skills, and powerful tools that will profoundly change your relationships and the course of your life for the better.

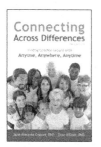

Connecting Across Differences, 2nd Edition
Finding Common Ground With Anyone, Anywhere, Anytime
By Jane Marantz Connor, PhD and Dian Killian, PhD

$19.95 – Trade Paper 6x9, 416pp, ISBN: 978-1-892005-24-3

Connection Is Just a Conversation Away!

In this fully revised second edition, Dr. Dian Killian and Dr. Jane Marantz Connor offer an accessible guide for exploring the concepts, applications, and transformative power of the Nonviolent Communication process. Discover simple, yet transformative skills to create a life of abundance, building the personal, professional, and community connections you long for. Now with an expanded selection of broadly applicable exercises, role-plays, and activities. Detailed and comprehensive, this combined book and workbook enhances communication skills by introducing the basic NVC model, as well as more advanced NVC practices.

Respectful Parents, Respectful Kids
7 Keys to Turn Family Conflict Into Co-operation
By Sura Hart and Victoria Kindle Hodson

$17.95 – Trade Paper 7.5x9.25, 256pp, ISBN: 978-1-892005-22-9

Stop the Struggle—Find the Co-operation and Mutual Respect You Want!

Do more than simply correct bad behavior—finally unlock your parenting potential. Use this handbook to move beyond typical discipline techniques and begin creating an environment based on mutual respect, emotional safety, and positive, open communication. *Respectful Parents, Respectful Kids* offers *7 Simple Keys* to discover the mutual respect and nurturing relationships you've been looking for.

Available from PuddleDancer Press, the Center for Nonviolent Communication, all major bookstores, and Amazon.com. Distributed by Independent Publisher's Group: 800-888-4741. For Best Pricing Visit: NonviolentCommunication.com

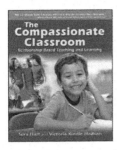

The Compassionate Classroom
Relationship Based Teaching and Learning
By Sura Hart and Victoria Kindle Hodson

$17.95 – Trade Paper 7.5x9.25, 208pp, ISBN: 978-1-892005-06-9

When Compassion Thrives, So Does Learning!

Learn powerful skills to create an emotionally safe learning environment where academic excellence thrives. Build trust, reduce conflict, improve co-operation, and maximize the potential of each student as you create relationship-centered classrooms. This how-to guide offers customizable exercises, activities, charts, and cutouts that make it easy for educators to create lesson plans for a day, a week, or an entire school year. An exceptional resource for educators, homeschool parents, child-care providers, and mentors.

The No-Fault Classroom
Tools to Resolve Conflict & Foster Relationship Intelligence
By Sura Hart and Victoria Kindle Hodson

$17.95 – Trade Paper 8.5x11, 256pp, ISBN: 978-1-892005-18-2

Students Can Resolve Their Own Conflicts!

The No-Fault Classroom leads students ages 7–12 to develop skills in problem solving, empathic listening, and conflict resolution that will last a lifetime. The book's twenty-one interactive and step-by-step lessons, construction materials, and adaptable scripts give educators the tools they need to return order and co-operation to the classroom and jumpstart engaged learning—from the rural school to the inner city, the charter school, to the home school classroom.

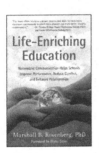

Life-Enriching Education
Nonviolent Communication Helps Schools Improve Performance, Reduce Conflict, and Enhance Relationships
By Marshall B. Rosenberg, PhD

$15.95 – Trade Paper 6x9, 192pp, ISBN: 978-1-892005-05-2

Maximize Every Student's Potential!

Filled with insight, adaptable exercises, and role-plays, *Life-Enriching Education* gives educators practical skills to generate mutually respectful classroom relationships. Rediscover the joy of teaching in a classroom where each person's needs are respected!

Available from PuddleDancer Press, the Center for Nonviolent Communication, all major bookstores, and Amazon.com. Distributed by Independent Publisher's Group: 800-888-4741. For Best Pricing Visit: NonviolentCommunication.com

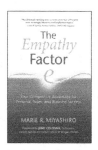

The Empathy Factor
Your Competitive Advantage for Personal, Team, and Business Success
By Marie R. Miyashiro, APR

$19.95 — Trade Paper 6x9, 256pp, ISBN: 978-1-892005-25-0

The Transformative Power of Empathy!

Marie Miyashiro explores the missing element leaders must employ to build profits and productivity in the new economy—Empathy. This book takes Dr. Marshall Rosenberg's work developing Compassionate Communication into the business community by introducing *Integrated Clarity®*—a powerful framework you can use to understand and effectively meet the critical needs of your organization without compromising those of your employees or customers.

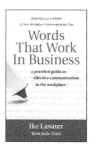

Words That Work In Business, Updated 2nd Edition
A Practical Guide to Effective Communication in the Workplace
By Ike Lasater With Julie Stiles

$15.95 — Trade Paper 5-3/8x8-3/8, 208pp, ISBN: 978-1-934336-15-1

Be Happier and More Effective at Work!

Words That Work in Business, 2nd edition, is a must-have guide to thriving in the workplace. Learn how to reduce workplace conflict and stress, effectively handle difficult conversations, have more effective meetings, give and receive meaningful feedback, and navigate power differentials, all of which serve to improve your productivity and fulfillment.

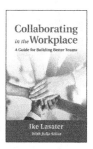

Collaborating in the Workplace
A Guide for Building Better Teams
By Ike Lasater
With Julie Stiles

$7.95 — Trade Paper 5-3/8x8-3/8, 88pp, ISBN: 978-1-934336-16-8

Foster Superior Collaboration!

What can individuals do to improve the ability of teams to collaborate and create powerful outcomes? *Collaborating in the Workplace* focuses on the key skills that research shows support effective collaboration and the practical, step-by-step exercises that individuals can practice to improve those skills. By using this book, people can work better together to create outstanding outcomes.

Available from PuddleDancer Press, the Center for Nonviolent Communication, all major bookstores, and Amazon.com. Distributed by Independent Publisher's Group: 800-888-4741. For Best Pricing Visit: NonviolentCommunication.com

Being Me, Loving You: *A Practical Guide to Extraordinary Relationships* **by Marshall B. Rosenberg, PhD** • Watch your relationships strengthen as you learn to think of love as something you "do," something you give freely from the heart.
80pp, ISBN: 978-1-892005-16-8 • **$6.95**

Getting Past the Pain Between Us: *Healing and Reconciliation Without Compromise* **by Marshall B. Rosenberg, PhD** • Learn simple steps to create the heartfelt presence necessary for lasting healing to occur—great for mediators, counselors, families, and couples.
48pp, ISBN: 978-1-892005-07-6 • **$6.95**

Graduating From Guilt: *Six Steps to Overcome Guilt and Reclaim Your Life* **by Holly Michelle Eckert** • The burden of guilt leaves us stuck, stressed, and feeling like we can never measure up. Through a proven six-step process, this book helps liberate you from the toxic guilt, blame, and shame you carry.
96pp, ISBN: 978-1-892005-23-6 • **$7.95**

The Heart of Social Change: *How to Make a Difference in Your World* **by Marshall B. Rosenberg, PhD** • Learn how creating an internal consciousness of compassion can impact your social change efforts.
48pp, ISBN: 978-1-892005-10-6 • **$6.95**

Humanizing Health Care: *Creating Cultures of Compassion With Nonviolent Communication* **by Melanie Sears, RN, MBA, PhD** • Leveraging more than twenty-five years nursing experience, Melanie demonstrates the profound effectiveness of NVC to create lasting, positive improvements to patient care and the health care workplace.
112pp, ISBN: 978-1-892005-26-7 • **$7.95**

Parenting From Your Heart: *Sharing the Gifts of Compassion, Connection, and Choice* **by Inbal Kashtan** • Filled with insight and practical skills, this booklet will help you transform your parenting to address every day challenges.
48pp, ISBN: 978-1-892005-08-3 • **$6.95**

Practical Spirituality: *Reflections on the Spiritual Basis of Nonviolent Communication* **by Marshall B. Rosenberg, PhD** • Marshall's views on the spiritual origins and underpinnings of NVC, and how practicing the process helps him connect to the Divine.
48pp, ISBN: 978-1-892005-14-4 • **$6.95**

Raising Children Compassionately: *Parenting the Nonviolent Communication Way* **by Marshall B. Rosenberg, PhD** • Learn to create a mutually respectful, enriching family dynamic filled with heartfelt communication.
32pp, ISBN: 978-1-892005-09-0 • **$5.95**

The Surprising Purpose of Anger: *Beyond Anger Management: Finding the Gift* **by Marshall B. Rosenberg, PhD** • Marshall shows you how to use anger to discover what you need, and then how to meet your needs in more constructive, healthy ways.
48pp, ISBN: 978-1-892005-15-1 • **$6.95**

Teaching Children Compassionately: *How Students and Teachers Can Succeed With Mutual Understanding* **by Marshall B. Rosenberg, PhD** • In this national keynote address to Montessori educators, Marshall describes his progressive, radical approach to teaching that centers on compassionate connection.
48pp, ISBN: 978-1-892005-11-3 • **$6.95**

We Can Work It Out: *Resolving Conflicts Peacefully and Powerfully* **by Marshall B. Rosenberg, PhD** • Practical suggestions for fostering empathic connection, genuine co-operation, and satisfying resolutions in even the most difficult situations.
32pp, ISBN: 978-1-892005-12-0 • **$5.95**

What's Making You Angry? *10 Steps to Transforming Anger So Everyone Wins* **by Shari Klein and Neill Gibson** • A powerful, step-by-step approach to transform anger to find healthy, mutually satisfying outcomes.
32pp, ISBN: 978-1-892005-13-7 • **$5.95**

Available from www.NonviolentCommunication.com, www.CNVC.org, Amazon.com and all bookstores. Distributed by IPG: 800-888-4741. For Best Pricing Visit: NonviolentCommunication.com

ABOUT THE AUTHOR

Based in Belgium, Thomas d'Ansembourg is a former lawyer and legal advisor, and has worked for more than a decade managing support to at-risk youth. First published in French in 2001, *Being Genuine* is now a European bestseller with more than 200,000 copies in print. *Being Genuine* has also received the 2003 festival of authors of psychology of Nimes award.

It was in his one-on-one work with youth that d'Ansembourg connected to a fundamental aspect of the Nonviolent Communication process—that all destructive behavior stems from unmet needs. As d'Ansembourg worked with and listened to young people, he began to realize that most of their so-called deviant behaviors actually represented a series of unmet basic needs, such as identity, acceptance, closeness, respect, safety, and recognition.

Using Dr. Rosenberg's principles and methods, as well as those of Carl Rogers and Thomas Gordon, the author has led numerous workshops and seminars in Europe, Morocco, and Québec. He is a certified trainer in Nonviolent Communication. He also provides private NVC consultations with individuals, couples, and families. He and his wife, Valérie, have three daughters, Camille, Anna, and Jiulia.